Unknown anonymous

Rochester New Hampshire Selectmens Records 1794 1806

Unknown anonymous

Rochester New Hampshire Selectmens Records 1794 1806

ISBN/EAN: 9783743454798

Manufactured in Europe, USA, Canada, Australia, Japa

Cover: Foto ©Thomas Meinert / pixelio.de

Manufactured and distributed by brebook publishing software (www.brebook.com)

Unknown anonymous

Rochester New Hampshire Selectmens Records 1794 1806

The Selectmens Record for the Town of Rochester for the Year 1794 &c

Mordica Varney's	Dr.	453 in £ 3 " 15 " 6	By paid Jotham Nute the p
Dr. Samuel Plumer's	Dr.	660 in £ 5 " 10 " 0	an order to Amos Main for 3 " 3 " 4 1/2 Dr. Samuel Plumer 1 " 6 " 0 Simon Torr 1 " 3 " 0
Thomas Davis's	Dr.	521 in £ 4 " 6 " 10	one to Joseph Walker for 2 " 7 " 5 one to Gershom Horn for 1 " 19 " 5 }

3

The Town of Rochester's Accounts for the Year 1793 Returned in Constable, Collectors and Selectmens hands March 2[illegible] 1794

	£	s	d
In Collector Paul Hartfords hands for 1781 —	25	10	7
In Collector Hosea Roberts's hands for 1781	25	18	4
In Collector Thomas Roberts's hands for 1787	8	1	0
In Constable Benjⁿ Dame's hands for 1787 £165–12–8 Convolledated in —	127	4	6
In Collector James Hows hands for 1788 in Specie and Certificates —	494	15	7
In Collector Howard Henderson's hands for 1788 £490:4:1 Convelledated —	272	1	4½
In Collector Thoˢ Roberts's hands for 1789 in Specie	259	14	5
In Collector Elijah Varney's hands for 1789 —	44	18	—
In Collector Peter Cushing's hand for 1790 —	189	8	2
In Collector Danˡ Wingate's hands for 1790 —	137	7	1
In Collector Hatevil Knight's hand for 1792 —	212	10	4½
In Collector Elijah Varney's hands for 1792 —	182	2	4
Raised in Collector Danˡ Wingate's State List for 1793 —	134	19	4
Raised in Sᵈ Wingate's Parish List for 1793 —	45	5	7
Raised in Collector Jotham Nute's State List for 1793	145	1	4
Raised in Sᵈ Nute's Parish List for 1793 —	56	17	10
Received of Capᵗ Samuel Nute in part of the Mortgage on John Nute's farm —	42	5	10
Received of the Selectmen for 1792 in Cash —	12	2	—
Received of the Selectmen for 1792 in Notes Indents and Orders —	57	9	6
£	2559	15	3

The way Sᵈ Money is laid out and Paid

	£	s	d
Paid the State Treasurers Extent against the Town for 1787 in full in Specie —	257	17	0½
Paid Daniel Libby Depᵗʸ Sherriff his fees for Serving Sᵈ Extent —	2	19	2
Paid the State Treasurer in part the Tax for 1788 Specie —	127	10	—
Paid the County Treasurer in part the Tax for 1792 —	27	10	8
Paid Benjⁿ Palmer and others for paying their District School Master in 1790	2	9	3
Paid Widᵒʷ Molly Meservey for paying her Disᵗ School Master in 1790	2	11	2
Paid Benjⁿ Copps and others for paying their Disᵗ School Master in 1790	1	10	3

4

	£	s	d
Paid Ensⁿ Johⁿ Carson & others for paying their District School Master in 1790 —	3	9	6
Paid Joˢʰ Plumer & others for payᵍ their Disᵗ School in 1790	1	8	9½
Pᵈ Deaⁿ Saml Plumer & others for payᵍ their Disᵗ Schooling 1790	2	2	7½
Pᵈ Wᵐ Trickey & others for paying their Disᵗ School in 1790	1	10	6
Pᵈ Mark Miller & others for paying their Disᵗ School in 1790	1	17	11
Pᵈ Caleb Varney & others for payᵍ their Disᵗ Schooling 1790	3	—	2
Pᵈ Benjⁿ Chesly and others for payᵍ their Disᵗ School in 1790	2	17	3½
Pᵈ Col David Place & others for payᵍ their Disᵗ School in 1790	3	12	6
Pᵈ Ephᵐ Kimball & others for payᵍ their Disᵗ Schˡ in 1790	3	1	4½
Pᵈ Joseph Pearl & others for payᵍ their Disᵗ Schˡ in 1790	1	3	
Pᵈ Amos Ham & others for payᵍ their Disᵗ Schˡ in 1790	1	13	9½
Pᵈ Paul Jenness & others for payᵍ their Disᵗ Schˡ in 1790	1	10	10
Pᵈ Capᵗ Danˡ McDuffee & others for payᵍ their Disᵗ Schˡ in 1790	4	5	8½
Pᵈ Capᵗ John Brewster & others for payᵍ their Disᵗ Schˡ in 1790	—	15	10
Pᵈ Thoˢ Ham & others for their paying their Disᵗ Schˡ in 1790 —	2	14	1½
Pᵈ Capᵗ Saml Nute & others for payᵍ their Disᵗ School in 1790 —	4	3	10
Pᵈ Edmund Tebbetts & others for payᵍ their Disᵗ Schˡ in 1790	2	8	—
Pᵈ Saml Leighton & others for payᵍ their Disᵗ Schˡ in 1790	2	9	6
Pᵈ Isaac Wentworth & others for payᵍ their Disᵗ Schˡ in 1790	1	19	2
Pᵈ Benjⁿ Meader & others for paying their Disᵗ Schˡ in 1790	2	10	1
Pᵈ Jotham Twombly & others for payᵍ their Disᵗ Schˡ in 1790		11	6
Pᵈ Esqʳ Plumer & others for payᵍ their Disᵗ School in 1790	3	5	—
Pᵈ Major Perkins & others for payᵍ their Disᵗ Schˡ in 1790	1	11	—
Pᵈ Johⁿ Hayes & others for payᵍ their Disᵗ Schˡ in 1790	3	—	2
Pᵈ Danˡ Wingate & others for payᵍ their Disᵗ Schˡ in 1790	—	14	2½
Pᵈ Colᵒ Roberts & others for payᵍ their Disᵗ Schˡ in 1790	2	18	3
Pᵈ Simon Torr for 2 Days trying to procure Money for the Treasurer —	—	8	—
Pᵈ David French & others for payᵍ their Disᵗ Schˡ in 1792	3	9	5
Pᵈ Colᵒ Roberts for paying his Disᵗ School-master in 1792	4	6	3
Pᵈ Elliat Cartland for keepᵍ Schˡ in Col Place Disᵗ in 1792	5	1	1
Pᵈ Danˡ Dame keepᵍ School in Capᵗ Danˡ McDuffee Disᵗ 1792	3	6	—
Pᵈ Esqʳ Wingate for his paying his Disᵗ School in 1792	3	—	—
Pᵈ Jacob Main for keepᵍ Schˡ in Lieu Downing Disᵗ in 1792	4	14	[illegible]
Pᵈ Josʰ Horn for keepᵍ School in Thoˢ Ham Disᵗ in 1792	3	14	8
Pᵈ Stepⁿ Brewster for keepᵍ Schˡ in Amos Place Disᵗ 1792	2	5	—
Pᵈ Josiah Main for keepᵍ Schˡ in Colᵒ McDuffee Disᵗ in 1792	4	3	7
Pᵈ Danˡ Rogers & others for payᵍ their Disᵗ School in 1792	3	16	[illegible]
Pᵈ Capᵗ Saml Nute for boarding the Schˡ master in his Disᵗ in 1792	2	2	7
Pᵈ Benjⁿ Meader & others for payᵍ their Disᵗ School in 1792	3	3	9
Pᵈ Silas Dame for keepᵍ Schˡ in Deacon Plumer Disᵗ in 1792	2	13	9
Pᵈ Amos Main for keepᵍ Schˡ in Dnᵒ How's Disᵗ in 1792	4	6	3
Pᵈ Peter Cushing for payᵍ Schˡ master in Majʳ Perkins Disᵗ 1792	3	4	[illegible]
Pᵈ Benj Briant for keepᵍ Schˡ in Capᵗ Nute's Disᵗ in 1792	3	3	[illegible]
Pᵈ Benj Wingate for keepᵍ Schˡ in Esqʳ Dame's Disᵗ 1792	3	12	[illegible]

	£	s	d
Pd Joseph Pearl & others for pay'g their Dist. Sch. in 1792	1	12	7
Pd Nat. Knight for keep'g Sch. in Col. Goodwin's Dist. 1792	3	6	–
Pd Moses Roberts Jr for keep'g Sch. in Capt. Adams Dist. 1792	3	14	9
Pd Paul Jerres for pay'g Sch. Mas. in Aaron Ham's Dist. 1792	2	6	8
Pd Joseph Drown for pay'g Sch. Mas. in J. Ham's Dist. in 1792	2	10	7
Pd Cons. Nute for warning poor People out of Town in 1792	–	8	–
Pd Selectmen for writing 4 Warrants to Warn poor out of Town in 1792	–	6	–
Pd Wid. Han. Evans for a Road through her Land as apprised	1	13	–
Pd Aaron Wingate Esq. as a Committeeman in 1792		12	–
Pd Capt. Dan. Hayes his Serv. as a Lott Layer in 1792	1	4	–
Pd Jacob Hanson his Acct as overseer of the poor in 1792	1	5	3
Pd Joseph Thomson Jr agreeable to a former Vote of the Town	1	7	8
Pd Col. John Waldron as a Surveyor runing out the Road by Siew Downing's	–	6	–
Pd Paul Place to Redeem a piece of Land Illegally Assessed Sold at Cushing's Vendue		9	–
Pd Capt. Moses Roberts for Supp'g Committee on Parsonage House	1	–	–
Pd Edward Rollings a Bal. Due to Selectmen for 1792	2	12	5
Pd Peter Cushing his Acct for Sawing Plank for Norway Plain Bridge	5	5	11
Pd an Order given by former Selectmen to Josiah Main for Service as Town Clerk in 1787	–	18	–
Pd Josiah Main his Acct for Drawing & return'g Surveyors & making a return of State and County Officers in 1792	4	–	–
Pd Hubartus Neal his Acct as a Committeeman in 1792	1	8	–
Pd Col. Roberts for Coll'g the Tax in 1789 in full	3	14	–
Pd Pelatiah Cartland as an Auditor in 1789	–	12	–
Pd J. Cartland for keep'g Sch. in Aaron Ham's Dist. in 1792	–	8	2½
Pd Elij. Varney for Coll'g the Tax in 1789 in full	7	10	–
Pd Jacob Hanson his Services as an Auditor in 1792	–	12	–
Pd J. Hanson a Note against the Town given by former Selectmen	–	15	3
Pd Hunkin Colbath for a road throu his Land in part	6	–	–
Pd Selectmen for time Settling with the People on 10 Rod Road	1	16	–
Pd Selectmen for writing & exchanging 4 Deeds	–	6	–
Pd Selectmen for Runing the line between Capt. Dan. McDuffee & Jer. Folsoms Land	–	18	–
Pd Selectmen for runing the Line between Rochester and Dover	–	12	–
Pd Selectmen for runing the Line between Rochester and Somersworth	–	12	–

	£	s	d
Pd for Runing the Line between Rochester and Barrington in 1792	2	0	–
Pd Selectmen & Surveyor for runing the Line between Rochester and New Durham	1	10	–
Pd Selectmen & Surveyor for runing the Line between Rochester and Middleton	1	10	–
Pd Selectmen & Surveyor for runing the Line between Rochester and Wakefield	1	10	–
Pd for time & Expences laying out a Road from Meaderborough Road to Wm Holmes Grist mill and so on to Barrington Line	–	18	–
Pd Benj. Chesley & others for Building a fence for Col. Joshua Wingate as a Compensation for a Road throu his Land	5	6	–
Pd Wm Atkinson Esq. the Cost of Presentment for bad highway	1	17	10
Allowd an abatement of Nath. Hartford's Tax for 1792	2	15	3
Pd to Individuals for repairing the Bridge by John Furbush	2	9	–
Pd Rev. Joseph Haven's Salary in full to March 25 1793	115	0	–
Pd Rev. Joseph Haven's Salary in part after March 25 1793	33	0	[illegible]
Pd Dan. Libby (by agreement) his extra fees for relevying an Extent on Collector Hendersons Property	2	2	–
Pd Dr Paul Libby his Services as an assessor in 1792 & 1793 in full	–	18	–
Pd Coll. Daniel Wingate for Coll'g the Tax in 1790 in full	3	12	–
Pd the overseers of the Poors bill in part for 1793	–	7	1
Pd Col. McDuffee & others for pay'g their Dist. School Mas. in 1792	2	6	6
Pd Joshua Lane his Services as a Lott Layer in 1793	1	16	–
Pd Cons. Dea. Jewett for warning poor out of Town in 1793	–	15	4
Pd J. Rich. Place for an abatement of Nathan Hoag's Taxes in 1784	–	12	–
Pd J. Rich. Place as an Overseer of the Poor in 1792	–	6	–
Pd Peter Horn for Supp'g the Comm. in the Parsonage House	1	5	11
Pd Enoch Horn for a Road throu his Land in full	1	4	–
Allowd the abatement in Cons. Benj. Dame's List for 1787 Specie	12	18	8
Allowd the abatement in J. Dame's List for 1787 Certificates	2	16	6
Pd Cons. Benj. Dame for Collecting the Tax in 1787	7	10	–
Rectifyed a mistake made by former Selectmen with Benjamin Dame	2	16	6
Pd James Knowles Esq. for taking the acknowled. of Deeds	–	7	2
Pd Maj. Rich. Furber for a Road throu his Land as apprised by Committee	1	4	–
All. an abatement of Henry Burzell Tax illegally Assessed	1	11	–
Pd Simon Torr for 3 Journeys to Exeter Settling with Treasurer	1	4	–
Pd Tho. Footman the poundage on a Note of hand that Benj. Dame held against the Town and the abatement in his List when extended	–	12	2
To a Loss sustained by an Act of Congress taking place regulating Crowns & gold when we had Cash in hand (for the Treasurer	[illegible]	[illegible]	10
To £26..8 in Indents Sold at 11/6 pr £ which makes a Difference of	11	5	[illegible]

	£	s	d
(7) Allow'd the abatement in Col. Thos. Roberts List for 1789 in Specie	8	8	1
Allow'd the abate in Col. Elijah Varneys List for 1789	12	6	3
Allow'd the abatement in Collector Howard Henderson's List for 1788 in Specie	9	19	4
Pd Selectmen for time and expence Settleing with the Old Collectors	3	–	–
Allow'd the abatement in Collector Danl Wingate's List for 1790	4	14	1
Rectify'd a mistake made by the Selectmen for 1790 with Collector Henderson	1	5	–
Made abatement on Wm. McNeale List for 1778 of Joseph Brown Jr. John Jennes Joseph Jones & Moses Meader's Ministers Tax	–	7	9
Pd for two Books for the use of the Town, one for the Town Clark the other for Selectmen	1	10	–
Pd Jabez Dame Esqr a Note against the Town in	7	4	–
Pd Selectmen for making State List & Counterpart	3	12	–
for making Surveyors Lists & Dec. Surveyors	1	10	–
for making School Lists & Destricting the Schools	2	–	–
For taking an Inventory and making a return to the General Court	4	11	–
Selectmen Services throu the Year Settleing and Paying the School Destricts arranging Town Accounts &c	5	–	–
Writing Paper throu the Year	–	9	–
Pd an Abatement of Danl Rogers Taxes in Benjn Dames List for 1788	1	9	10
Pd the Auditors for 1793 their Services in full	1	4	–
Pd the Selectmen for runing & establishing the Line between Rochester & Barrington in 1793 in full	2	10	–
Pd the Selectmen for going to Durham to Search the Records	–	6	–

Remains in Collectors & Selectmens hands

	£	s	d
In Collector Paul Harfords hands for 1781	25	10	7
In Collector Thos. Roberts hands for 1787	81	17	8
In Collector James Hows hands for 1788 in Specie & School	49	15	7
In Collector Thos. Roberts hands for 1789 in Specie	166	4	7
In Collector Peter Cushing's hands for 1790	120	1	3
In Collector Hatevil Knight hands for 1792	147	14	2
In Collector Elijah Varneys hands for 1792	63	2	4
In Collector Jotham Nutes hands for 1793 State Tax	145	1	4
In Collector Danl Wingates hands for 1793 State Tax	134	19	4
In Selectmens hands in Notes Orders & in Indents	150	14	4

	£	s	d
In Collector Jotham Nutes hands for 1793 Parish List	56	17	10
In Coll. Daniel Wingates hands for 1793 Parish List	45	5	7
	£ 2544	12	6
In the Selectmens hands in Cash	15	2	8
	£ 2559	15	3

A true state of the Town's Account both Debt and Credit throu the Year and Presented to the Town this 31st Day of March 1794.

William Palmer
Richard Furber
Simon Torr } Selectmen

Having Cast the Counterpiece and Cast the foregoing Account and Examined the Same they appear to be well adjusted as they are handed to us by the Selectmen this 31st Day of March 1794

Jabez Dame
Jacob Hanson } Auditors

Voted to accept of the within Account as Read by the Clark in the Audience of the Meeting

Town

November ye 10th 1794 Receiv'd of Howard Hander
9) son two hundred Dallars and Indorced the same
on his Note of Land

Lt Richard Place Debtr to four Dollars pd to
Howard Handerson to be allow'd out of his acct
as overseer

Novembr 10th 1794 Receiv'd of Moses Young
Eleven Pounds Six Shilling & Eight pence
on Nutes Mortgage

Receiv'd of Mr Benjn Lame £15: 0: 0

Novembr 24th 1794 Receiv'd of Collectr Elijah
Varney the follow payments (viz)
Selectmens orders amounting to for 92 tax £21: 6: 0

Novembr 24th 1794 made the following settlement on
Mr John Nutes Mortgage (viz) for 86

allow'd an abatement of Ebenr Places taxes	£2: 3: 6½
allow'd Joseph Pearls Junr taxes abated	0: 11: 6
and abated Moses Drown's taxes	0: 7: 8
took Moses Young's & others Notes for	82: 6: 8
took up a Note given by former Selectmen for abateing the widow Barbers taxes on Intrest	17: 0

Decembr 8th 1794 Receiv'd of Collector Elijah
Varney £2: 4: 3

Jany 26th 1795 Receiv'd of Collectr Elijah
Varney the following payment (viz) in Cash £3: 17: 4
in orders Mr Havens & Mr Mains 3: 19: 4
total £ 7: 16: 8

February 2d 1795 Receiv'd of Collector Hatevil
Knight the following payment (viz) Cash £6: 0: 0

in Mr Havens orders	30: 19: 3
pd for Majr Furber for Services	2: 8: 2
pd for Collecting said 92 List	4: 0: 0
allow'd abatements in his List	6: 5: 7
Selectmens orders for School for 92 List	56: 0: 6
total	105: 13: 6

February 5th 1795 Receiv'd of Doctr James
How the following payment for 1788 tax

State Treasurers Receipt for	£209: 10: 6
Selectmens order	6: 10: 0
on Majr Furbers act	0: 12: 0
total	£ 216: 12: 6

and Likewise gave him a Receipt
for the abatements made in his
List amounting to in Certificates £24: 8: 0
and in Specie 11: 14: 1

10 March
Paid Zeblon Davis three Dollars on count
of a peace of Land for a Road through his Land
as prised by the Comitey - 0: 18: 0

March 14th 1795 made the following settlement with
Collector Daniel Wingate (viz)

in orders & former Receipts	£ 125: 4: 10
allow'd abatements for 1793 in full	6: 9: —
allow'd abatements for 1790	8: 8
His Receipt in Cash	48: 17: 6
which is Just the amount of his 1793 List	180: 5: 0

March 23 made the follow settlement with Collector
Anthony Perry viz — 1794 tax

Selectmens orders amounting to	£12: 1: 6
Mr Havens orders	7: 19: 2
in Cash	19: 6
total	21: 0: 2

March 24th 1795 gave a Receipt to Lt Richd Place
for £25: 11: 11 in part of his List for 1794 which
compleats the payment of his bill as overseer of the poor

Joseph Holmes	458	3.16.4	one in favor of John Bakker in full	3.16.4
Abner Hodgdon	286	2.7.8	one given out in favour of Abner Hodgdon for in part one in favour of Benjamin Page for in full	0.16.7 1.11.1 2.7.8
Docr James How	999	8.6.6	one in favour of Daniel [illegible] for [illegible] in full	8.6.6
Joseph [illegible]	534	4.9.0	An order in favor of Simeon Folsom for in full	4.9.0
Joseph Giles	287	2.5.4	Doct Josiah Mann two pound five shillings and four pence in full	2.5.4

Enoch Wingate	348	2..18..0	[illegible]
Richard Walker	513	4..3..6	one to Joseph Walker in full
Daniel Wingate	304	2..10..8	[illegible] in favour of Daniel Wingate

Pursuant to a vote of the Town of Rochester
We have examined the Towns accounts
and Col. Thos. Roberts Rate lists & Receipts for
the years 1785 and 1786 and after
mature Consideration are of Opinion
that his receipt for £61.17.10d ought
to be allowd towards his tax for 1787 &
that there remains due from him
fifty Seven pounds Ten Shillings for the year
1785 and £4.6.10 for 1786 according
to the face of his Lists & Warrants
Rochester 16 March 1795

57..10..0
4..6..10
£61..16..10

Aaron Wingate
James Howe
Richd Dame

Which Sum We the Subscribers have Consolidated
at Twenty one pounds fourteen shillings [illegible]

£21..14..0

Recd a Note for the sum

Aaron Wingate }
James Howe } Committee
Richd Dame }

William Palmer }
Richd Furber } Select men
Simon Torr }

Agreed to by Thos Roberts Coll

15 The Towns Account for 1794 Both Debt and Credit as Returnd March 30th 1795

Pr Credit

	£	s	d
In Collector Paul Harfords hands for 1781	25	10	7
In Collector Thomas Roberts hands for 1787	81	17	8
In Collector James Homs hands for 1788 in Specie & Certificates 499.15.7 which Consolidated	227	18	4
In Collector Thos Roberts hands for 1789 in Specie	166	4	7
In Collector Peter Cushings hands for 1790	120	1	3½
In Collector Hatevil Knights hands for 1792	147	14	2½
In Collector Elijah Varney's hands for 1792	63	2	4
In Collector Joatham Nutes hands for 1793	201	19	2
In Collector Daniel Wingale's hand for 1793	180	4	11
Received of Selectmen for 1793 in notes orders and 12/ in Indents	150	14	4
Received of Selectmen for 1793 in cash	15	2	8½
Rais'd in Collector Richd Places list for 1794 State tax	134	5	5
In Sd Places town list for 1794	49	17	10
Rais'd in Collector Anthony Peavys State list 1794	127	10	6
In Sd Peavy's town list for 1794	38	-	9
Received in full of the Mortgage on John Niles farm	115	14	5
Recd of David Twombly & Ensn Corson for Timber Sold them by vote of Town & appraisd	16	4	-
Recd of Joseph & Beard Plumer for Timber Cutt on School Lott as returnd by Committee	12	-	5
Recd of Dodavah Scates for Timber cut on School Lott Settled by Selectmen	-	12	-
Recd for Interest on Notes of hand		18	-
Recd for Rent on town Lotts for 1794	1	19	-
Recd and to be paid of Saml Palmer for timber Cut on School Lott as returnd by the Committe	14	8	-
	1892	-	1

The Selectmen are to pay the whole bill of cost on John Niles Mortgage & Expences that shall arise thereon

16 The way Sd Money has been laid out & paid

To Pr Debt

	£	s	d
Paid the State Treasurer in full for the tax for 1788	315	13	
Pd State Treasurer in part for the tax for 1789	84	18	
Pd County Treasurer in full for 1792	14		
Pd Revd Joseph Haven's Salary in full to March ye 26. 1795	126	19	4
Pd Amos Places Destrict School master for 1792	–	10	6
pd Eleazer Hodgdon; for paying Dest School master 1792	—	3	-
pd Benjamin Furbers Destrict School master 1792	2	12	5
pd Samuel Gray's Destrict School master 1792	1	3	1
pd Ensn Ichabod Corson's Destrict School master 1792	2	10	2
pd Thos Davis & others for paying their Destrict School for 1792	3	16	6
pd Mark Miller & others for paying their Destrict School 1792	2	15	—
pd Richd Walker & others for paying their Dest School 1792	3	7	2
pd Thos Pinkham Destrict School master for 1792	3	13	4
pd Capt Daniel Hayes Destrict School master for 1792	3	17	—
pd Wm French Darling for keeping School in Paul Jewetts Destrict for 1792	–	13	—
pd Capt Beard Plumer's Destrict School master 1792	4	17	5
pd Deacn Saml Plumers Destrict School master 1792	2	13	9
pd Edmund Tebbetts Destrict School master 1792	3	7	2
pd Ensn Ichd Corsons Destrict School master in full 1792	2	10	2
pd Jabez Dame Esqr Destrict School master for 1793	4	3	9
pd Capt Jeshurun Allen Destrict School master 1793	2	0	4
pd Anthony Peavys Destrict School master for 1793	3	10	6
pd Ebenr Horn Junr Destrict School master for 1793	4	4	-
pd Benja H. Evans Destrict School master for 1793	-	13	5
pd Lt Saml Downings Destrict School for 1793	4	5	
pd Joseph Joyles Destrict School for 1793	2	12	9
pd Saml Palmer Dist School master for 1793	5	0	-
pd Jonathan French Dest School master 1793	-	9	—
pd Lt Wm Wingate Dest School master 1793	3	5	
pd James Knowles Esq Dest School master 1793	2	–	11
pd Ensn David Leighton's Dest school mast. 1793	4	7	8
pd James Knowles Esq Destrict in full for 1793	3	5	11
pd Moses Jennes Destt School master for 1793	2	14	-
pd Benja Furber's Destt School master for 1793	2	11	8
pd Benja Meders Destrict School master 1793	-	9	—
pd Moses Jennes Dest School master for 1793	2	3	-
pd Paul Jennes Destrict School master 1793	2	6	9
pd Israel Hams, Destrict School master for 1793	5	7	6
pd Saml Grays Destrict School master 1793	1	7	[illegible]
pd Capt Daniel McDuffee's Dest School master 1793	3	10	[illegible]

	£	s	d
Paid Saml Leighton Destrict School for 1793	3	3	
Paid Lt Joshua Holmes Destrict Schoolm 1793	2	14	9
Paid Paul Jewett Dest School master 1793	3	4	1
Paid Col Thos Roberts Dest Schoolmaster 1793	1	3	–
pd Col John McDuffee Dest Schoolmaster 1793	7	13	4
pd Col Thos Roberts Dest School master 1793	2	8	–
pd Capt Beard Plumer Dest School master 1793	5	16	6
pd Col John Goodwin's Dest Schoolmaster 1793	7	10	–
pd Capt Joshua Allen's Dest Schoolmaster 1793	2	8	
pd Ensn Ichabod Corsons Destrict School master 1793	2	–	1½
pd Decn Saml Plumer Destrict School master 1793	1	–	–
pd Richd Walker Dest School master for 1793	4	14	10
pd Caleb Wakehams Dest Schoolmaster for 1793	3	3	8
pd Moses Horn's Dest School master for 1793	2	7	5
pd Decn Saml Plumer Schoolmaster 1793	3	7	
pd Ichabod Hayes Dest School master 1793	1	19	5
pd Mordecai Varney Dest Schoolmaster 1793	3	15	6
pd Col John McDuffee Dest School master 1794	6	17	
pd Col John Goodwin's Dest School master 1794	1	10	
pd Col John Goodwin's Dest Schoolmaster 1793	1	10	–
pd Danl Wingates Dest Schoolmaster 1794	2	10	8
pd Capt Moses Roberts Dest School master 1794	2	13	6
pd Capt Saml Nutes Dest Schoolmaster 1794	4	16	4
pd Benja Furbers Dest School master 1794	2	13	5
Paid Selectmen for making School lists & Deducting Schools	2		
Do. for making Ratelists & Counterparts —	3	12	– 4
Do. for making Surveyors lists & Destributing of Surveyors	1	10	
Do. for Writing Warrants for 2d highway tax	–	18	
Do. for taking Inventory for 1794 —	2	8	–
~~Paid for Writing [illegible]~~			
To £15 :17 : presedents Order sold at 15/on the pound which makes a Difference of	3	15	4
Paid Dr James How for services as Assessor 1794	–	9	–
pd an Abatement in Dr Hows Nonresident list 1788	–	14	3
pd Jacob Ellis for a road thro' part of Varney Lot	1	15	–
pd Col David Place as a Committee for laying out a road on the neck		6	–
pd Col Thos Roberts for Collecting Tax in 1787	3	–	–
Allowd the abatement in Col Roberts List 1787	20	10	8
pd Dr How a Surveyor running line between Rochester and Barrington	1	10	
[illegible] Hayes for services as Lott layer 1793	1	16	

	£	s	d
Paid Jacob Hanson for Supplying Poor in 1793	–	6	0
pd Moses Horn Jr his bill as overseer of poor 93	1	13	10
pd John Rindge for Supplying poor in 1793	–	7	6
pd Capt Danl Hayes his services as Lottlayer 1794	2	2	–
pd Constable John Bergen for carrying poor out of town 1794	–	12	–
pd Dr How ~~the Loss he sustained~~ [illegible] up the Certificate part of his List as reported by a Committee appd for that purpose	8	5	9
pd Dr How the poundage that he pd on the abatements in his list. 1788	–	8	6
Paid an abatement made on Col Roberts Non resident list 1786	1	1	
Paid Col Palmer to redeem a piece of Land illegally sold at Lt Richd Places vendue to Wm Hendersons in 1784	9	–	–
Paid the Expences of the Referees settling with said Palmer	–	18	
Paid Jeremy Folsom the balance of his account for going to Boston for the Town	2	7	2
Paid John Whitham for a road through his land		15	
Paid an Order given by former Selectmen to Enoch Hoyt for carrying a poor child out of Town	–	12	
Paid John Brown for making a Coffin for Nich Hammond		8	
Paid Haley Knight for Collecting taxes in 1792	4		
Allowd the abatements in Collector Haley Knights list for 1792	8	17	7
Paid John Baker for Supplying poor 1793	–	5	
pd Ensn Ichd Corsons account as Lott layer for 1793	1	16	–
pd Ensn Corson's Acct for paying James Coleman for haling lime from Dover for town use	–	7	6
pd Ebenr Horn for Supplying poor in 1793	–	6	
pd the Committee for Dividing the town	3		
pd Lt Anthony Peavy for timber for bridges		10	6
pd Gilbert French for a road through his Land	3		
pd James Horn for a Road through his land	3	18	
pd Majr Perkins the expences letting out town lotts	–	5	6
pd the Expences of the Committee Dividing the town	1	14	6
pd the Expences of Lemuel Wakeham at Maj Perkins	–	8	
pd Hunkin Colbath in full for a road thro' his land	3		
pd Saml Leighton for a road thro' his land in full	6	–	
pd Josiah Main for Drawing & returning 19 Juror	1	18	
pd Josiah Main for returns for State & County Officers in full 1793 —	1	12	
pd Jonathan Dame his account as a Surveyor 1793	1	2	6
pd Elijah Varney for Collecting taxes in 1792	6	12	
pd Zebulon Dame for a road thro' his land in full	–	18	
pd Majr Furber for services as Lott Layer for 1792 & Assessor for 1792 in full	2	19	
pd Esqr Wingate as a Committee in settling with Col Thos Roberts		12	
Paid Josiah Main in full for his services as town Clerk in 1794	4		
pd Daniel Wingate for collecting taxes for 1793 in full	[illegible]		

	£	s	d
Paid Dependence Bickford for timber for Swing glass bridge	2	8	
pd Lt Anthony Peavy for a road thro his land	3	–	
pd Mercy Main in ~~part~~ of a Note against the town	7	6	2
pd John Swain for a road thro his land in full	1	10	
pd Moses Hayes Jr for supplying the State with Beef in 1782	3	6	
pd the Overseers of the poor's Bill in full for 1794	47	4	1
pd Constable Elijah Varney for warning poor out of the town	–	14	–
pd Abatements in John Nutes List for 1785 and 1786 in full	4	18	9½
Gave up a Note of hand against Jacob Chamberlin which appears to have been paid but handed to us as good	2	19	6
Paid Richd Dame's Account in full for keeping School, Services as Lotlayer and otherwise	11	10	
Allowed a Receipt of 61.17.10 in Specie to Col Roberts list for 1787 which sum was credited in his List for 1785 as certificates which makes a Difference of —	40	2	10
Allowed the abatements in Dr Hows List for 1785	23	18	1
Allowd the abatements in Danl Wingate List for 1790	–	8	8
Allowd the abatements in Collector E. Varneys List for 1792	5	7	11½
Allowd the abatements in Collector D. Wingate List for 1793	6	9	
Paid the Selectmen for time & Expences in taking care of School Lott appraising timber &c	2	2	
pd Selectmen for running out the Road from New Durham road to the Stenrod road by Land of ~~John~~ Bickford &c & paying Surveyor	–	18	
pd Selectmen for a Journey up to Gilmantown to prevent presentment on bad roads		18	
pd Majr Furber for 200 Brick for parsonage house		6	
pd for writing paper thro the year		9	
pd Selectmen for writing & Exchanging 4 Deeds		7	
Do for writing warrants to warn 25 poor out of town	–	12	
pd Major Furber as a Committee man procuring Train field	–	18	
pd Jacob Hanson his Account as Committee man 1793 &c	1	4	
pd the Auditors for their Services in 1794 in full	1	10	
pd the Selectmen for their Services through the year paying School Districts settling with Collectors arranging town accounts and so forth in full	5	–	
pd Wm Palmer time & Expences searching the records at Exeter to find Moses Hayes Jr receipt for Beef	–	9	
pd State Treasurer in part for the tax for 1790	19	2	6
pd Jabez Dame Esqr District Schoolmaster for 1792	–	14	3
pd Capt David Leighton District School for 1794	4	9	–
pd Joseph Thompson Jr for a Road thro his Land in full	1	4	
pd Col David Place for timber for Walkers bridge so called	2	6	6
pd Time & Expences waiting on the Committee rectifying mistakes in Col Roberts List 1787	1	16	
pd Selectmen for writing Collectors bonds & making [illegible]	–	12	–
pd Dr How as a Committee man settling with Col Roberts	–	12	
pd Wm Palmer for Journey to Exeter to settle with Treasurer	–	12	
	1069	0	9t

Outstanding in Collectors & Selectmens hands	£	s	d
In Collector Paul Harfords hands for 1781	25	10	7
In Col Thomas Roberts hands for 1789	74	10	–
In Collector Peter Cushings hands for 1790	120	1	3½
In Collector Joatham Nutes hands for 1793	101	19	2
In Lt Richd Place's hands for 1794	148	5	11
In Lt Anthony Peavy's hands for 1794	144	11	–
In Selectmens hands in Notes & 12 pr Indents	173	1	
Total	787	19	0
Cash on hand	1069	0	9t
Town Debt	1856	19	9
Town Credit	1892	0	1
More cash on hand	35	0	3½
	1	10	
	36	10	3½

A True State of the Towns accounts both Debt and Credit through the year and presented this 30th Day of march 1795

William Palmer }
Richd Furber } Selectmen
Simon Torr }

Having cast the Counter-pins and the foregoing accounts and Examined the same and they appear to be well adjusted ~~[illegible]~~ Except 9/ too much pd Capt Danl Hayes as Lotlayer in 1794.

Jacob Hanson }
Richd Dame } Auditors

Voted to accept of the above Account as was read by the Clerk in the Audience of the Meeting

---

Rochester November 24th 1794

Received of the Selectmen of Rochester their receipt in full of all Lists committed me to collect and in full of all Abatements made on said Lists & do hereby promise not to call for any more abatements & engage to Indemnify the town from all Suits Actions or expences that may arise by virtue of any Lists heretofore committed me to collect as witness my hand

John Nute

A true Copy —
Att. Richd Dame

April 27th 1795 made the following Settlement with Collect^r Jotham Nute — (viz)

Selectmens orders amounting to £9: 19: 9

Mr Havens orders 2: 8.

total £ 12 : 7 : 9

June 6th 1795
Made a Settlement with Collector Anthony [illegible] as follows

Select Men's orders amounting to £ 14. 8. 9

in Parson Havens Order 2. 3

Rec^d in Cash 4. 5. 6

18. 16. 0

June 6th 1795 Made Settlement with Jotham Nute as follows Selectmens Order 2. 2. 0

Joseph Havens Order 2. 0. 10½

Rec^d in Cash 1. 4. 7

£5. 7. 5½

July 11th Rec^d of Collector Jotham Nute in Cash 12 Dollars 3. 12. 0

Octr 6. made a Settlement with Peter Cushing and made abatements to the amount of 8. 13. 5

and in Orders 2. 8

Novr 26 made a Settlement with Co^l Thos Roberts and Rec^d in Treasurers Receipts & Selectmens 40. 7. 11

Joseph Jackson's Order 2. 6. 8

Allowed Abatements for 1789 5. 17. 9

for Copying & Advertizing nonresidents list 0. 15. 7

Allowed the Sum rec^d of [illegible] of nonresidents Taxes for 1789 & not by him allowed to Roberts 5. 8[illegible]

Rec^d in Cash 15 Dollars 4. 10. 0

And took his Note for 22. 15 in full for his List 1789 54. 2. 9

Novr 31 Settled with Collector Richd Place

rec^d in County Treasurers Receipts £9. 6. 0

In [illegible] Orders 34. 18.

Cash 6

Gave a Receipt for 1794 50. 4

[illegible] Rec^d of [illegible] Young 40 Dollars 12. 0. 0

Novr 25 The Remainder being 60 Doll. 18. 0. 0

And the Interest thereon 1. 11. 6

31. 11. 6

Jany 25. 1796 Then made a Settlement with Col Anthony Peavy in Orders &c 18. 0. 3

Jany 25. 1796 Then Settled with Co^l Richd Place and Rec^d in Orders 8. 12. 8

In Cash 5. 15. 4

Precept from the State Treasurer for 1795 — 495.

Of which Lt Place is to pay 250

Danl Wingate 125

James Hayes 120. 44 — 495.

March 21 Rec^d of Daniel Wingate Dol. Cts.

in Cash 97. 35

In Selectmens Orders 52. 84

p^d Maj^r [illegible] 14. 75

Gave a Receipt for 164. 94

March 21st of Lt Place in Specie 8 Specie Order 61 Dol^s & 8 Cents in part of his List 1795

March 21st Received of Lt Richd Place Dol. Cents

in Cash 56: 27

Selectmens orders 29: 78

D^o for repairing Parsonage house 21 56

overseers of poors bill 38 14

Gave a Rec^t for 1795 List 144 75

for Collecting 30 53

176. 08

March 22 1796 Rec^d of Anthony Peavy £ £

In Specie Orders & for Collecting his List 22 6

In Abatements 3 6

Also in Cash 7 1

And gave a Receipt for 32 14

March 22 Rec^d of Peter Cushing Doll. cent.

State Treasurers Receipt 125. 17

Selectmens Note 11

136. 17

March 25th 1796 Then Settled with Ens^n James C. Hayes Doll. Cents

Capt Plumer Dist School in full 26 98

Capt Plumer Order for Road 10 —

p^d State Treasurer 96 —

Cash 62 15

p^d Abatement in his List 1795 1 63

for Collecting [illegible] 10 [illegible]

And gave a Receipt in full for his List & for 211 Doll. & 76 Cents 211 76

25 Rec^d of Jotham Nute Doll. Cts.

D^o [illegible] Abatement of Jo^n [illegible] Tax 1788 2 —

for Warning poor out of Town in 1794 in full 8 —

In Cash 19 17

And gave a Receipt for 29 17

Jonathan Heard Jr	1	·	1	1	·	4	·	·	·	·	·	·	·	·	·	·	·	·
Richmond Henderson	1	·	2	·	·	·	·	·	·	·	·	·	·	·	·	·	·	·
Ensn Nathaniel Hayes	1	2	·	1	1	1	1	·	·	·	·	·	1	2	·	12	50	2
John Hammlet	·	·	2	·	·	·	1	·	·	·	·	·	1	3	12	·	·	·
Moses Hammet	1	2	1	1	1	·	·	·	·	·	·	·	·	·	·	·	64	·
Ephraim Hammet	1	·	·	·	·	·	·	·	·	·	·	·	·	·	·	·	·	·
Capt Alexander Hodgdon	2	4	3	1	·	2	1	·	1	·	·	t	1½	15	14	35	190	·
Joseph Heard 3d	1	·	·	·	2	·	·	·	·	·	·	·	1	·	12	·	65	·
Stephen Heard	1	·	1	1	·	1	·	·	·	2	·	·	·	·	·	·	·	·
Nathaniel Horn Junr	·	·	2	·	1	1	·	·	·	·	·	·	·	2	8	12	30	12
Paul Harford's Son	1	·	·	·	·	·	·	·	·	·	·	·	·	·	·	·	·	·
Richard Hayes	1	·	2	·	4	·	·	·	·	·	·	·	2	6	8	10	98	·
Tristram Heard	·	2	1	1	1	·	1	·	·	·	·	·	3	6	20	10	·	·
Joseph Hanson	1	·	·	·	·	·	·	·	·	·	·	·	·	·	·	10	·	·
Timothy Heard	1	·	1	·	1	·	·	·	·	·	·	·	1	3	·	10	40	·
Parker Hopkinson	2	·	1	·	·	·	·	1	·	·	·	·	·	·	·	·	·	·
Reuben Hunniford	1	·	·	·	·	·	·	·	·	·	·	·	·	·	·	·	·	·
Ebenezer Horn	1	·	1	·	·	·	·	·	·	·	·	·	·	·	·	·	·	·
Joshua Hayes	1	·	·	·	·	·	·	·	·	·	·	·	·	·	·	·	·	·
Joseph Haynes	1	·	·	·	·	·	·	·	·	·	·	·	·	·	·	·	·	·
Samuel Ham	1	·	1	·	2	·	·	·	·	·	·	·	·	·	·	·	·	·
John Hanson Jr	1	·	·	·	·	·	·	·	·	·	·	·	·	·	·	·	·	·
Enoch Hoit Junr	1	·	·	·	·	·	·	·	·	·	·	·	·	·	·	·	·	·
Theodore Hodgdon	1	·	·	·	·	·	·	·	·	·	·	·	·	·	·	·	·	·
James Horn of Dover	·	·	·	·	·	·	·	·	·	·	·	·	·	·	24	·	62	·
Joseph Heard Junr	2	2	2	1	2		1						1½	2	·	10	45	·
Paul Jennes	1	·	2	4	2	2	1	·	·	·	·	·	2	7	8	10	29	·
William Jennes	1	·	3	2	3	1	1	·	·	1	·	·	3	7	16	20	17	1½
Moses Jennes	1	·	1	2	·	2	1	·	·	·	·	·	1	4	8	10	55	·
Aaron Jennes	1	·	2	2	·	2	1	·	·	·	·	·	1	4	8	10	55	·
David Jennes	1	2	2	1	1	3	1	·	·	·	·	·	1	5	4	·	60	·
Joseph Giles	1	2	2	1	3	1	·	·	·	·	1	·	3	5	8	15	118	·
Isaiah Jenkins	1	·	3	2	2	·	1	·	·	·	·	·	1½	3	8	10	55	·
Jonathan Jennes	1	2	2	·	·	·	·	·	·	·	·	·	1	2	4	·	26	·
Samuel Jennes	1	·	·	2	·	·	1	·	·	·	·	·	1	1	·	·	59	·
Daniel Jennes	2	·	2	2	4	3	1	·	·	·	·	·	2½	6	12	10	8	·
Wm Jennes Junr	1	·	·	·	·	·	·	·	·	·	·	·	·	·	·	·	·	·

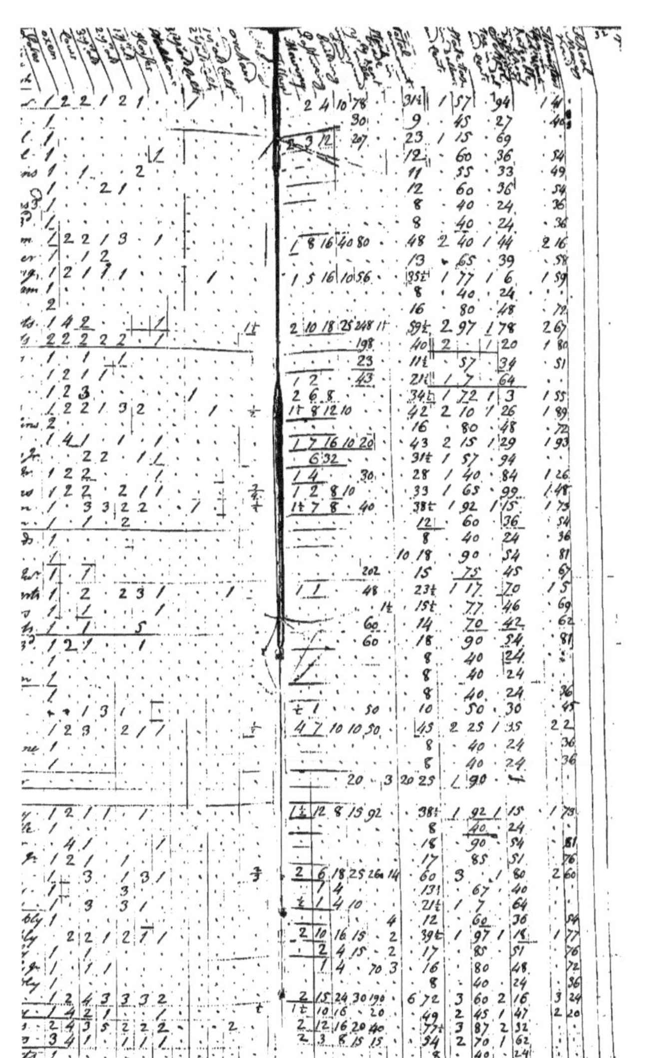

…y and …hant for Hali[illegible] first Parish	Polls, Oxen, Cows, stock (as entered)	[illegible]	[illegible]	Total	[illegible]	[illegible]	[illegible]
…l Tebbets	2 3 2 1 . 1 . 1	2 6	12 10 15	49	2 45	1 17	
…d Tebbets	2 2 2 . 1	1 4	12 15 10	38	1 90	1 14	
…el Tebbets	1 2 2 . 1 1	2 8	10 10 10	39	1 95	1 17	
… Tebbets	1 . 1 . 2		15	11½	57	34	
… Tebbets	1 2 1		16	16½	82	49	74
…s Tebbets	1 . 2			12	60	36	
…ezer Tebbets	1 2 1			16	80	48	72
… Tebbets	1			8	40	24	
…d Tebbets Jr.	1 2			14	70	42	
…h Tebbets Berwick		1 6	8	11½	57		
… Varney	1 . 1 . 4	1 4	4 . 26 1½	28	1 12	67	
…h Varney	2 . 2 1 . 1 1	2 2	6 15 48 1½ 2	38	1 92	1 15	
…zer Varney	1 . 1 . 3 . 1	2 5	12 12 60 1½	32½	1 62	97	
… Varney Jr.	1 2 . 2		61	18½	92	55	
…s Varney	1 2 . 2 1 1 2	2 5	6 10 20 1	33	1 65	99	
…iah Varney	1			8	40	24	
…s Varney	1 2 3 . 5 1 1	1 4	8 10 36	40	2	1 20	
…as Varney 3d	. 1			2	10	6	
… Varney 3d	1 . 1			10	50	30	
…las Varney	1 . . . 1			10	50	30	
…h Varney Jr.	1			8	40	24	
…as Varney Jr.	1 2 1 . 2 . 1	1 2	4 . 40	27½	1 37	82	
… Varney Dover		1 2	38	4	20		
…l Varney Dover			4 . 12	2	10		
…n Wentworth	. 1 . . 1	½	. 15 16	9	45	27	40
… Wentworth	1 2 . 3 2 2 1	1½ 9	16 10 40	44½	2 22	1 33	1 98
… Wentworth	1 . 3		74 . 8	24	1 20	72	1 8
… Wentworth	1 . 1 3 . . 1	1½ 7		27	1 35	81	1 21
…el Wingate	. 2 1 . 1 3	2 12	16 15	32½	1 62	94	1 46
… Witherill	1 . 1 5 . 1 1 . . 1	2 3	12	34	1 70	1 2	1 53
…e Willand	1 2 2 1 . 2	1	39	22½	1 12	67	1 1
…d Wingate	1 2 3 2 2 1 1	1 2 12	16	31½	2 57	1 54	2 31
…n Wallingford	1 2 2 2 . 1 1	¾ 1 4	12 10	34½	1 72	1 3	1 55
… Wallingford	1			8	40	24	36
…im Walson	1			8	40	24	36
…r Whitehouse	1 . 1 . 2			12	60	36	54
…my Whitehouse	1 . 1 . . 1	½	4 . . 2	18	90	54	81
…er Whitehouse	2 . 2	¼	4 10 10	23½	1 17	70	
…a Whitehouse	1 . . 1			9½	47	28	42
…h Waldron Dover	1 . . 1	½ 1½ 4	8 10 86	15½	77		
… Whitham	1 . . 2 1	1 1	4 . 18	14½	72	43	64
…n Whitehouse	1 . 1 1		26	12	60	36	54
… Whitehouse	1 . 1			10	50	30	45
…a Wiggins	1			8	40	24	36
… Walson	2 . 1			18	90	54	81
… Waldron	1 . 1 2 2 . . 1	1 2	4 . 226	27	1 35	81	1 2[illegible]
…a Wingate	1 . 1 . 1			11	55	33	49
… Wingate	2 . 1			18	90	54	81
…s Wentworth 3d	1 . 2 3 3 2 1	1 8	8 12 12	38½	1 92	1 15	1 73
… Willand	1			8	40	24	36
… Willand	1			8	40	24	36
…Witherill Jr.	1 . 1 . . 1			14	70	42	62

Doormages in the first parish as agreed on for 1795.

	Rate		
Squamanagonnick		Jabez Dame Esqr. Tanner	4
Upper Sawmill	18	Hatevil Knight Stock	6
Corn Mill	24	Maj^r. Silv^r. S. Pratt D^o.	6
Lower Sawmill	12	Parker Hopkinson	12
Norwayplains		John Kent Saddler	2
Upper Sawmill	18	John Rindge Stock	10
Cushings Sawmill	24	Capt. Saml. Storer Stock & [illegible]	20
Cushings Cornmill	12	Joseph Hanson Stock	8
Nat^l. Horn's Cornmill	12	John Odiorne Saddler	3
M^c.Duffee & Dames Fulling m^l	20	Josiah Wentworth Bl^k.sm	8
Garlands Sawmill	18	Anthony Whitehouse Tan^r	2
Jacob Hanson Bl^k.smith	3	Elijah Varney tanner	2
Peter Horn Bl^k.sm^th	6	Simon Torr tanner	6
Caleb Jackson Tanner	4	Joshua Lane Stock	4

The above Doormages agreed on by the Assessors and Selectmen in 1795 and Entered with other Estate in the foregoing List of Taxes —

Drawbacks from foregoing List	State Dol.	State cents	School Dol.	School cents	Minist. Dol.	Minist. cents
Peter Horn's Doormage taken off	-	30	-	18	-	27
Parker Hopkinson overrated one horse	-	20	-	12	-	18
Ezekiel Tebbets Deceas^d	1	95	1	17	-	
William Henderson Overrated	—	15	—	9	—	13
L^t. Edward Rollins 1 ox Lost		15		9		13
Stephen Wentworth 1 Cow lost		10		6		9
James N. Hodgdon's parish Tax						45
Abraham Pearl overrated 1 horse		20		12		18
Wid^o. Martha Pike's parish Tax					1	50
Benj^a. Roberts One horse Lost		20		12		18
John Nute 1 Cow Lost		10		6		[illegible]
Elijah Whitham's parish Tax						64
Moses Hayes 3^d. parish Tax						58
Henry Tebbets Dec^d		40	-	24	-	36
Stephen Downs Dec^d		40	—	24	—	36
Nathaniel Horn^s Mill rated		60	-	36	-	52
George Hayes lost a horse		20	-	12	-	18
John Roberts 3^d. parish Tax	—	—	—	—	—	81
Jo^nathan place overrated 5		25		15		22
James Coleman for his brother	1	92	1	15	1	73
Reuben Cook Dec^d		40		24		36
Maj^r. Silv^r. S. Pratt remov^d		90		54		81
Jacob Quimby remov^d		80		48		72
Joshua Ellis a poor		50		30		49
Josiah Folsom a poor		60		36		54
Stephen Tebbets a poor		40		24		
Hezekiah Clortman overrated		5		3		
Tristram Heard overrated		25		15		22½
The foregoing allowed March 21.1797	11	2	6	61	11	65

Richard Place

Warrants for Collecting the foregoing Lists

State of Newhamp^r. Strafford Ss. } To Leiu^t. Richard Place Collector of Taxes for the Lower parish in the Town of Rochester for the year 1795 — Greeting —

By virtue of a Law of this State Directing Selectmen to raise money for the Support of Schools. And in pursuance of a precept from the Treasurer of said State to raise money for a State Tax and in pursuance of Sundry votes of this Town to lay out and purchase roads. For the Support of the poor and other Town Expenses Through the year 1795

(L.S.) You are hereby required in the name of the State aforesaid to Levy and Collect of all the persons named in the foregoing List herewith Committed you to Collect. the Sums Set to their names in Silver or gold or in orders drawn by the Selectmen of Rochester. And you are hereby Directed to pay the the State Treasurer the sum of Two hundred & fifty Dollars. by the last Day of December next. and the whole of the remaining Sum in said list to the Selectmen by the Twentieth Day of March next. And if any person or persons shall neglect or refuse to pay their Taxes herein assessed. after Legal warning or notice you are to take the Same by Distraint and Sale as the Law Directs and for your Lawful proceedings this shall be your Sufficient Warrant Given under our hands and Seals in Rochester this 11th. Day of July 1795

Rich^d. Dame
Rich^d. Furbush
W^m. Palmer

Select men of Rochester } & Assessors

State of Newhamp^r. Strafford Ss. } To Leiu^t. Richard Place One of the Collectors of Taxes for the Town of Rochester for the year 1795 Greeting

By virtue of Sundry votes of the town of Rochester for raising money for the Support of the Gospel & other parish Expenses —

(L.S.) You are hereby required in the name of said State to Levy and Collect of all persons named in the foregoing List herewith Committed you to Collect the Sums Set to their names in Dollars and Cents and pay the same in Cash or parson Havens Orders to the Selectmen in office by the first Day of March next Ensuing And if any person or persons shall neglect or refuse to pay their said taxes after Legal warning or notice you are to take the same by Distraint and Sale as the Law Directs & for your Lawful proceedings this Shall be your Sufficient warrant Given under our hands & Seals in Rochester this 29th. Day of September 1795

Rich^d. Furbush
Willm. Palmer

Select men of Rochester } & Assessors

Rochester May 5th 1797 Then we the Subscribers Richard Furbush Jr. and Rich^d. Dame Selectmen of Rochester Tendered Ten Dollars to Dependance Stafford in full for a Road laid out by a Committee Round Sandy Hill So called below his house Tendered in presence of Howard Henderson Elijah Varney and Leiu^t. Samuel Downing which Sum s^d. Dependance Declined taking

Richard Dame
Rich^d. Furbush Jr. } Selectmen

No. 4 William Jennes	450	13.50	[illegible] pd March 1799
No. 5 Capt. Samuel Nute	577	17.32	Bar'd pass't Nute Dols. 17.32 cents in full and Israel Ham [illegible] the List
No. 6 Ensn. Ichabod Corsen	572	17.16	May 1 1797 [illegible] Tebbets [illegible] for [illegible] Dollars by Direction of the Committee [illegible] paid Benj. Tebbets by Directors order
No. 7 Capt. Joshua Allen	462½	13.87	pd Micah Allen the Cash in full March 21 1796 By order of the Committee who [illegible] the List
No. 8 Col. John Goodwin	845	22.10	an order Given to Captn Shannon

No.	Name		Amount	Payment	
No. 7	Samuel Gray.		5..20	Paid five Dollars and twenty Cents to Samuel Mills in full	5
No. 8	Joseph Holmes.		7..9	February the 18d 1797 then Given an order to John Brock for four Dollars fifty three Cent which is in full for Joseph Holmes District and John Murrays	4
No. 9.	John Murrey.		9..53	one Given out for twelve Dollars part for Joseph Holmes District joyntly out of Both — —	12
No. 10.	Edmund Tebbets.		11..61	an order in favour of Edmund Tebbets for Eleven Dollars and Sixty one Cent in full — — — — —	11
No. 11.	David French.		12..18	January the 19 1797 one order Given to Ebenr. French for Twelve Dollars and Eighteen Cents in full. — — —	12
No. 12.	Samuel Lighton.		7..36	January 30d 1797 an order to Jonathan [illegible] for Seven Dollars thirty six Cents in full —	7

No. 4 Joshua Harford	13.6	order given to Levy Jones for
No. 5 Enoch Wingate	12.15	paid Enoch Wingate for keeping School
No. 6 James Berry	14.22	March 19th 1799 Paid by Benj Staler by the Committees order for paying them Dam'd
~~Settled~~		
12		

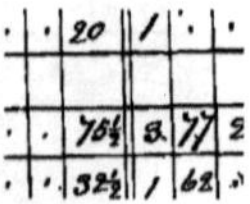

.	.	20	1	.	.
.	.	76½	3	77	2
.	.	32½	1	62	[illegible]

.	74	13	70	2	22	1	89
.	2½	.	.	.	.	.	6
.	27½	1	37	.	82	.	68
.	28	1	40	.	84	.	70
.	28	1	40	.	84	.	70
.	24	1	20	.	72	.	60
.	18½	.	92	.	55	.	46
.	8	.	40	.	24	.	20
			40		24		20
.	20½	1	2	.	61	.	.
.	15	.	75	.	45	.	37
.	27	1	35	.	81	.	6[illegible]

1	·	2	· ·	3	4	1	·	·	·	·	·	1	5	12	10	10A
1	·	3	2	·	1	1	·	·	·	·	·	1	6	12	10	80
1	·	·	·	1	1	1	·	·	1	·	·	1	V	4	10	34

Samuel Richards Jr	4	Places Sawmill	16
Jonas C. March (Blackfs)	8	Waldrons Cornmill	8
Benjamin Jones Blacksmith	3	Holmes Cornmill	12

The above Damages Listed in the foregoing List with the Tax [illegible] as agreed on by the Assessors & Selectmen

Drawbacks in 2d Parish	State		School		Parish	
Benjamin Furber overrated 4		20	—	12	—	10
Paul Demerit overrated 11		55	—	33	—	
Alexand Berry Lost 3y old 1t		7		4		3
Charles Knight Lost 1 Cow		16		6		5
Samuel Leighton poll Tax	1	2	—	61	—	
James Runnels for building bridge	1	30	-	78		
Chandler Peavy	—	40	—	24		
	3	64	7	18		18
[illegible] 30th 1797 then settled	7	18				
[illegible] Wingate [illegible] dollars	5	82				
[illegible] John Gray Junr						38
William Allard						40
Alexander Berry						36
Samuel Beck						30
John Beck						25
Samuel Drown						78
Ebenezer Horn Jr						80
Samuel Hammons						25
William Horn						60
Enoch Horn						35
Joseph Horn						27
Daniel Kimball						20
Joseph Leighton						73
Andrew Leighton						66
Hanson Libbey						20
James Rand						22
Joseph Young						30
Allowed March 20th 1798					7	05

Errore [illegible] Anthony Peavy

State of Newhampshire } To Daniel Wingate one of the Collectors for
Strafford Ss. } the Town of Rochester for the year 1795 Greeting

By virtue of the Law of this State Directing the Selectmen to raise money for the Support of Schools & other necessary affairs and in pursuance of a precept from the Treasurer of this State Directing the town to raise a Sum of money for the State. You are hereby Directed required in the name of the State of Newhampshire to Levy & Collect of all the persons named in the foregoing List herewith Committed you to collect the Sums set to their names in Dollars & cents or in orders Drawn by the Select men of Rochester. And you are Directed to pay the State Treasurer one hundred & twenty five Dollars by the first Day of December next and the remainder by the Twentieth Day of march One thousand seven hundred & Ninety six to the Select men in Office. And if any person or persons Shall neglect or refuse to pay their taxes after Legal warning you are to take the Same by Distraint & sale as the Law Directs and for your Lawful proceedings this Shall be your Sufficient Warrant. Given under our hands & Seals in Rochester this 27th Day of June 1795

(L.S.)

Richd Dame
Richd Furber Jr } Select men of Rochester
Willm Palmer } Assessors

State of Newhampshire } To Lt Anthony Peavy one of the
Strafford Ss } Collectors of the Town of Rochester for the year 1795 Greeting

By virtue of Sundry votes of the Town of Rochester for raising money for the Support of the Gospel and other parish Expences. You are hereby required to Levy and Collect of all persons named in the foregoing List herewith Committed you to Collect the Sums set to their names in Dollars & cents and pay the same in Cash or Select mens Orders to the Selectmen in Office by the first Day of March next Insuing. And if any person or persons Shall neglect or refuse to pay their said Taxes after Legal warning you are to take the same by Distraint & Sale as the Law Directs and for your Lawful proceedings this Shall be your Sufficient Warrant. Given under our hands & Seals in Rochester this 29th Day of September AD 1795.

(L.S.)

Richd Furber Jr } Select men Rochester
Willm Palmer } Assessors

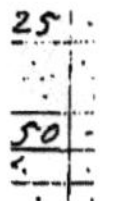

.	55
1	55
.	70
.	62

… assess'd in the		3d Parish in 1795	
… Stock in Trade	8	S. Palmers Sawmill ..	20
…d Stock &c ..	3	Ed. J. Palmers Sawmill	18
…h Stock &c ..	2	Watsons Sawmill ..	16
…mill	24	P. Jewells Sawmill ..	16
…n mill ..	24	P. Jewells Corn mill ..	8

…ade in the foregoing List	State Dol.	State cent	School Dol.	School cent	Parish Dol.	Parish cent
…t State and School ..	-	50	.	30	.	.
…parish State & School ..	.	52	.	31		
…d March 25th 1796	1	2	-	61	.	.
…arish parish		.		-	-	26
…dwin parish		.	-	.	-	21
…nth parish				30		

State of Newhampshire } To Constable James C. Hayes one of the
Strafford ss } Collectors of the Town of Rochester for the year 1795 Greeting

(L.S.) By virtue of a vote of the Town of Rochester for raising money for the Support of the Gospel and other parish Expences you are hereby required in the name of said State to Levy & Collect of all persons named in the foregoing List herewith Committed you to Collect the sum set to their names in Dollars and Cents and pay the same in cash to the Select men in Office by the first Day of march next and if any person or persons shall neglect or refuse to pay the said Taxes after Legal warning or notice you are to take the same by Destraint & Sale as the Law Directs and for your Lawful proceedings this shall be your Sufficient Warrant Given under our hands & Seals at Rochester the 29th Day of September AD 1795 Richd Furber } Select

Willm Palmer } men

…mitt }	2	79	80	20
…m }	3	60	40	2½
…mer.	3	14	50	3
…rk }	2	15	100	6

Town Account for 1795 — 6 — Credit

		Dollars	Cents
In Collector Paul Harford's hands	1781	85	10
In Collector Thos Roberts hands	1789	248	33
In Collector Peter Cushings hands	1790	400	21
In Collector Jonathan Nutes hands	1793	339	85
In Lt Richd Places hands	1794	494	33
In Lt Anthony Peavys hands	1794	481	83
In Select mens hands returned in Notes & 12 Indents		576	83
Cash returned by Select men for 1794		121	72
Recd for Rent of Town Lotts		10	59
Recd of Hatevil Knight for the priviledge of Collecting nonresident Tax		5	50
Recd of Trespassers on School Lott		4	50
Rais'd in Collector Richard Places List	1795	691	74
Rais'd in Collec Daniel Wingates List	1795	371	44
Rais'd in Collec James C Hayes List	1795	211	76
Recd Interest on Notes of Hand		5	24
Rais'd in Hatevil Knight Nonresident List	1795	92	58
		4081	55

The way sd Money has been laid out

		Dollars	Cents
Paid State Treasurer in full for 1790		184	76
pd State Treasurer in full for 1789		134	56
pd State Treasurer in part for 1795		370	44
pd County Treasurer in full 1794		128	14
pd Esqr Wingate District School in full	1792	4	73
pd Esqr Dames Dist School in full	1793	13	95
pd Col Places Dist School in full	1793	16	66
pd Deacn Plumer Dist School in full	1793	3	83
pd Saml Grays Dist School in full	1794	4	59
pd Deacn Plumer Dist School in full	1794	17	79
pd Esqr Dames Dist School in full	1794	27	75
pd Capt Beard Plumer School in full	1794	18	23
pd Joseph Holmes Dist School in full	1794	12	72
pd Col Places Dist School in full	1794	14	72
pd Abner Hodgdon School in ~~part~~	1794	2	77
pd Col Godwin his School in full	1794	16	53
pd Richd Walker School in full	1794	14	25
pd Paul Jenness Dist School in full	1794	8	18
pd Lt Anthony Peavys Dist School	1794	11	78
pd Ensn Corsen's Dist School in full	1794	16	94
pd Capt Allens Dist School in full	1794	13	43
pd Capt Allens Dist School in full	1795	13	87
pd Enoch Wingate School in full	1794	9	66
pd Benn Meders Dist School in part	1794	6	—
pd Edmund Tebbets School in full	1794	10	67
pd Benjamin Evans Dist School in full	1794	4	25
pd Col Thos Roberts School in full	1794	11	81
pd Mordecai Varneys School in full	1794	11	91
		1104	92

Debtor Continued

		1104
pd Saml Grays Dist School in full	1795	5
pd Edmund Tebbets School in full	1795	11
pd Lt Anthony Peavys School in full	1795	14
pd Ben Meders School in part	1795	6
pd Paul Jenness School in part	1795	6
pd Joseph Iles Dist School in full	1794	7
pd Benn Furber Dist School in part	1795	12
pd Joseph Jones Dist School in full	1795	11
pd Col McDuffees School in full	1795	30
pd Israel Hams Dist School in full	1795	17
pd Gilbert French Dist School	1792	5
pd Gilbert French Dist School in full	1793	4
pd Gilbert French Dist School in part	1794	5
pd Lt Downings Dist School in full	1794	12
pd Saml Palmers Dist School in full	1794	11
pd Capt Beard Plumer Dist School in full	1795	21
pd Jonathan Wentworths Dist School in full	1795	13
Paid Capt Samuel Runnels for building a Stone bridge at Places mill & other Expenses for same		39
pd Select men for letting out sd Bridge and Settling the Same		3
pd Esqr Atkinson in full for two presentments on highways		27
pd Benjamin Varney Towards a road thro his land		5
pd Stephen Whitehouse in full for a road thro his land		35
pd Committee & Surveyor in full for laying out a road by Aaron Hams		7
pd Committee in full for laying out a road round Holmes mill pond		3
pd Committee & Surveyor in part for Laying out & making return of a road by Isaac Twombly		3
pd Committee for Dividing the Lower parish into Schoolhouse Districts & giving out Lists		9
pd Jacob Hanson in full as Assessor	1795	1
pd Committee for Dividing Southwest parish for Schoolhouses & giving out Lists		5
pd Committee for Dividing North East parish for Schoolhouses & giving out Lists		4
pd James Place in full for a road thro his land		10
pd Moses Chamberlin in full for a road thro his land		12
pd Jacob Hanson in full for a road thro his land		10
pd Limuel Jackson in full for his part of a road through the Davis Lot		7
pd Ephraim Kimball in full for his Services as Lotlayer & Committee man 1795		4
pd Capt Daniel Hayes his Services as Lotlayer	1795	8
pd Simon Torr for his Service as Lotlayer in 1795 and Committee man		8
pd Collector Lt Richd Place the 4 per Cent agreed on for the money he has Collected & paid in for 1795		19
pd Abatement of Jonathan Nutes Taxes in Dr Howe List for 1788		2
pd Abatement [illegible] allowed by former Select men in John Nutes List for 1781 · 1785 · 1786		17

Debtor Continued 1795

Abated Amos peasley (Daniel Lom & Jedediah Hill?) Taxes in L. Places List 1784	5	3
pd Esqr Dame a note of hand given by former Select men in full	73	91
pd Lt Anthony peavy for Collecting Taxes in full for 1794	20	—
pd Peter Cushing for Collecting Taxes in 1790	11	—
pd Allowd Abatements in P Cushings List 1790	28	90
pd Anthony peavy his account in full for timber for Dock brook bridge and	15	50
Warning a poor out of Town &c.	1	17
pd Ensn Corsen his account in full as lotlaying in 1794	8	—
pd Josiah Main in full for services as Town Clerk in 1795	15	—
pd Joshua Lane for Erecting post Guides in part	4	25
pd Joseph Tucker & others their account for Supplying Widow Waymoth with wood &c.	4	77
pd Ebenezer Horn for Supplying poor 1793	2	—
Abated Dodavah Garlins Taxes in Barnabys (Holdings?) List for 1793	7	—
Abated Dodavah Garlins Taxes in Lt Places List in 1794	4	22
pd Lt Rollins in full to redeem a piece of Land Illegally assessed in 1778	12	—
pd Lt Place in full for his services as Overseer of the poor in 1793	7	50
pd Dearborn Jewett for Clearing out the meeting house after June Court	1	50
pd Abatements in full in Wm McNeals List 1778 & 1780	6	37
pd Esqr Wingate as Committee man in full 1795	—	50
pd Col McDuffee in full as Committee man running ten rod road in 1795	4	—
pd Col McDuffee in full for procuring Trainfield	3	—
pd Ephm Kimball as assessor & other services in 1794 in full	2	—
pd Josiah main in full for a book for the Town	2	—
~~pd Mr ... in full for procuring ... for ... Town ...~~		—
pd Mercy main & Hannah Main the balance in full for Three notes of hand they held against the Town for one Hundred Dollars on Interest	81	25
The Select men for taking the Inventory 1795	10	—
The Select men for Laying out & making return of a road by Benjamin Wentworths	2	—
pd Select men for settling with people for the roads on each side of the Long marsh by Solomon Drown James places &c.	4	—
pd Committe for Laying out a road from Haines mills & settling with people Concerned in it	3	—
pd Select men for prosecuting Joseph Thompson for obstructing highway & settling the same	2	—
Select men for Journeys to Gilmantown Town to settle for presentment on bad high ways in full	2	—

Debtor Continued

pd Committee for running out and Settling with Trespassers on Third Division School Lot	5	—
pd Selectmen for time & Expences letting out Town Lotts in full	3	50
pd for Making Ratelist & counterpart for State & School Taxes	10	—
pd for Destributing & giving out School List 1795	7	—
pd for making Surveyors List & Destributing Surveyors	6	—
pd for agreeing with Collectors & taking bonds	3	—
pd Select men Services Settling with Collectors paying Schoolmaster & arranging Town accounts	20	—
pd Select men for recording Inventory & ratelists for Town Clerk	3	—
pd for making Non resident List	4	—
Allowd Abatements in Anthony peavys List for 1794	11	7
Allowd Abatements in Col Roberts List for 1789	19	64
pd Col Roberts for Copying & advertising non resident List at Easter 1789	2	60
Allowd Col Roberts the Sum recieved of the reciever of non resident Taxes & not by him allowd to said Roberts in 1789	—	91
paid Moses Horn to redeem a piece of Land Illegally assessed in 1789	1	50
pd Joseph Clark Esqr his services as Committee man in Esqr Dame & Moses Hayes Case	—	50
For Writing paper through the year	1	50
pd Select men for Writing & Exchanging 17 Deeds	4	25
pd Capt Plumer in full for a Road thro his land	10	—
pd Ensn James C Hayes in full for a Road thro his land	5	—
pd Ensn James Hayes in full for Collecting his State and School List for 1795	15	—
Allowd Drawbacks in P Hayes List 1795	1	63
pd Lt Edw Rollins in full as Committee man procuring Trainfield 1794	3	—
pd Jotham Nute for Warning Sundry persons out of Town in 1794 and Carrying Limuel Wakeham out of Town	8	
pd The balance of a Note of hand Given by parson Havens to release John Wentworth from Imprisonment	1	
pd Overseers of the poor's bill in full for 1795	39	15
pd Daniel Dame in full as assessor for 1795	1	50
	2676	10

Outstanding in Collectors Hands

		Doll	Cent
In Paul Harfords hands for	1781	85	10
In Peter Cushings hands for	1790	196	16
In Lt. Joathian Nutes Hands for	1793	171	6
In Lt. Anthony Peavys hands for	1794	249	99
In Lt. Richd. Places hands for	1794	177	92
In Collectr. Richard Places hands for	1795	184	50
In Collectr. Daniel Wingates hands for	1795	206	49
In Select mens hands in Notes & 12 P. Students		531	57
In Hatevil Knights Non resident List		32	58
		1835	37
		2076	10
		3911	47
Paid The Auditors in full for 1795		7	50
		3918	97
		4081	55
Balance Due from the Selectmen		162	58

A True account of The Towns accounts both Debt and Credit thro The year & presented this 28th Day of March 1796

Richd. Dame
Richd. Furbur
Willm. Palmer
Selectmen of Rochester

Rochester March 26th 1796
In auditing the foregoing account we find them well vouched & to our appearance true & Just as handed to us by the Selectmen.

Simon Torr
Edward Rollins
Ephm. Kimball
Auditors

Parish Tax & Account 1795

	Dol	Cent
Parish Credit Raisd in Collector Places parish List for 1795	307	60
In Anthony Peavys List for South West Parish for 1795	73	75
Raisd in Ensn. James C. Hayes parish List for 1795 in North East parish	40	45
	421	80

Parish Debtor

	Doll	Cent
pd Parson Havens Salary in full to March 25 1796	266	66
pd Parson Havens's account for repairing parsonage house. boarding Workmen &c	14	73
pd John Plumer Jr. Esqr. Account for Board for Parsonage house in full	4	22
pd John McPlace for work on parsonage house	2	-
pd Thomas Brown for work on parsonage house	17	34
pd Moses Horn for Articles for parsonage house	2	20
pd Tobias Twom[illegible] priviledge [illegible] as adjudged by a Comittee	18	-
pd for Making parish Taxes in Each parish	5	-
pd the 4 pr Cent for Collecting first parish Tax and paid in for 1795	11	[illegible]
pd Dearborn Jewell in full for Taking Care of the meeting house & Cleaning the Same	2	50

Outstanding in the Parish accounts

	Dollr.	Cen
In Coll. Richd. Places hand for 1795	20	93
In Coll. Anthony Peavys hand for 1795	73	75
In Coll. James C Hayes hands for 1795	40	45
	135	13
paid out	343	65
paid out & outstandg	478	78
Raisd 1795	421	80
Ballance Due to Selectmen	56	98

A True account of the Parish accounts both Debt & Credit thro The year as presented this 28 Day of March 1796

Richd. Furber Jr. Select men
Willm. Palmer

In Auditing the foregoing we find them well vouchd accurate and to our appearance true and Just as exhibited to us by the Selectmen this 26 Day of March 1796

Simon Torr
Edward Rollins
Ephraim Kimball
Auditors

March 28th 1796
The Town Voted to accept of the within Accounts as was read by the Clerk in the audience of the Meeting

attest Josiah Main Town Clerk

	Dolls	Cent.	m
Precept from the County Treasurer Dated March 10th 1796 for [illegible]	73	20	5

Settlements made with Collectors 1796

	Dolls	Cents
May 27 Rec.d of Moses Young 78 Dollars being the balance of the principal of his second note for John [illegible] Farm & 8 Dollars & 61 Cents Interest	78	61
July 6 1796 Rec.d of Hatevil Knight the whole of his Nonresident List for 1795	32	58
Oct.r 19 Rec.d of Moses Young toward last note	20	—
Oct.r 31 Rec.d of Elijah Varney in full of his note	13	48
—— of Peter Cushing Cash 20 Dol. p.d Esq.r Palmer 20	40	—
Nov.r 7th Rec.d of Lt. Rich.d Place	10	12
Nov.r 28th Rec.d of Elijah Varney of 96 List	21	8
Feb.y 1st 1797 Peter Cushing in Cash —— 20.0 made abatement in his List be- 20.0 took Mr B. Rollins' note for 116:16 total 136:16 which appears to be in full of his List	156	16
February the 11th 1797 then the Selectmen Received fifty Dollars of Ensign James McDuffee for the fourth Division Lot of Land Drawn to the Right of Grammer Schoole in Rochester and Deeded the same to Ben. Rollings as it will appear by his Receipt	50	
Feb.y 27th Received of Col. Varney Mr Havens orders —— 51.82 Col. Place for Schoolhouse —— 30.30 Jacob Hayes for road 43 —— & in Cash 50.10 and 3 Doll.s p.d Joseph Heard for a Road total 172.22 [illegible] 175.22	172	22
December 26th 1796 [illegible] Place Col. [illegible] Place's Order for [illegible]	16	15
Eben.r Wingate's order for part of Dea. Plumer's School [illegible]	16	76
Samuel [illegible] for Capt. [illegible] 1795	19	80
[illegible] for Jn.o Tanner for 3d [illegible] 179[illegible]	9	12
[illegible] Place for [illegible] Town Clerk 1796	10	00
John Tanner for part of [illegible] Hayes [illegible]	8	14
Levi Jones for Joshua Hayford's D.o 1795 full	13	6
[illegible] for Col. Place D.o 1795 in full	17	62
[illegible] Jun.r toward Bridge [illegible]	10	19
Joseph Walker for Tho.s Davis [illegible] 1794 in full	14	17
[illegible] Discounted [illegible] Major [illegible]	4	27
Cash	4	00
And gave a Rec.t for 1795 List for	130	5
March 19 1797 Rec.d of Col. Thomas [illegible] [illegible] for keeping School in Col. Place [illegible] 1796	15	00
p.d by way of Jacob Hanson to Maj. [illegible]	30	30
Paid [illegible] toward the Bridge	22	90
Paid Anthony [illegible] towards Court house frame	12	41
Abatement [illegible]	12	18
in Cash	10	
Notes held against him 1st 72.34 2d 75.83 Interest on both notes 11.86 159.73	117	79
Rec.d Col. Robert's note for the Balance [illegible]	46	74
[illegible] 30 Rec.d of Elijah Varney the Balance of [illegible] School	9	6
Capt [illegible] as Committee man in 1795 [illegible] Receipt in full 1796	73	20
Cash	6	
And gave a Receipt for	89	26

Jan.y 30th 1797 Settled with Dan. Wingate
Rec.d State Treasurer Rec.t for 1795 in full
Maj. [illegible] Rec.t 49.46 & Taxes Discounted 2.37
By p.d Hatevil Knight on Jos. [illegible] acc.t
for Collecting 15 D. Abatements 5.89
Cash paid the 19th Instant
which with 165 D. paid last year is the balance in full of his List for 1795

Feb.y 27 1797 Rec.d [illegible] State
Levi Jones Order for keep.g school in [illegible] 1795
Capt Hayes on John Carney's acc.t
[illegible] Havens' order
Abatements allowed
Cash
And gave a Receipt for

March 20th 1797 Settled with Ens.n James Hayes
Rec.d Capt Benj.a Plumer's Dist. School order [illegible] Wingate & Jones
Capt Plumer for Building a Bridge [illegible]
p.d Capt Plumer for paying Benjamin Rollins
p.d John Twombly for Bridge timber in full
p.d Enoch Wingate for keeping his Dist. School 1795
p.d James Berry for pay.g Benj.a Rollins [illegible]
p.d Capt Dan.l Hayes for John Carney's expences
p.d Levi Jones for keep.g Rich.d Walker Dist. 1795
p.d D.o in part for D.o in part for 1796
p.d the 6½ percent for Collecting
p.d Taxes for Esq.r Palmer & others [illegible] allowed
Abatements allow
Cash
And gave a Rec.t in full for his List 1796

D.o Settled with Elijah Varney and Rec.d
Joseph Tucker for supplying wood to said [illegible]
Capt Brewster's School order in part 95 & 96 lists
p.d Joseph Heard for his p.t Capt Brewster 95 & 96 lists
p.d Jacob Hanson for supplying [illegible] Alley
p.d Joseph Havens' order in full
p.d Abatem.ts allow.d Hatevil Knight of nonresident 1792
p.d Eben Wingate for Simon Torr's Dist. in full 1796
Cash

Settled with [illegible] Place and [illegible]
Hatevil Knight [illegible] on Joseph [illegible] acc.t
Joseph [illegible] p.d of his School money for 1795 & 96
p.d John [illegible] for p.t [illegible] Dist. 1796
p.d Benj.a Rollins 27.60 for [illegible] 179[illegible]
Abatements in 94 List 18.56 in 95 [illegible] 29.18
The Balance for Collecting 1795 List [illegible]
[illegible] Taxes Discounted [illegible] Cash
[illegible] a Receipt being the Balance of 1795 and [illegible]

March 21st Settled with [illegible] Holmes [illegible]
[illegible] School [illegible] List for 1796
[illegible] for 1796
[illegible] Laughton's Dist. 1795
[illegible] 1796
p.d for carrying [illegible] Committee out of town &c.
p.d for Building Bridge at [illegible] pond
p.d John [illegible] the Balance [illegible] Jos. Holmes' Dist. 1795
p.d [illegible] Hayes [illegible] for a [illegible] for [illegible]
p.d [illegible] Dist. School for 1796
p.d [illegible] supplies for William Horn
p.d [illegible] Murray's Dist. 1795
p.d for Collecting 10.93 p.d Maj. [illegible] 10.86
p.d Cash
and gave a Rec.t for 1796 List for

Settled with Jotham Nute and Rec.d
p.d Elijah Horn for a Road the balance in full
p.d Capt Dan.l Hayes Dist. School for 1795 and 1796
p.d Simon Torr on Jos. [illegible] acc.t
p.d for Collecting 25 D. Abatements made this day 4.09
p.d Capt Dan.l Hayes' [illegible] 1796 in full
Cash by Taxes Discounted
And gave a Rec.t for 1793 List for [illegible] 29 Cents

10	·60
8	·48
27	1·62
10	·60
12	·72
8	·48

Name	1	2	3	4	5	6	7	8	9	10	11	12	13	14	15
John M[illegible]	1						1								
Dn. Paul Libby	1	4	2	1	2	1		½		2	6	16	15	74	4[illegible]
David Langley	2	2	2	1	1	2	1			2	6	8		100	4[illegible]
Clement Libby	1		1			1									10
Joshua Lane	1						1								1[illegible]
Col. T. McDuffee Esq.	1	4	4	3	1	2	2		1½	3	20	32	40	240	9[illegible]
Capt. Wm. McDuffee	1	4	3	1	1	4	½			1	8	20	20	45	5[illegible]
Majr. James McDuffee	1	4	5		2		1	½	½	8	10	18	30	105	70
Capt. Danl. McDuffee	1	2	1	4	3	4	½	½		8	17	40	30	120	8[illegible]
Lt. John McDuffee 3d	1														8
Saml. McDuffee	1														8
Jacob McDuffee	1	2	2			1	¾				6	16		35	3[illegible]
David McDuffee	1														[illegible]
Benja. Meder	1	2	4			1	1			2	4	8	15	40	38
Nathl. Meder	2	2	4			1	1			1½	5	12	10	20	47
Joseph Meder	2	2	1	2	1	3	1			1½	6	8	12	117	4[illegible]
Jonathan Meder	1		2		2	1	¾	¾		1	5	8	10	34	3[illegible]
Francis Meder	1		3		2					2	6	12	15	20	3[illegible]
Lemuel Meder	1						1							40	13
Josiah Main	1		1	3	2	2	1	½		1	3	10			32
Amos Main	1		1		1	1									11
Wid. Sarah Morison		2	2		1	1	1			1½	4	8	10		25
Wm. McNeal	1		2	3	4	1	¾	½	½	2	6	8	10		38
James McDuffee Jr.	1		3		2	2	¾			1	7	12	10	40	35
William Messor	1														8
Majr. Jothn. Merron															
Capt. Saml. Nute	1		1			1	1		½		2	4	15		21
Richd. Nutter		2	2				1	½		½	2	8			20
Winthrop Nutter	1		2		1						2	4			16
Jotham Nutter	1	2			1	1				1	1			28	18
Richd. Nutter Jr.	1		1												10
Richd. Nutter 3d	1														8
John Nutter	1														8
Stephen Nutter	1														8
John Nute		2	2		1										7[illegible]
John Odiorne	1		1				1		3 Stock						17
John Plumer Esq.	2	4	5	2	2	3	2	1½		4	18	40	45	217	10[illegible]
Dr. Saml. Plumer	1		2	2	3		1	½		2	12	16	30	220	51
Lt. David Place	1	4	3	1		2	1			3	12	32	25	70	67
Barnabas Palmer	1		1					½			1	8	30	100	20
Ebenr. Pearl	1	2	2	3	1	3	1	½	1	2	6	16	15	36	47
John Place	1		2					½		1½	8	12	10		28
Jonn. Place	1	2	1		1		1								21
Benja. Palmer	1												40		12
Lt. Richd. Place	1		1	3	1		1			1	4	12	15	100	33
John Mt. Place	1	2	2		1		1	½		1	2	8	10		31
Paul Place	1	2	1	1		1				1	4	12			28
Dr. Saml. Perry	1						1								12
Levi Pickering	1		1												10
James Pickering	1	2	2	2			¾			½	6	16		57	37
Lt. James Place	1		1	1		6		½		4	16	16		80	44
Daniel Page	1	4	3	5	2	3	1	½		2	10	16	20	78	64
Joseph Page	2	2	3	2	4	1	1			½	10	12	10	46	57
Benjamin Page	1						[illegible]							[illegible]	[illegible]

Richards	1	2	1	3	·	·	1	·	·	1½	4	8	20	10	35	2.10	1.75
Randall Jr	1	2	1	1	·	2	·	·	·	1	4	·	30	·	24	1.44	1.20
Richardson	1	2	2	2	2	2	1	·	·	1½	7	12	40	·	42½	2.55	2.13
Richardson	1	·	1	2	·	·	·	·	·	·	·	·	26	·	13½	.81	.68
Richards	1	·	1	·	·	·	·	·	·	·	·	·	·	·	10	.60	.50
Roberts	1	·	1	·	4	·	1	·	·	·	1	·	58	·	20½	1.23	1.03
Roberts	1	·	2	2	3	1	2 yds	·	·	1	1	·	48	·	23½	1.41	1.18
Rogers	1	·	2	·	·	2	1	·	·	·	·	·	·	·	17	1.02	.85
Roberts Jr	1	·	1	·	·	·	1 yd	·	·	·	·	·	215	·	17½	1.05	.88
Roberts 3d	1	2	1	·	2	1	·	·	·	·	·	·	·	·	19½	1.17	·
[illegible]	1	·	·	·	·	·	·	·	15 [illegible] trade					·	23	1.38	1.15
Rollins	½	2	1	·	·	1	·	·	·	1	2	·	90	·	17	1.02	.85
Robinson	1	·	·	·	·	2	·	·	·	·	·	·	·	·	9	.54	·
Robinson	1	·	·	·	·	·	·	·	·	·	·	·	·	·	8	.48	·
Tenell	1	·	·	·	·	·	·	·	·	·	·	·	·	·	8	.48	.40

By virtue of Sundry Laws of s^d State directing & impowering [illegible] to raise money for the support of Schools Repairing highways & other necessary expences and in pursuance of a precept from the County Treasurer to raise a sum of money for said County —

15 You are hereby required in the name of said State aforesaid to Levy and Collect of all persons named in the foregoing List herewith Committed you to Collect the sums set to their names in Dollars and Cents which sums you are to collect in Silver & Gold or orders drawn by the Selectmen of Rochester for the time being and you are hereby directed to pay the [illegible] Treasurer Seventy Dollars by the Last Day of [illegible] next and the whole of the remaining sum to the Selectmen of Rochester by the Twentyth Day of March next. And if any person or persons Shall neglect or refuse to pay their Taxes after [illegible] warning or notice you are to take the same by Distress [illegible] as the law Directs and for your Lawful proceedings [illegible] your Sufficient Warrant Given under our hands and [illegible] Rochester this 12th Day of September in the year of our [illegible]

[illegible] Farrer } Select
[illegible] Turber [illegible] } men
of Rochester
Zaphra[illegible]

Warrant for Parish Tax[illegible]

State of Massachusetts } To Elij[illegible] of the Collector of Taxes for the
Strafford [illegible] } Town of Rochester for the year 1796 Greeting

Pursuant to Sundry order of this Town for Raising money for the support of the Gospel and other parish expences & for raising & collecting

15 the same. You are hereby Directed & Impowered in the name of s^d State to Levy & Collect of all persons named in the foregoing List herewith Committed you to Collect the several sums set to their names in Dollars and Cents and pay the same to the Selectmen or else pay Two hundred & Sixty six Dollars & Sixty seven Cents to parson Haven & the remainder to the Selectmen by or before the Twentyth Day of March next Ensuing. And if any person or persons shall neglect or refuse to pay his or their Taxes after legal warning or notice you are to take the same by Distress & Sale as the Law Directs and for y^r Lawful proceedings this Shall be your Sufficient warrant Given under our hands & seals this Twelfth Day of September in the year of our Lord 1796

Richd Turber [illegible] } Select
Willm Palmer [illegible] } men

Name																	
[illegible] Wingate																	
Edward Wingate	1	-	-	3	-	1	1	-	-	1	6	8	-	7½	29½	1:77	:74
John Walker	1	2	3	2	-	2	[illegible]	-	-	1	6	8	-	30	37	2:22	93
Aaron Wingate	2	-	4	3	4	2	[illegible]	-	-	2	15	26	29	56	75½	4:53	1:59
[illegible] Wingate	1	2	1	1	2	1	[illegible]	-	-	1	7	12	10	30	39	2:32	97
Willm Whitehouse	1	-	4	-	3	2	1	-	-	1	8	8	10	29	38	2:25	
Nath. Whitehouse	1	-	-	1	-	-	—	-	-	-	-	-	-	-	9½	2:87	24
Tom Winkley	1	-	2	3	3	2	1	-	-	2	8	8	10	20	39½	2:37	99
Tom Winker	7	2	2	1	2	-	[illegible]	-	-	1	6	8	10	30	36½	2:1	84
Nath. Watson	2	-	4	-	3	1	1	-	-	2	10	16	40	96	56	3:36	1:40
Daniel Watson	1	2	3	-	2	2	1	-	-	2	6	8	10	62	40½	2:43	1:1
Thomas Watson	1	2	2	2	3	2	—	-	-	1	6	8	-	80	37½	2:25	- 94
Tom Watson	1	2	1	1	-	2	—	-	-				-		18½	1:11	46
Samuel Wingate	-	-	1	-	-	-	—	-	-	1	2	4	-	-	-	:39	-
Joseph Young	1	-	1	1	2	-	—								13½	81	- 34

Abatements	Dollars	[illegible]
Isaac Libby	72	30
Geo Leighton	90	38
John Twombly	81	00
John Murray	10	
Moses Hanford	70	00
Thomas Davis	60	40
Israel Hanson	48	20
Allowed Mar 24 98	431	
Except J. Murray	10	
	421	

Doomages in the forgoing list

	Dollars
Jonas C. March Stock in Trade	8
Lemuel Richardson	—
Saml Holmes Corn Mill	12
Col John Waldron Sawmill	16
Ditto Corn mill	8

Samuel Gray 00, 51 cents. Abatements further made see page 88 —

Rochester May 1st 1797 Then agreeable to a Return on Record We tendered Ten Dollars to The Widow of John Whitehouse Decd and further offered to pay her Taxes by Discount for 1796 [illegible] on Elijah Varney, but four Dollars and Twenty [illegible] in full Compensation for the Road as laid out on their land at the Southeasterly end of their lot. Tendered in presence of Samuel Roberts which she neglected taking at that time.

Richd Dame } Selectmen
Richd [illegible] } for 1797

Rochester June 1st 1797 Then Run out a piece of a Road or turn of a Road that Benjamin Dame Says is on his land above his house on the same that he purchased of Samuel Morrow at a Sandy bank of which he was never possessed and to prevent Disputes in future Tendered him One Dollar in full therefor in presence of Simon Torr Ensn Ichabod Corson Jos. Hurd and [illegible] Downing

Tendered on behalf of the Selectmen by Richd Dame [illegible]

No.	Name	Amount		Paid
No 3	Col John McDuffee	31.98	By the [illegible] paid the Cash to Jacob Main	39.00
No 4	Willm Jennes	11.32	pd Richd Dame in full for Keeping sd School	11.32
No 5	Israel Ham	16.45	March 21 gave Israel & Stephen Ham an order on Elijah Varney for and Amos Main by their order on Varney for the Balance	5.17 11.28 16.45
No 6	Ensn Ichd Corsen	17.75	paid Benjamin [illegible] by the [illegible] order	17.75
No 7	Lieut Jotham Allen	14.83	paid the Cash to Levi Jones by order of the [illegible]	14.83
No 8	Peter Cushing	23.00	an order given to Capt Shannon in full. Willm Shannon afterwards kept said School in 1799	23.—
No 9	Col David Place	18.97	Paid Amos Main in part. Paid the Committee the Balance	15.00 3.97
No 10	Aaron Ham	13.41	gave an order on Ichd Corson for Palatiah Cartland for the whole Feby 26. 1798	13.41
No 11	Simon Torr Jr	20.14	Gave Ebenr Wingate an order on Elijah Varney for the whole	20.14
No 12	Capt John Brewster	5.20	Gave Capt Brewster an order on Varney; Joseph Dame an order 2d place; Joseph Heard [illegible]	1.65 2.50 1.05 5.20
No 13	Abner Hodgdon	8.49	March 25th 1797 Gave Daniel Dame an order on Richard Place for the whole	8.49
No 14	Benja Meder	17.37	pd Cash to Benja Cann by Com[illegible] order; Oct 1797 Paid School Dame by Com order; pd John Magner by Com order; pd John Magner by Com order	4.90 7.09 3.84 1.68 17.37
No 15	Capt Dan. McDuffee	19.57	Gave John Tanner an order on Richd Place for the whole March 28. 1797	19.57

Name			Payment		
Captn Daniel Hayes's	13	68	pd the whole to Joatham Nute for the District by order of the Directors —	13	68
Richard Walker's	17	23	paid Levy Jones — John Tanner —	9 7 17	16 77 23
Captn Beard Plummer's	22	32	paid Levy Jones 8 Dol. — Caleb Wingate 14.32	22	32
Joshua Hartford's	13	—	paid Levi Jones thirteen in full for the list by order of the Directors	13	00

[illegible] } To Ens^n James C Hayes Collector of taxes in the North East District in Rochester for the year 1796. Greeting

By virtue of A Law of this State Dividing & Impowering Selectmen to raise Money for the Support of Schools — and in Persuance of a Precept from the County Treasurer to raise Mone for the use of Said County — & by virtue of Sundry votes of this town to raise Money for the Support of the Gospel to lay out & Purchase High ways &c —

You are hereby Required in the Name of the State of New Hampshire to Levy and Collect of all the persons Named in the foregoing List herewith Committed you to Collect the Sum set to their Names in Dollars & Cents and pay the whole of said amount to the Selectmen of Rochester or their order by the twentieth day of March Next, and if any person shall Neglect to pay their taxes after Legal Notice, you are to take the Same by Destress as the Law Directs — and for your Lawful Proceedings this shall be your Sufficient Warrant Given under our hands and Seals at Rochester this twelfth day of Septr 1796

Richd Furber } Selectmen of Rochester
Willm Palmer }

Town account 1796 Credit

		Doll	Cents
In Collector Paul Harford's hands	1791	85	16
In Peter Cushings hands for	1790	196	16
In Ens. Jotham Nutes hands for	1793	171	6
In Lieut. Anthony Peavy's hands	1794	249	99
In Lieut. Rich. Place's hands for	1794	177	92
In Lieut. Rich. Place's hands for	1795	184	50
In Daniel Wingates hands for	1795	206	49
In Hateal Knights Nonresident list	1795	37	58
Notes & 2 Poll Indents Returned by Selectmen	95	531	57
Cash returned by the Selectmen	1795	162	58
Receiv'd in Elijah Varney's list	1796	522	38
Receiv'd in Joseph Holmes list	1796	293	1
Receiv'd in Ens. James C. Hayes list	1796	169	62
Rec'd of Committee for sale of Town Lotts		50	
Rec'd Interest on Notes of hand		325	59
Rec'd for the Rent of Town Lotts		14	21
Rec'd for a piece of Road sold Moses Hanson		12	
		3084	76

The way said money has been laid out

		Doll	Cents
Paid the balance of State Treasurer in full	1795	125	00
Paid the County Treasurer in full	1796	73	20
Paid for Building Guptins mill bridge in full		109	00
Paid Selectmen time & expence letting out and settling for sd Bridge		6	—
Paid for Build. a Bridge over Holmes Mill pond on Meders bro. Road by Joseph Holmes		62	—
Paid Selectmen for laying out a Road over sd pond and letting out sd Bridge in full		3	—
Paid Jacob Hayes in full a Road thro his land as appraisd by a Committee		40	—
Paid sd Committee & Selectmen attending them		3	33
Pd Jos. Ricker the sum allowd him for bounty money by the Committee as a Soldier		50	—
Pd the Committee for settling with sd Ricker		6	—
Paid Solicitor Atkinson his demand for Indictment on Wakefield Road & for neglect of Post guides		9	25
Paid for build. a Bridge on sd Road		25	—
Paid Selectmen time & expence at Dover & Gilmanton to stop & settle presentments		1	50
		513	28

		Doll	Cents
Paid Samuel Hanford for a Road to Guptins Bridge		5	00
Paid Selectmen for laying out sd Road & return		2	—
Paid Jos. Hoare 3d for a Road thro his land		15	00
Paid Col. J. Place's acct for Bridge plank in full	96	16	25
Paid Joh. Corson Jun. in full for the road thro Davis lott		3	95
Pd Lt Anthony Peavy towards building Court house		66	—
Pd Maj. Furber for Baize for the Courts use		2	50
Pd Benjn Rollins towards building Court house		400	30
Pd Levy Jones for keeping School in Ens. Corsons Dist	1793	10	89
Pd Benjn Meders Dist the ballance in full for	1794	5	48
Pd Benjn Canney for keeping School in Benjn Meders Dist	1795	9	62
Do. in part for keeping School in Benjn Meders Dist	1796	1	90
Pd Benjn Furbers District in ful for	1794	4	62
Pd Captn Danl McDuffee the whole of his Dist for	1794	12	40
Pd Captn Saml Nute for laying out a road by Jonathan Hayes Corner	1795	1	—
Pd Joseph Walker for keeping Sch. in Danl Hayes Dist	1794	14	17
Pd John Tanner for keeping Sch. in Coll. Roberts Dist	1795	2	62
Pd Simon Torrs District in full for	1795	19	6
Pd Danl Dame for keeping Sch. in Danl McDuffee Dist	1795	19	80
Pd Amos Main for keeping Sch. in Coll. Places Dist	1795	17	62
Pd Esqr Dames District in full for	1795	26	22
Pd Esqr Wingate Dist in part for	1795	8	14
Pd Coll. McDuffees Dist in full	1796	32	—
Pd Coll. Places Dist in full	1796	78	97
Pd Joshua Harfords Dist in full	1795	43	6
Pd Captn Plummers Dist in full	1796	22	32
Pd David Frenchs Dist for	1794	10	20
Pd David Frenchs Dist for	1795	12	18
Pd David Frenchs Dist in full for	1796	11	40
Pd Enoch Wingates Dist in full for	1795	12	15
Pd Captn Brewsters Dist in full for 1795 &	1796	10	7
Pd Simon Torrs Dist in full for	1796	20	14
Pd Richd Walkers Dist for	1795	8	—
Pd Richd Walkers Dist in full for	1796	17	23
Pd Captn Allens Dist in full for	1796	14	83
Pd Saml Grays Dist in full for	1796	5	38
Pd Joseph Holmes Dist for	1795	4	33
Pd Saml Leightons Dist for	1795	7	36
Pd Saml Leightons Dist for	1796	9	18
Pd John Murrys Dist for in full	1796	18	64
Pd Edmond Tebbets Dist for in full	1796	13	20
Pd John Murrys Dist for the Balance	1795	4	50
Pd Willm Jennes Dist for in full	1796	11	32
Pd Willm Jennes Dist for in part	1795	11	18
Pd Captn Danl Hayes Dist in full for	1796	13	68
Pd Captn Danl Hayes's Dist for	1795	11	47
Pd Benjn Furbers Dist in full	1795	6	10
		[illegible]	[illegible]

	Dollars	Cents
pd John Twombly for timber for ye bridge by his house	4	—
pd Thoms Pinkham to settle the Complaint for insufficiency of the road	10	—
pd for the support of the poor in 1796	26	25
allow abatements in Col. Roberts's list for 1787 & 1789	12	18
pd Howard Handerson for Collecting the tax in 1788	25	—
pd Joseph Thomson Junr for a road thro his land in full	7	—
pd Joseph Holmes the 5 pr Ct agreed on for Collecting money	10	99
pd Esqr Sias as a referree settling trespass on Rd Lottin	4	
pd Peter Cushing for baize, making benches, house room, &c for the use of the Court	10	—
pd Committee for selling the 4th Divn School Lott	3	—
pd Selectmen for laying out a road by Edward Varney	3	—
pd for laying out a road from the fulling mill to Wakefield road	2	—
pd for laying out a road by James Roberts	3	—
pd for letting out town lott & expences	2	67
pd for time & expences agreeing with Collector & writing Bond	5	25
pd for time & expences making Preparations for the Court	5	—
pd for Running out a road for Ichd Corsons [illegible]	1	—
pd for taking Inventory in 1796	10	—
pd for making rate lists & Counterparts	10	—
pd for making ~~making~~ Schl lists & Destricting Schools	10	
pd for making Surveyors lists & Destricting Surveyors	8	50
pd Leut Elijh Horn for a road thro his land the balance	5	—
pd Ensn Jotham Nute for Collecting the tax in 1793	25	—
allow abatements in J Nutes list for 1793	26	85
pd Captn Danl Hayes for Services as a lott layer 1796	2	—
pd Simon Torr for Services as a lott layer in 1796	2	—
pd Selectmen for serving Town Clerk with a Copy of Inventory rate lists &c for 1796	5	—
for Writing paper thro the Year	1	50
for Writing of Deeds for Roads for the Towns use	1	34
Give up a Note against George Place on acct of some abatements made in his list for 1781 & not allowed	5	90
pd Jona Flagg to redeem a piece of land illegally assessed in Doctr Hows Non Resident list for 1788	3	—
pd Some extra expences in Joshua Ellis Case vs N Durham	2	—
allowd abatements in Peter Cushing list for 1790	20	—
allow abatements in Hatevil Knights Non resdt list 1795	2	9
allow abatements in Lt Richd Places list for 1794	18	56
allow abatements in sd Places list for 1795	17	64
allow abatements in Ensn Hayes list for 1796	2	25
allow abatements in Danl Wingates list 1795	5	82
pd Danl Wingate for Collecting tax in 1795	15	[illegible]

	Dollars	Cents
pd Constable Joseph Holmes for Carrying a poor person out town & recording Warrant	2	—
pd Lt Richd Place for Collecting tax in 1794	23	59
pd Benja Palmer for time & trouble Cleaning & taking Care of the meeting house in full for 1796	6	
	93	20
	513	28½
	918	33
	414	31
pd out	2059	12
out standing	915	1
total	2974	13
	3084	76
pd the Auditors in full for their Services for 1796 / Cash on hand	110	63
	9	
Due from the Selectmen	101	63

Outstanding in Collectors hands

		Dollars	Cents
In Paul Harfords for	1781	85	10
In Collector Lt Anthony Peavys hands	1794	249	99
In Lt Richd Places hands for	1794	107	85
In Collector Elijah Varneys hands	1796	100	30
In Coln Joseph Holmes hands	1796	62	88
In Selectmens hands in notes & Credit		309	69
		915	1

A true Statement of the Towns acct both Debt & Credit thro the year as kept by us
March ye 25th 1797

Thomas Darnel
Richd Furbush } Select men
Willm Palmer

In Auditing the foregoing Accounts we find them well vouched accurate and to our appearance honest true & just as exhibited to us this 25th Day of March 1797

Edward Rollins
Beard Plumer } Auditors
Jonas C. March

Parish accounts 1796 — Credit

		Dol	Cents
Returned in Richd Places hands	1795	20	93
In Lt Anthony Peavys hands	1795	73	75
In Ensn James C Hayes hands	1795	40	45
Raisd in Elijah Varneys List	1796	343	15
Raisd in Joseph Holmes List	1796	80	37
Raisd in Ensn James C Hayes List	1796	55	71
		614	36

	Dol	Cents
Debt pd Selectmen for making Lists and Counterparts and Recording the same	5	-
Allowd Abatements in Richd Places List 1795	11	65
pd the Balance due to the Selectmen of 1795	56	98
	73	63

out Standing in Collectors & Selectmens hands	Dol	Cents
In Lt Anthony Peavys hands for 1795	73	75
In Ensn James C Hayes hands for 1795	40	45
In Collectr Elijah Varneys hands for 1796	343	15
In Collectr Joseph Holmes hands for 1796	80	37
In Collector James C Hayes hand 1796	55	71
In Selectmens hands in orders	73	46
	666	89
paid the present year	73	63
	740	52
	614	36
Balance due to the Selectmen	126	16

a true Statement of the Parishes account both Debt & Credit for the year as kept by us
March ye 25th 1797 Richd Furber Jr, Willm Palmer } Selectmen

In Auditing the foregoing accounts we find them well vouched accurate & to our appearance honest true & just as exhibited to us March 25 1797
Jonas C March, Edward Rollins, Benja Plume } Auditors

Precept from the County treasurer for 1797		Dol	Cents
Ichabod Corson Jr	for 1st parish	59	80
Joseph Holmes	for 2d Do	30	—
by James C Hayes	for 3d Do	20	—
		109	80

May 22. 1797 then appointed Ichabod Corson Collector of Town & Parish Taxes for the year who accepted the same & gave bonds accordingly

Settlements — 1797 — with Collectors

	Dol
April 24th 1797 Recd of Elijah Varney	
Joseph Havens Recd & order for	37
Peter Cushings Tax for 1796 Due last year	5
And gave a Receipt for 1796 list for	42
May 29 Recd of Elijah Varney	
pd David Tebbits Jr for keeping School in Ensn Corsons Dist 1795	16
pd Silas Dame for Jona Wentworths Dist 1796	14
pd Amos Main for Israel Hams Dist in part 1796	11
pd Joseph Haven as pr Receipt	22
pd Moses Horn for Benjamin Rollins	9
pd Majr Furber by Saml Jenness Tax	2
pd Josiah Main for Richard Dame	2
pd Cash	24
And gave a Receipt for	102
Do Settled with Lieut Anthony Peavy & there: his account for part of a Day with Lt Hayes his act	
his act for notifying people to attend Town meeting	1
By Cash paid Major Furber	10
pd Benja Pages Dist School for 1795 in full	5
By Commttees order for Courthouse frame paid the before	204
Abatements allowd John Gray Dever [illegible]	1
and gave a Receipt for	221
and took his note for the balance of his list 28.34	
August 7th Recd of Joseph Holmes in Cash	30
By Majr Furbers Rect	4
gave a Receipt for	34
August 28 Recd of Elijah Varney	
pd Majr Furber Moses Jenness Tax	2
pd Zebulon Dame towards keeping Town Cattle a pen	4
pd Benja Rollins towards Courthouse	4
pd Howard Henderson towd Taking Inventory	4
pd Joseph Haven as pr Receipt	103
pd in Cash	24
pd Benja Rollins the 21st Instant	3
And Gave a Receipt for	147
October 2 Recd of Ichabod Corson Jr in Cash	5
Cash pd Samuel [illegible] 15.1 Cash by [illegible]	17
pd to Majr Furber 1.17	1
and Gave a Receipt for 1797 list	23
Do Settled with Capt Brewster & L Rollins a Committee for Parsonage Barn Their accounts pd	5
Gave Capt Brewster an order on Ichd Corson Jr for	3
and paid the Balance to Benj Rollins by his order	1
	5
November 11th Recd of Ichabod Corson Jr	
Col David Place order from Benja Rollins	12
Benjamin Varney Jr order for a Road at [illegible]	3
Elisha Wentworth for work on Wakefield Road	3
Benja Whitehouse for Shoes for Wd Weymouth	1
Joshua Lane in part for post Guide & the balance	2
Taxes for Sundries & cash to Richd Dame	14
and Gave a Receipt for 1797 List one dollar mistake before	40
Novr 27. Received of Ichabod Corson Jr	
Benja Rollins order for	184
Decr 25 Recd of Ichabod Corson Jr in Cash for 1797 list	5
and took up the above Receipt & gave one for	189
Decr 25 Recd of Joseph Holmes by pd Majr Furber	19
By Capt Daniel Hayes Receipts & Note	14
Abatements 8.25 and Cash 7.43	15
and gave a Receipt in full for the list for	49
Capt Daniel Hayes District & Schoolhouse	

95

Settlements with Collectors 1797

	Dollars	Cents
12 m° Received of Lieut. Anthony Peavey		
An order of Lt Tim° Roberts for keeping E Alley	15	00
his services as Auditor for 1796	1	00
his account for work on Neddenham Road	7	00
his acc.t for opening Roads as Committeeman	2	00
agreed to endorse on his note	25	00
Jan.y 1. 1798. Rec.d of Benj.a Dame		
Lt Anthony Peavey's order for a Road	10	00
D° for timber for Dock bridge	1	75
For to Redeem a Note for keeping Rich.d Hammet 1790	1	92
Abatement of Ephm. Ham's Jr. Tax 1787	1	67
Interest that he has paid for the above Deduction	4	
Receipted in part of his note	19	34
Jan.y 2. Rec.d of Co. Thomas Roberts		
Abated James Varney's Tax in 1787 & Interest till now	2	1
A Deed given up for a disputed piece of Land	1	43
his note 46.94 Interest 2.55 is 49.52	3	44
paid 3.44		
and took a new note for — 46.08		
Jan.y 29 Rec.d of Lieut Rich.d Place		
p.d Eben.r Horn for Timber for Courthouse	1	50
p.d John Tanner for Capt Dan.l McDuffee's Dest. 96	19	96
p.d Daniel Dame for Aaron Wingate's Dest. 95	8	49
D° D° 1796	9	49
D° for assessor 1796	2	60
Drawback for Isaac Libbey's Taxes for 1774	2	43
D° Morris Ellis Tax for 1794 & 95	1	67
and gave a Receipt for	45	54
Feb.y 2.d Rec.d of Ichabod Corson Jr. p.d B. Rollins	108	81
p.d Joseph Meder for appraising Schoolhouse	1	50
p.d Dr. Saml Plumer for a Road Thos. Meserve lott	12	00
p.d Paul Dame Jr. for an order given his father 1785		94
+ p.d Maj.r Furber. Winthrop Nutter Tax 1797	2	46
p.d Isaac Pearl for wood for Wid.o Waymouth	1	55
p.d Joseph Tucker for D°	2	17
p.d Cash	7	60
And gave a Receipt for 1797	137	03
Feb.y 26 Rec.d of Ich.d Corson Jr. Cash	15	00
p.d Col. John McDuffee Towards his Courthouse bill	17	97
p.d Joseph Clark Esq.r D° his Taxes	3	99
p.d John Brown part of a note	1	00
p.d Lt Timothy Roberts towards keeping E Alley	8	84
p.d Richard Cross for Maj.r Furber's order	10	00
p.d Israel Ham in p.t of his Destrict 1796	5	17
p.d D° in p.t D° 1797	12	00
× p.d Mark Huntress for Maj.r Furber's order	2	00
p.d Edward Cole by order of Courthouse Com.ee	3	42
p.d Capt. John Brewster for parsonage barn sup.	3	52
p.d D° for work on said barn	2	00
p.d Saml Jenness Tax by Maj.r Furber's order	2	97
p.d Benj.a Hayes Tax for Capt. Plumer	3	7
p.d Benj.a Rollins 4.29 more cash to me 2.25	6	54
p.d for removing pound to training field	7	00
p.d Maj.r Furber's order	4	
and gave a Receipt for	108	49
[illegible] 19 1798 With James C. Hayes [illegible]	41	18
Abatement 96. 1.18. p.d Benj.a Nute 40	5	43
for Collecting 96. 3.62. p.d Esq.r Wingate 1.31	31	53
p.d Capt. Plumer 30. a Clark 1.53		
	78	14
Receipted for 96 list 55.71 in full —		
and part of 95 list 22.43 in part —		
78.14		

96

Settlements with Collectors

	Dollars	Cents
9th Rec.d of Ens.n James C. Hayes in Cash	75	09
Abatements for 97 2.78 p.d County Treasurer 20.	22	78
p.d Esq.r Wingate towards Courthouse	2	69
p.d Jotham Nute for Benj.a Rollins	8	49
p.d Jacob Main for Capt. Plumer's Dest. 97	22	00
p.d Saml Wentworth Jr. for John Plumer Esq.r	2	00
p.d Jonath.n Tuttle for Capt. Dan.l Hayes Dest.	14	40
p.d Joseph Walker for Ich.d Hayes Dest.	17	06
p.d Capt. Plumer for Benj.a Rollins	6	02
p.d Capt. Plumer 21 Dol. D° 12. D° 15.30	48	30
p.d for work on Middleton Road as p.r order	14	51
p.d for D° on Wakefield Road as p.r order	19	75
p.d Josiah Main for Paul Jewett Dest. 96 & 97	35	81
p.d Benj.a Rollins 2 Dol. p.d Capt. Plumer 1.25	3	25
p.d for collecting 14.25 p.d Isaiah Varney for a Road [illegible]	16	35
p.d John Brown 2.50	2	50
and Receipted in full for 97 list	311	90
March 21 Rec.d of Ich.d Corson Jr. p.d Maj.r Furber	4	80
p.d John Wagner's Jr. Benj.a Meder's Dest. 96	3	84
p.d Amos Main Tax for 1777	1	45
p.d Zebulon Dame for keeping Tom Cook a poor	5	36
+ p.d Maj.r Furber 1.30. Ich.d Corson for Roads & 7.12	8	42
two former Receipts Given up	12	45
p.d David Heard for Widow Waymouth	2	07
p.d Benj.a Rollins 9.57 Lt Tim.o Roberts 21.61	31	18
and gave a Receipt for 1797	69	57
23 Settled with Joseph Holmes Rec.d Cash	21	00
his Destrict for 96 7.74 John Murray's 97 10.83	18	57
John Murray for opening Roads 97	1	00
Lt Peavey's Dest. 96. 15.54 ins.t for 97. 8.50	24	04
for work on [illegible] Road under John Murray	20	00
Wm. Ham for his father's support	3	93
Robt. Wadleigh Knight for Timber for Dock bridge	8	87
Esq.r Wingate for Courthouse as Com.ee [illegible]	10	31
Maj.r Furber 30 Doll. p.d Eph.m Kimball for Jo. Brown	33	17
p.d Jo. Haven Jr. for keep.g Joseph Jones Destrict 96	11	16
p.d Ens.n Saml Knowles for wood for Wid.o Crocket	6	67
p.d Cash Some time past 18.75 to Jon Dame & 5.20 to	23	95
p.d Maj.r Furber Dest. School 97	20	73
p.d David Watson for a Road thro his land	40	00
p.d County Treasurer 30 D. p.d Wid.o Austin p.r order	34	67
p.d for supplying Wm. Ham a poor person	3	81
Abatement 96 list 4.21 Charles Knight 97 1 Dol.	5	21
p.d for Collecting Capt. Dan.l Hayes Schoolhouse Tax	1	50
p.d the Balance for Collecting 96 tax	3	14
p.d for Discounting Taxes for work on Road under [illegible]	40	00
whole p.d this Day — 330.74	330	74
2 former Receipts given this year — 44.00		
374.74		
Receipted in full the balance for 96 list — 62.88		
& 80 in part for 1797 list — 311.86		

Surveyors of highways Destricts

Heard Roberts $55.64	
Jacob Ellis Do. 50.57	
Cpt. Tho. Roberts $43.43	
Joshua Knight $78.45	
Joseph Hanson $83.44	
Jonathan Heard 81.93.	
Lt. Saml. Downing $62.34.	
Stephen Ham $50.70	
Stephen Whitehouse $40.78	March the 1798 Returned in full $40..78
Francis Alleder $71.12	
Cpt. David Pi[illegible] $50.24	
Joseph Page $41.77	
James Pickering $41.56	
William Hen[illegible] 33.85	
John Tebbetts 33.54	
John Trickey Jun 29.87.	

Surveyors in Northeast Parish

Samuel Varney D. 42,22.	
Jotham Nute 22 Doll. 98 Cent	
Enoch Varney D. 11.80	
Dudley Burnham D. 30.07	
Ephraim Twombly Jr. D. 31.00	
Joshua Harford D. 10.79	
Samuel Ricker D. 25.92.	
Joseph Plumer D. 76.57	
Gilman Jewett D. 60.58 -	
The Second Parish	
~~Daniel Varney~~ Dol. 65 - 46 Cents	March the 23d 1798 Returned in full $65..46
Moses Varney 26 - 48 Cents	Returned in full. $26..48
Samuel Gray 18 - 23 Cents	Returned in full $18..23
Jonathan Wentworth 58 - 57 Cents	
James Runnels 42 - 31 Cents	
Ichabod Hayes 60 - 58 Cents	
Edmond Tebbets 47 - 22 Cents	
John Murrey 38 - 5 Cents	
Gilbert French 16 - 27 Cents	Returned all worked out. - 15.27
Lt. A. Pinney $86.11	

Nonresident Tax 1797

Original Proprietors Names	Division	Number	Quantity	Ratable	Tax Dollars & Cents
James Burgin	2	46	88	5	50
Lieut John Woodman	2	86	160	4	40
Lieut John Smith	2	103	140	4	40
Eli Demerit	2	71	90	3	30
Ditto	3	34	35	1	10
Capt Timothy Gerrish	1	85	60	2	20
Col Richard Waldron	1	130	60	2	20
Capt Francis Matthes	3	63	87	2	20
Lieut Joseph Jones	3	92	140	5	50
Archibald McPhedris	2	12	200	6	60
Ditto	4	116	10	½	5
Capt Thomas Tebbetts	2	49	172	5	50
Capt Paul Gerrish	3	15	140	4	40
William Furber	2	3	140	8	80
Lieut Tristram Heard	2	18	65	2	20
Capt Timothy Gerrish	2	113	240	6	60
Capt John Downing	3	55	140	3	30
Samuel Penhallow	2	32	100	5	50
Richard Wibird Esqr	2	90	160	4	40
Ditto	3	113	140	3	30
Thomas Packer Esqr	3	73	140	4	40
Clement Hughes	2	76	60	2	20
John Usher	3		140	4	40
Henry Tebbets & John Tebbets	3	43	111	3	30
Philip Chesle, Jos. Chesle & Jon. Chesle	3	26	94	3	30
Jos. Chesle, Saml Chesle & John Williams	3	29	46	1	10
Joseph Richer, Geo. Richer & Joel Rollins	3	37	82	2	20
John Frichey, Tho. Frichey, Hatevil Nutter	2	91	84	2	20
Ditto	3		82	2	20
Benj. Mason, Wm Dame & John Layton	2	89	70	1½	15
Nath Randal, Saml Randal & Wm Randal	3	36	140	4	40
John Sias, James Burnham, John Sias Jr	3	46	46	1	10
Eben Tuttle, Wm Twombly & Jas Guppy	3	23	104	2	20
Saml Heard, Jas Heard & David Watson	2	107	228	5	50

School Destricts for first Parish 1797

Destricts	The way said Money has been laid out	Dolls Cents
No 1 Thos Roberts 11.91	pd Levi Jones by Directors order March 18. 1800	11.91
No 2 Jabez Dame Esqr 23.34	Paid March 1799 the whole to Daniel Dame by Directors order	23.34
No 3 Col John McDuffee 34.45	pd John Plumer Jr Esq for the Committee Gave Jo. Bickford an order on Jab. Corson pd the balance to Jno. Plumer Jr Esq	29.0[illegible] 4 1.4[illegible] 34.4[illegible]
No 4 Willm Jennes 13.10	March 1799. Paid the Directors for paying their Schoolmaster the whole	13.10
No 5 Israel Ham 16.00	Decr 25. 1797. Gave Israel Ham an order on Jab. Corson for and to Dependence Bickford on Do	12.00 4 16
No 6 Ensn Jabz Corson 18.45	[illegible] Gave Micah Allen an order on J Horne Jr [illegible] See 1801 acct for last sum	1.[illegible] 17.36 18.45
No 7 Capt Joshua Allen 18.19	gave an order on Collector Corson to Micah Allen for the whole [illegible] 13th 1800 [illegible] this order was taken [illegible] See 1801 acct	18.19
No 8 Joseph Clark Esqr 25.11	paid Benja Allen for [illegible] wood by order of the Directors paid Joshua Lane by Capt Plumer gave Joshua Lane an order on Jabez Corson Jun. for the balance	4.[illegible] 9.50 11.3[illegible] 25.11
No 9 Col David Place 20.43	[illegible] by Com. order [illegible] for boarding Schoolmaster	14.43 6 20.43
No 10 Paul Jennes 15.34	Gave Pelatiah Caulland an order on Jab. Corson Jr for Paid Schoolmistress by Directors order Paid Saml [illegible] Jr by Directors order	6.66 7.50 1.18 15.34

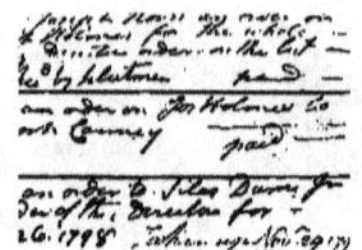

Holmes for the whole
order on the list —
paid —

an order on Jos Holmes to
paid

an order to Silas Dunn for
of the Directors for —
26. 1798 Nov 29 179

...iah Wentworth Do.	2	Ditto upper Corn mill
...ence Tebbets Do.	2	Ditto Lower Cornmill
...mon Torr Do.	2	Garlins Sawmill
...ebz Dame Esq Tanner	2	

...New Hampshire } To Ichabod Corson [?] appointed Collector of Taxes for the ...
...fford ss } in the Town of Rochester for the year 1797. Greeting
...within of Sundry Laws of said State. Directing & Empowering
...to raise money for the Support of Schools, preaching
...other necessary expences. and in pursuance of a precept
County Treasurer to raise a Sum of money for said County
You are hereby required in the name of said State to levy
all persons named in the foregoing list herewith committed
Collect the several Sums set to their names in Dollars
...ich Sums you are to Collect in Silver and Gold or order Dr...
...by the Selectmen of Rochester for the time being and
...by Directed to pay the County Treasurer fifty nine Dollars
...ty cents by the first Day of December next and Two h...
...llars to the Selectm... [illegible]

112

State of New Hampshire } To Joseph Holmes appointed Collector
Strafford ss } of taxes for the south west parrish
In the town of Rochester for 1797 Greeting —
By Virtue of Sundry Laws of Sd State Directing & impowering Selectmen to raise money for the Support of Schools & procuring highways and other necessary Expences and in persuance of a precept from the County treasurer to raise a sum of money for the use of Sd County

[illegible] you are hereby Required and directed in the name of the State of New Hampshire to Levy and Collect of all the persons named in the foregoing List herewith Committed you to Collect the several sums set to their names in dollars and Cents which sums you are to Collect in Silver or Gold or orders drawn on you by the Selectmen of Rochester for the time being and you are hereby Directed to pay the County Treasurer thirty dollars by the first day of December next and one hundred and fifty dollars to be ~~[illegible]~~ paid the Selectmen for the time being by the first day of December next and the bale of the Remainder of the List by the Twentyth day of March next to the Selectmen in said Town in office and if any person or persons shall neglect or Refuse to pay their said tax after being Warned or notised you are to take the same by Distress and for your Lawfull proceedings this shall be your Sufficient Warrant Given under our hands and seal in Rochester this 3d of May in the year of our Lord ~~AD~~ 1797 Richd Dame } Select
Richd Furber Jr }
Beard Plumer } Men

State of New Hampshire } To Joseph Holmes of Rochester in Sd State
Strafford ss } and County Collector of taxes by a vote of Sd Town directing and impowering Selectmen to raise money for the support of the Gospel in the South west parish
[illegible] in Sd town. you are hereby required in the name of Sd State to Levy and Collect of all the Persons named in the List of parrish taxes the several sums set to their names in Gold or Silver carried off in dollars & cents. and you are hereby Directed to pay the same to the Selectmen by the first day of March next in the year 1798 and you are to have for Collecting the sum of three and a half Pr Cent that is to say three Dollars and fifty cents on the hundred if paid in by Sd time if not to pay six Pr Cent for all the money out standing or in your hand and for your Lawful proceedings this shall be your Sufficient Warrant Given under our hand, and Seal at Rochester in the year of our Lord one thousand seven hundred & Ninety seven August the 28th Richd Furber Jr } Select
Beard Plumer } men

1797

Inventory and Com…

Inhabitants Names	[illegible]	Oxen	[illegible]	
Thomas Applebee	1	-	-	1
James Berry	2	1	2	2
James Berry, Jr	1	1	2	5
William Berry	1	-	-	-
Francis Berry	1	-	-	-
Jr John Bergin	1	-	-	-
Isaac Brant	1	0:3	-	2
John Wakfin	1	-	-	1
Ridley Hamham	1	1	2	2
William Mesirl	1	-	-	-
Moses Chamberlain	1	-	-	2
Ivan Carson	1	-	-	1
Samuel Chapman	1	-	-	2
~~George Cook~~	1	-	-	1
Benjamin Carson	1	-	-	1
Joshua Carson	1	-	2	1
Ebenezer Carson	1	-	-	1
Joseph Cop	1	-	-	-
Hezekiah Cole	1	-	-	-
John Downs	1	-	2	1
Jonathan Dore	1	-	-	1
Daniel Dore	1	-	-	1
Hezekiah Dore	1	-	-	1
James Dore	1	-	-	1
Nathan Durbin	1	-	2	4
Miles Davis	1	0:2	-	1
Ens. John Frith	1	1	-	1
Thomas Furber	1	-	-	1
John Fishall	1	2	-	2
Jeremiah Gooding	2	1	2	4
James Gooding	1	-	-	1
Daniel Grant	1	-	-	1
William Gooding	1	-	-	-

[illegible]	–	[illegible]	[illegible]	[illegible]
5	–	11½	1:15	–
8	–	17	1:70	–
0	–	35	3:50	0:86
02	–	56	5:60	– –
20	15	64	6:40	– –
0	10	30	3:00	0:75
[illegible]	–	14	1:40	– –
[illegible]	–	16	1:60	– –
–	–	11	1:10	– –

Inhabitants Names														tax D C	tax D C	tax D C
Obediah Whitham	1	-	-	-	2	1	3	-	-	-	—	-	13½	1:35	0:34	1:25
John Whitham	1	-	-	1	2	1	-	-	-	-	26	-	14½	1:45	0:36	1:35
Geo. Wentworth	1	-	2	1	-	-	-	-	-	-	60	-	17½	1:75	0:44	1:59
Stephen Wentworth Jr	1	:3	-	2	1	3	3	-	2	8	60	-	27½	2:75	0:69	2.57
Jno. Wentworth Jr	1	-	-	2	-	-	5	-	-	-	61	-	16	1:60	0:40	1.50
Caleb Wakeham	1	1:3	2	5	2	3	-	1	7	16	150	15	57	5:70	—	5.34
William Wentworth	1	1:1	2	1	-	1	1	-	1	-	35	-	20	2:00	0:50	1:89
Enoch Wingate	1	1:	-	1	-	2	2	1	3	5	149	13	35	3:50	0:88	3:27
Otis Wentworth	1	-	-	-	-	-	2	-	-	-	-	-	9	0:90	0:23	0:84
David Wallingford	2	-	2	3	1	5	1	1	7	8	121	10	51	5:10	1:28	4:77
Enoch Wentworth	1	-	-	1	-	-	-	-	2	4	48	-	15	1:50	0:38	1:40
Isaac Wooster	1	1:	-	1	-	-	-	-	-	-	—	-	14	1:40	0:35	1:31
John Willand	1	-	-	-	-	-	-	-	-	-	-	-	8	0:80	0:20	0:75
Ephm. Wentworth	1	-	-	2	2	-	-	-	-	-	-	-	15	1:50	0:38	1:40
Daniel Wentworth	1	-	-	-	-	-	-	-	-	-	-	-	8	0:80	0:20	0:75
Ichabod Wentworth	1	0:2	-	2	5	1	1	1	2	-	130	-	30	3:00	0:75	2:81

State of New Hampshire Strafford ss. } To James C. Hayes appointed Collector of taxes for the upper north East part of the Town of Rochester 1797. Greeting

By virtue of sundry Laws of the said State impowering Selectmen to raise money for the support of Schools, procuring high ways, & other necessary expences, & in pursuance of a precept from the County Treasurer, to raise a sum of money for the County of Strafford, You are hereby required in the name of the State to levy & collect of all persons named in the forgoing list, the sums set to their names in Dollars & Cents, which sums you are to collect in silver, or gold, or Orders drawn on you by the Selectmen for the time being, & you are to pay the County Treasurer twenty dollars by the first day of December next, and also you are to pay the Selectmen one hundred dollars by the first day of Octbr. next, & the whole of the remaining sum by the twentieth day of March next, & if any person or persons shall neglect or refuse to pay the said taxes, after legal warning, or notice, you are to take the same by distraint, & sale as the Law directs, & for your Lawfull proceedings, this shall be your sufficient Warrant.

Given under our hands & seal this 9th day of May AD 1797.

Richd. Dame
Richd. Furber Jr. } Select
Beard Plumer } Men

State of New Hampshire Strafford ss. } To Capt. James C. Hayes, appointed Collector of Taxes for the Town of Rochester, for the year 1797, Greeting,

Pursuant to sundry votes of the Town of Rochester for raising money for the support of the gospel & other parish expences, & for raising & collecting the same you are hereby required in the name of sd. State, to levy & collect of all the persons named in the foregoing list, the sums set to their names in Dollars & cents, & pay the whole sum in Dollars & cents, or Silver & Gold, or Select Men's orders, by the first day of March next, & if any person or persons shall neglect, or refuse to pay after legal warning, or notice, you are to take the same by distraint & sale as the Law Directs, & for your Lawful proceedings this shall be your sufficient Warrant.

Given under our hands & seal at Rochester this 9th day of May in the year of our Lord 1797.

Richd. Furber Jr. } Select
Beard Plumer } Men

Abatements in foregoing list

Jeremiah Fisher a poor	1.10	25
Capt. Daniel Hayes a Cowlost	20	5
Lt. Elijah Horn an ox lost	30	7½
allowd March 19. 1798	1.60	
Benond Varney for [illegible] Varney	80	
		20

Beard Plumer	
Betjorn	20
James Berry parish	1.11
James Berry Jr. Do.	1.25
Wm. Berry Do.	20
Ezekiel Berry Do.	20
Moly Davis Do.	38

Towns accompt 1797 Credit

In Collector Paul Harfords hands for 1781
In Lieut. Anthony Peavys hands for 1794
In Lieut. Richard Places hands for 94
In Elijah Varneys hands for 96
In Joseph Holmes hands for 96
Returnd in Notes & Indents by Selectmen 96
Raisd in Ichabod Corsons Jr. list 97
Raisd in Joseph Holmes list 97
Raisd in Ensn. James C. Hayes list 97
Raisd in Lt. Anthony Peavy nonresident list 97
Recieved of Committee for selling town lotts
By Sundry Notes Given to fulfil Contracts about the Courthouse &c
~~Recievd Interest on Notes of hand~~
Cash Recieved of the Selectmen 1796
Recd. of Anthony Peavy for Collecting Non resident tax

The way said Money has been laid out

Paid the County Treasurer in full for 1797
pd. Court house Committee's bill in full 2259.22 the balance paid this year in full
pd. Howard Henderson for taking Inventory 1789
pd. Benjamin Varney Jr. for a Road thro his land
pd. Joshua Lane the Balance in full for [illegible]
pd. Col. Jno. Robert to redeem a piece of Land Sold in 1790
pd. Benj. Dame to redeem a Note given by Selectmen 179[illegible] for keeping Nich. Hammett
pd. Joseph Meder & Benja. Rollins for appraising a School house in Capt. Daniel Hayes District
pd. Dean. Saml. Plumer for a Road thro Messervi Co[illegible]
pd. Lieut. Anthony Peavy as Assessor 1795
pd. Lt. A. Peavy for a Road allowed by Selectmen 9[illegible]
pd. Lt. Peavy for Timber for Dock bridge 1794
pd. Ichabod Corson Jr. for removing pound
pd. Jona. Richards for a lock for the pound
pd. Lt. A. Peavy for waiting on Settlayers 1796
pd. Daniel Dame in full as Assessor 96
pd. for Supplies for the poor thro the year past
pd. Referees and time & expence settling Jacob Hanson & Messrs. Chamberlain Case
pd. David Watson for a Road thro his Land
pd. Time & Expence Settling for said Road
pd. Committe in first Parish for opening Road
pd. Do. in South west Parish for opening Road
pd. Selectmen Settling line at 2d. Dn. School lott
pd. for runing Road by Ephm. Plumer to Newdur[illegible]
pd. for runing & settling a Road by Willm. Wentworth
pd. for vewing Road by Joseph Holmes & Wm. Whitehou[illegible]
pd. Ichabod Corson for a Road at the end of his la[illegible]
pd. Enoch Varney in part for a Road thro his lan[illegible]
pd. Paul Dame to redeem an order given 1763
pd. Lieut. Edw. Rollins for Bark for Court 1797

pd Israel Hams Dest in full for 96		
pd Israel Hams Dest for 97 in part	16	45
pd Capt Daniel McDuffee, Destrict for 96	12	—
pd Ens. Ichabod Corsen, Dest for 95 in part	19 / 16	97
pd Enoch Wingate, Dest. in full for 1796	12	81
pd Benja Meders the Balance for 96 in part	10	84
pd Abner Hodgdon, for 94. 95 & 96	23	16
pd Jonathan Wentworths Destrict for 96	14	34
pd Ichabod Hayes Dest. for 95	17	06
pd Paul Jewett Dest for 96. & 97	35	81
pd Joshua Harfords Dest for 96 & 6 Dol. for 97	19	00
pd Capt Daniel Hayes Dest for 97	14	40
pd Capt Plumer Dest in part for 97	22	00
pd Norway Plains Dest. in full for 95 & 96	45	10
pd Joseph Jones Dest in full for 96	11	16
pd Lt Anthony Peavy Dest in full for 96	15	54
pd Joseph Holmes Dest in full for 96	7	74
pd John Murrays Dest in full for 97	10	83
pd Benja Furbur Dest in full for 97	20	73
pd Lt Anthony peavys Dest in part for 97	8	50
	336	21
pd for Recording Counterparts Nonresident list &c	5	00
pd Selectmen for agreeing with James Runnels & others for repairing Newdurham Road	2	50
pd for time & Expence attending Court at Gilmanton to prevent Complaints from town's [illegible]	2	00
pd for laying out and settling a Road from New Durham Road to Ten Rod Road by Paul Demerit's	3	00
pd Selectmen Giving out Schoolhouse lists and settling about Schoolhouses Several Districts	4	50
pd Selectmen Time and expence settling Courthouse Committee bill & making payments	9	00
for agreeing with persons to take poor persons & for settling their Bills	3	00
for writing & exchanging 14 Deeds for Roads	3	50
pd time laying out & settling for a Road from the Ten Rod Road to Meadows Road by Benja Furber	5	00
pd Selectmen for taking Inventory 1797	10	00
pd Do for making Whole list & Counterpart	10	00
pd Do for Surveyors lists & Destricting Surveyors	10	00
pd Selectmen for Destricting & giving Schoollists	8	50
pd Do for Nonresident list & giving out	3	00
pd Selectmen for procuring Collectors & bonds	4	00
pd for writing paper thro the year	1	50
Selectmens Services thro the year settling with Collectors paying Schools & other Services	20	—
Allow Abatements in Howard Hendersons list 88	3	24
Do in Lieut Anthony Peavys list for 94	1	19
Do in Col Tho Roberts list 87	2	01
Do in Benjamin Dames list 1793	2	18
Do in Lieut Richd Places list 1794	4	10
Do in Joseph Holmes list for Capt Danl Hayes School house	8	25
Do in Ens. James C. Hayes list for 1797	1	60
Do in Ens. Jotham Nutes list for 1793	3	73
pd Ens. Ich. Corsen his acct for Supplying Eph. Alley in 1796 omitted in his account that year	1	12
pd Ens. James C. Hayes in full for Assessor 1797	1	00
pd Committee for apprizing Road by Benj Furber	1	50
pd Wid. Witherel in part for a Road at the South east Corner of her Land	3	41
pd Elijah Varney for Collecting Tax in 96	18	00
pd Abatement in E. Varneys Town list 96	8	76
	5??	03

pd Lt Anthony Peavy his bill for warning people called town meeting
pd for Collecting money for Capt Danl Hayes School house
pd Joseph Holmes the balance for Collecting 96 list
pd the Comttee time & Expence Selling Town Lots
pd Paul Demerit in full for a road thro his land
pd Benjamin Chesle in full for Do thro his land
pd Daniel Page in full for a road thro his land
pd Benjamin Hayes for a road in full
pd Robert & Edward Knight in part for timber for the Dock bridge 1797
pd Money advanced to repair Roads in Sundry parts
pd Ens. James C Hayes in full for Collecting Town Tax 97
Allow Abatement in Jos Holmes Town list for 96
pd John Murry in full as Assessor 97
pd Benja Rollins in part for loss sustained for want of payment according to Contract
pd Interest for money hired more than we received
paid the Auditors for their Services this year

the whole amount paid by Selectmen is 27[illegible] 2[illegible]

out Standing in Collectors &c
In Collector Paul Hartfords hands for 1781
In Elijah Varneys hands for 96
In Ichabod Corsen Jr Hands for 97
In Joseph Holmes hands for 97
In Selectmens hands in Notes & 2d Indents
In Lieut Richd Places hand for 1794
In Lt Anthony Peavys Nonresident list for 97
Due from Lt A Peavy for Privilege of Collecting
Due on Esq Moses Connor's Execution
the whole amount outstanding in Collectrs hands is

paid out & outstanding in Collectors hands is
the whole amount Received by the Selectmen
which leaves a balance due to the Selectmen
and 29.50 [illegible] a mistake in Courthouse Charge

A true statement of town accounts both [illegible] thro the year as kept by us
Rochester March 26th 1798

Richd Dame
Richd Furbush
Beard Plumer

In Auditing the town accounts for the year we find them well vouched accurate and to our appearance honest true & just as exhibited to us this 26th of March 1798

Simon Torr
Jonas C. March
William Palmer

Parish accounts 1797 first Parish

Town C^r In Elijah Varneys hands 96	343	15
Raised in Jchabod Corsons hands 97	325	30
Rec^d of Selectmen 1796 in orders &c	73	46
the whole amount Received by the Selectmen	741	91
The way said money has been laid out		
Paid Joseph Haven in full for 1796	266	67
paid the Committee in full for repairing Barn	9	01
p^d Selectmen for 96 the balance due them	126	16
p^d for making & recording parish list	2	50
p^d Elijah Varney abatement in 96 list	5	26
p^d Elijah Varney for Collecting 96 tax	12	
the whole amount paid by the Selectmen is	421	60
Outstanding in Jch^d Corson Jr hands 97	325	30
the whole that was paid & outstanding is	746	90
the whole Received in was	741	91
which leaves a balance Due to Selectmen of	4	99

Upper Parish account Credit 1797		
In Collector Anthony P^d Rawys hands 95	73	75
In James C Hayes hands for 95	40	45
In Joseph Holmes hands for 96	80	37
in James C Hayes hands for 96	55	71
Raised in Joseph Holmes list for 97	77	32
Raised in James C Hayes list for 97	58	89
the whole amount Received by the Selectmen	386	49
The way said money has been laid out		
p^d Jacob Kimball in full for preaching	96	00
p^d Rev Mr Page for preaching in full	8	00
p^d Esqr Wingate a Journey to Hopkinton	4	00
p^d D^o one Journey to Berwick for minister	1	50
p^d Wentworth Hayes D^o	1	50
p^d Benjamin Scales D^o to Kittery	2	00
p^d Lieu^t Ephraim Perkins for boarding minister	3	00
p^d Selectmen for making rateish &c	4	00
p^d James C Hayes for Collecting 96 Tax	3	62
p^d L^t A Rawys for Collecting 95 tax in full	7	08
Abatement in P^d Rawys 95 tax list	7	05
D^o in James C Hayes 96 list	1	18
	138	93
Cent to the 1st Parish to pay Mr Haven	30	
the whole amount paid by the Selectmen is	168	93
Outstanding in James C Hayes 95 list	18	02
remain in Joseph Holmes hands 96	53	87
remains in Joseph Holmes hands 97	77	32
remains in James C Hayes hands for 97	58	89
the whole that was paid and now outstanding is	208	10
	168	93
in Selectmen's hands [illegible] a note of hand	372	03
against Lt Anthony Rawy for 30.62	336	49
in Selectmen's hands for 1797 Forty doll^s	40	4

121

A true Statement of the foregoing Parishes account thro the Year as kept by us this 26th day of March 1798

Richd Furber Jr } Select
Beard Plumer } Men

In Auditing the Parishes accounts for the Year 1797 we find them well vouch^d accurate and to our appearance honest and just as exhibited to us by the Selectmen this 26 day of March 1798

Simon Gorr }
Jonas C March } Auditors
Willm Palmer

Notes Given to fullfill Contracts about Courthouse &c. 1797

	Dollars		
X One to Capt Saml Storer for	170.00	X Paul Dement	X 15.00
D^o Joseph Hanson	115.83	X Benj^a Chesle	X 34.00
X Balance of one to John Brown	X 25.61	X Daniel Page	X 7.00
X One to John Plumer	X 48.08	X J. Plumer Esq	X 3.55
X D^o to John McDuffee	X 48.08	X Wm Ham J^r	X 7.67
X One to John Plumer Jr	X 36.00		67.22
X One to John McDuffee	X 20.00		540.32
X One to Benj^a Rollins	X 76.71		$ 607.54
	540.32		

these (most are paid in full) –

Supplies for the Poor in the foregoing account for 1797

Supplied Eph^m Alley in full to April 1798 –	61.25
Wid^o Waymoth in full to March 26. 1798	27.75
Aaron Wentworth in full to D^o	10.38
William Ham funeral and all except then	32.41
Wid^o Crocket in full to March 26 98	11.00
Wid Dorras Dealing Expence & removing in full	23.00
Timothy Gerrish in full to March 26 98	6.84
Zebulon Dame for keeping a poor Child in part	12.00
	179.33

We the Subscribers as Selectmen & Auditors in the Second & third Parishes in Rochester do agree that it is our Opinion that at this 23 March 1798 the two parishes above mentioned have each paid their respective parts or proportion towards [illegible] for preaching in s^d parishes & at this date are fully even each parish having their proportion &

Jonas C March } Select
Beard Plumer } men

Richd Furber }
Wm Palmer } Auditors

March 27 1798 Rec^d of Ich^d Corsen J^r in cash	6.85
County Treasurers Rec^t charged to town last year's acc^t	59.80
George Hayes for work on the Road charged last year	2.25
Dependance Bickford for his Dest 97 in part	4.00
p^d Daniel Dame for keep^g David McDuffees Dest in full 97	20.19
+ p^d D^o as assessor for 97 in full	1.30
p^d Benj^a Hayes by Capt Plumers order	1.13
p^d Benj^a Rollins for p^t Norway plains Dest 97	4.58
and gave a Receipt for 1797 list	100.00
May 8 Rec^d of Ichabod Corsen J^r in Cash	2.00
+ Court house Comt^e order to John Osborne	0.86
and 19 Dollars received 27 of April last	19
and gave a receipt for 1797 list	21.86
May 28 Received of Ich^d Corsen J^r p^d Lieut Rollins	5.96
p^d Barker and Rindge for Benjamin Rollins rattle (?) lady	10.12
p^d John Brown order	6.00
p^d James Coleman by John Chalmers (?)	2.10
Paid Peter Cushing in part of Schoolhouse by order	20.00
x Paid Enoch Hoyt p^r order	3.34
Paid Simon Torr Esq in part of his Destrict for 1797	3.44
p^d Paul Dame Junr tax in p^t for Mas. keep^g School 97	5.3
p^d Barker & Rindge by order of Courthouse Committee	2.42
and gave a receipt for 1797 list	61.83
D^o Received of Joseph Holmes in Cash	4.35
p^d Benj^a Cheele in part of his note for a Road	3.10
p^d Capt Samuel Furber p^r order	1.75
p^d Enoch Burnham for Benjamin Rollins	7.83
p^d Jonathan Dame by selectmen order	10.50
p^d Edmund Tebbets School list for 1797	14.47
and gave a Receipt for	30.15
July 30th Received of Joseph Holmes in Cash	16.00
Benjamin Rollins order	2.50
and gave a Receipt for	18.50
September 24 Received of Joseph Holmes Cash	5.00
paid Jonas C. March this day by discounting tax	10.92
p^d D^o as p^r Receipt this day produced	6.10
p^d D^o for David Roberts	3.85
p^d John Brown p^r order	1.42
p^d D^o by Maj. Richd Furber	9.00
p^d Benj^a Furber by selectmen order	2.50
p^d Cash to selectmen the 4th District	2.00
and gave a Receipt for	40.79
D^o Rec^d of Ichabod Corsen J^r for repairing pound	3.00
p^d Benj^a Tebbets for keep^g Benj^m Corsen Dest for 95. 96 & 97	20.00
p^d Micah Allen for [illegible] 95 & p^t 96	18
p^d Nich^s Varney for board^g their school master 97	6
p^d John Magnes (?) in p^t for keep^g Capt Plumer Dest school 97	1.35
x p^d D^o for Elijah Varney p^r order of Magnes (?)	1.76
p^d Capt Plumer by way of John Fish (?)	8.98
p^d Benj^a Rollins [illegible] past not allowed till now	5.38
p^d Mr Hasford & Benj^a Tor (?) for keep^g School 1796 [illegible]	5.58
p^d James Coleman for keep^g [illegible] p^r receipt	14.51
p^d D^o [illegible] p^r receipt	4.93
p^d [illegible] Garland for keeping school in [illegible] 96	13.20
and gave a Receipt of 1797 list for	114.89
Ditto Rec^d of Ich^d Corsen J^r Joseph Hanson (?) order [illegible]	5.215
October 29th Rec^d of Ichabod Corsen J^r Cash	9.13
p^d Benj^a Palmer tow^ds cleaning meeting house 1797	2.66
p^d Solomon Brown the balance for keep^g Hannah Cheele	8.86
p^d Joseph Mann (?) for Paul Jewel Destrict	7.50
and gave a Rec^t for 1797 list for	28.15
D^o Rec^d of Joseph Holmes By p^d Silas Dame the balance for keep^g School in John Ham's Dest for 1797 and gave a Rec^t for 1797 list for the same	9.72
D^o Rec^d of Lt Richd Place By p^d Josiah Main for keep^g School in Main Road Dest for 1796	24.54
paid Zebulon Dame for keep^g poor Boy in part	9.20
and gave a Rec^t for 1796 list for	33.74
D^o Rec^d of Elijah Varney By p^d Josiah Main for services 98	1.52
paid John Brown towards Parsonage Barn	1.00
paid James Coleman for keep^g his Brother Willm	1.42
and gave a Receipt for 1796 list for	3.94

Decem^r 31 Rec^d of Ich^d Corsen J^r as Cash
paid Richd Cross (?) for cleaning Courthouse
p^d Nathl Meader for keeping poor
p^d Josiah Main for services for 1797 as Town Clerk
p^d for collecting 1797 tax in full of Town tax
p^d Abatements of 1797 lists in Town list
p^d Widow Witherell by Discount of her tax for Road
and Gave a Rec^t for the balance
of 1797 town list — 33.29
and part of 1798 town list — 41.67
D^o Rec^d of Said Corsen paid James Pickering for Parsonage [illegible] 74.96

D^o Rec^d of Lieut Ephraim Perkins
Paid Jon^a Dame for paying Saml Mills for Saml Grays District
p^d Paul Dennett for bridge plank for Norway plains bridge
p^d D^o in part of his Note given last year
p^d Joseph Jones for paying James Coleman's poor bill
p^d Joseph Holmes School list for 97 to John Beck (?)
p^d Benj^a Cheele in part of his note given last year
p^d Ezekiel Rickes (?) for laying out a Road by Haw hills
p^d John Murry for Services D^o
p^d Nathl Garland for paying Benj^a Rollins
p^d D^o for paying John Brown towards parsonage barn
p^d Nathl Meder towards keeping poor
p^d John Murrys Service as assessor 1798
p^d Benj^a Furber for paying Parish minister
and Gave a Rec^t in part of 98 list

D^o Rec^d of S^d Perkins parish orders for

D^o Rec^d of Joseph Holmes Cash
p^d George Melvels for keeping Ich^d Hayes Dest. 97
p^d William Hams Note Given last year
p^d Joseph Runnels for shoes for Wm Ham
p^d Silas Dame for keep^g Jon^a Wentworths Dest 97
Allowed Abatements of John Roberts & Jon^a Dames tax 97
p^d for Collecting 97 tax in full Town tax
p^d Abatements allowed in Town list 97
for Cash paid 26th of Novr last
And gave a Note for the balance of 97 town list
Gave a Rec^t in full for 1797 town list

March 18th 1799 Rec^d of Elijah Varney Cash
part of Taxes for Widow Waymouth
a Rec^t Given October 29 th last now Given up
he gave a Note for the balance of his list for 1796
And Gave a Rec^t in full of his 96 list

March 19th Rec^d of Benj^a Yeates Cash
State Treasurers Receipt
p^d for Work & Timber on N. E. pond bridge
John Plumer J^r Esqr Orders
p^d James Berrys School District in full 95
p^d Capt Plumers District the balance of 97
p^d D^o in full for 1798
p^d Joshua Hasfords Dest in part for 1797
p^d Capt Plumer 25.56 D^o 43.50
p^d Capt Daniel Hayes District 98
p^d for Collecting Town Tax 1798
abatements allowed in 1798 Town list
p^d Capt Plumer 22.75 D^o 7.49
and gave a Rec^t in full for 1798 Town list

D^o Rec^d of Ichabod Corsen J^r Cash paid March 22
Squamanegonnick (?) District in full for 1798
and Gave a Rec^t in part of 1798 list

Settlements with Collectors 1798

March 19th 1799 Rec'd of Lieut Ephm Perkins Cash	3.33
pd Edw & Robert Knight for timber for Dock bridge	15.08
pd Jon. Wentworth the District School in part for 1797 [illegible]	4.10
pd Jonas C March 38.95 pd Col. John Waldron for [illegible]	44.71
pd Joseph Carney Jr for keep'g Edmund Tibbets Dist. 98	15.36
pd John Ham's Dist in full for 1798	12.96
pd John Murry for work on the Road [illegible] order	12.00
pd Amos Main for Joseph Jones District in full 98	14.19
pd Saml Pinkham for timber for Places Bridge	8.25
pd Jonas C March 5.25 pd Geo Melcher for Jn. Hayes Dist	3.00 3.25
pd State Treasurer in full of his part for 1798	155.00
pd Eli Sumner in part of Gilbert French Dist. 97 & 98	6.00
and Gave a Rec't in part of his list from 1798	300.23
March 21st 1799 Rec'd of Ichabod Corson Jr	
John Plumer Jr Esq. order	37.08
pd James Coleman 7.80 pd Dr James How 5 Dollars	12.80
pd Jacob Hanson as assessor for 1798 Rich'd Dame 64	7.41
pd Benj Rollins for allowance for neglect of payment	3.43
pd Willm Jenness District 97 & 98 & part of 95	26.91
pd Capt Shannon in part of Norway plains Dist	6.66
pd Silas Dame for Capt Brewsters Dist in full 97 & 98	11.05
pd Simon Torrs Dist the balance of 97	10.56
pd Jabez Dame Esq Dist 97 23.34 pd R Dame 3.33	26.67
pd Stephen Hanford for keeping Ephraim Alley in pt	7.14
pd Do for David Langley by discounting Tax	7.00
pd Capt Plumer 8.67 pd Capt Moses Roberts 1 Doll	9.67
pd Col Places District in ~~full~~ part 98	3.00
allow'd Abatement of Caleb Jackson Tax 98 in pt	0.65
pd James Coleman for Caleb Jackson	1.50
pd Rich'd Dame 2.82 Norway plains Dist in pt 97 11.03	13.85
and Rec'd in part of 98 List	184.38

Settled with Lieut Rich'd Place

Paid John Place for work on Widow Waymouths house	.50
Abated Wentworth Twombly's Tax for 1795	1.00
paid Capt Beard Plumer	0.83
paid Zebulon Dame for keeping Tom Cook a poor	25.45
and Gave a Receipt in full of his list for 1795 for	27.78

Surveyors of highways Districts 1798

David Wingate

Col. Thos Roberts

Joseph Richards

Joseph Hanson

Moses Young

Lieut Saml Downing

Jacob McDuffee

Stephen Ham

Eleazar Ham

Paul Jenness

Joshua Holmes Jr

[illegible]

35-19

Entry	Account	Amount
No 4 William Jennes $ 13.00	paid the whole to the Committee for paying Their Master	13.00
No 5 Israel Ham $ 15.88	Gave an order to Israel Ham & others on John [illegible] Cowen for the whole Sept. 25. 1799 taken up	15.88
No 6 Ensign John [illegible] Cowen $ 17.44	Gave Micah Allen an order for [illegible] by the Comm[illegible] order on J[illegible] Cowen Paid Aug 1799 account March 13th taken up 1804 see 1st [illegible] account	4.64 7.88 4.96 17.48
No 7 Capt Joshua Allen $ 17.29	March 22d pd [illegible] for keeping said School by Director order pd by John [illegible] Cowen	17.29
No 8 Norway Plains 23.8	Paid Benj[illegible] Rollins by Com[illegible] order 1799 pd Enoch Hoyt Jr for wood [illegible] 1800 pd John [illegible] by Director order March 8 1800 Gave Enoch Hoyt Jr an order for [illegible] to Daniel [illegible] for the balance	2.[illegible] 7.3[illegible] 9.9 7.0[illegible] [illegible] 33.0[illegible]
No 9 Squamagonnee 20.77	Gave David Trombly an order on Jel[illegible] Cowen by Director order for Gave David Trombly an order for pd Daniel Hayes for wood all taken up	10.0[illegible] 7.44 3.33 20.77
No 10 Lieut James Plaice $ 15.73	Aug 26. 99. [illegible] Joseph [illegible] an order on [illegible] for [illegible] paid March 8th 1800 [illegible] keeping School by order of the Director pd Samuel [illegible] by Director order	8 4.1 7.9 3.6 15.7[illegible]
No 11 [illegible] Torr Esq $ 21.18	Aug. 26. 1799 Gave Simon [illegible] an order on Moses Hackford for do Sam[illegible] do David Langley do	9.63 9.33 2.21 21.1[illegible]
No 12 Capt Daniel McDuffee 21.06	March 18 1798 Gave an order on John Cowen Jr for the whole sum to Caleb Wingate Taken up March 18. 1800 by B. [illegible] allowed	21
No 13 Abner Hodgdon 9.06	Aug 26. 99. [illegible] an order [illegible] paid to Silas [illegible] for keeping said School	9

School districts Second Parish 1798

John Ham £ 12.96	Gave an order to Joseph Pittle on Lt Eph Perkins for —	12.9[illegible]
Gilbert French £ 7.05	Paid Eli Sumner by Committee order Paid Gilbert French the balance	3.6[illegible] 3.4[illegible]
Richard Furber Esq 20.82	Gave Benja Furber an order on Lt Richd Perkins for March 22d 1799 Gave Joseph Hanson Pr... on Perkins Jany 9 1800 pd ... Furber by Comt order	6.[illegible] 12.[illegible] 2.[illegible]
Daniel Canney 6.31 —	Paid the whole by Director order for paying their school	6.31
Wentworth Hayes	Jany 9 1800 pd Lt Anthony Pearcy by Direction order pd ... per ... pd Joseph ... Roberts by order	6.00 [illegible] 2.95
Joseph Emerson 8.37	Jany 9th 1800 pd the whole to ... Read by Directors order	8.37
Samuel Jones £ 14.19	March 19 1799 the list taken up and allowd to the Director —	14.19
Edmund Tebbetts 15.36 —	Gave Joseph Canney an order on Lt Eph Perkins for the whole by Direction order	15.36
John Murray £ 9.78	Paid the whole to Committee for paying the schoolmaster	9.78
Thomas Ham 6.21	paid March 4th 1800 to Jno Downe per order —	6.21
Jonathn Wentworth 17.88	March 18 1799 Gave the Director an order on Lt Eph Perkins for the whole taken up	17.88
Ichabod Hayes £ 20.22	March 18 1798 Gave orders in favour of Geo Melvil by Director order paid the whole to Geo Melvil	10.[illegible] 9.4[illegible] 20.22
School districts	Third Parish	
Enoch Wingate 15.00	March 18 1800 pd by Direction order by B. Scales —	15.00
Samuel Ricker 4.73	pd by Direction order March 18 1800 by B Scales	4.73
Paul Jewett 20.30	March 18 pd by Benja Scales and list given up by Direction order	20.30
Ensn John Fish 13.32	pd March 18 1800 by Benj Scales by Direction order —	13.32
Benja Scates	[illegible]	

Inhabitants Names	[illegible column entries]		Town Tax	Tax
Benjn Allen	1 2 5 1 1 1 ½ 1 5 8 15	80	18½	3.85
Micah Allen	1 2 2 2 2 1 1 5 12 5	58	42	4.20
Saml Allen	1 2 2 1 1 1 1 1½ 1½ 6 12 15	79	46½	4.65
Benjn Hamby Newington	1½ 16	80	10	1.00
[illegible] Brewster	1 2 2 1 2 1 1½ 6 8 25	60	39	3.90
Thos Brown	1 2 1 ⅔ 3 12 10	28	28	2.45
Wm Brown	1 ½	31	11	1.10
[illegible] Brown	1 1 10		17	1.70
[illegible] Brown	1 1 1 ½ 2 3 20 15	40	37	3.70
John Baker	1 2 2 1 [illegible] 15	170	30½	3.05
[illegible] Baker	1 2 2 1 2 3 8 20 20	90	55	5.50
Jos. Bickford	1 4 3 2 1 [illegible] 1 4 8 20	48	36	3.60
[illegible] Bickford	1 2 4 2 4 [illegible] ½ 4 18 10	72	41	4.10
John Bickford	1 2 1 2 5 1 1 4 7 18 10	105	64	6.40
[illegible] Bickford	1 2.5 3 3 1 [illegible]		11	1.10
[illegible] Brewster	1 1 2 1½ 4 8	50	32	3.20
Wm Bickford	2 4 2		10½	1.05
[illegible] Bickford	1 1		8	.80
S. B. Bruce	30	Stock 3	26	2.60
Dan. Barker	1 1 1		12	1.20
J. [illegible]	1 1		9	.90
Mar. Bickford	2	50	2	.20
Jas. Bickford Dover	2 16	52	10	1.00
Joh. Bickford Newington				
	½ 3 10 25	93	25½	2.50
[illegible] Cook	1 2 4 1 [illegible] 1 4 10 10	20	37	3.70
[illegible] Chandler	1 2 2 1 1 2 1 ½ 1 3½ 10 10	30	39	3.90
Ja. Coleman	1 2 3 1 2 1 1 60	70	32	3.20
[illegible] Cushing	1 2 1 2 1 4 8 16 10	34	56½	5.65
[illegible] Carson	1 4 4 2 1 1 2 12 30	4½	26	2.60
Jos. Clark Esq	1 2 1 2½ 6 16 15	50	73½	7.35
[illegible] Corson Jr	3 6 3 1 1 3 1 1 2 12 10	40	27	2.70
John Coleman	2 1 1 1 ½ 1 8 10	72	19	1.90
[illegible] Coleman	1 1 1¼ 1 4	50	29½	2.95
Abig. Clark	1 2 1 1 2 1 ⅔ 1½ 5 24 10	38	49	4.9[illegible]
James Clark	1 2 2 4 2 1 2 5 20 10	39	50	5.0[illegible]
[illegible] Cartland	2 2 3 2 1	14	11	1.1[illegible]
Dan Calf	1 1 1		10	1.0[illegible]
Rich. Cross	1 1 10	Stock 2	13	1.3[illegible]

.	.	1½	8	.	.30	11	1.10	.68
.	1	5	12	.		26	2.60	. .
½	2	12	28	25	123	64½	6.45	4.3
.	1	2	6	.	26	12	1.20	. .
.	1	2	6	.	66	26	2.60	. .
t	Parish		.	.	.	.	. .	1.75
1	2½	10	16	20	19	55½	5.55	. .
. .	1½	5	12	10	50	29	2.90	1.81
.	1	5	4	10	40	27½	2.75	1.71
½	2½	3	4	10	49	46½	4.60	2.87
1½	4	20	40	30	175	100	10.00	6.18
1	2	4	8	10	33	35	3.50	2.18
.	1	1	.	.	51	24	2.40	1.50

Joseph Knight	1		3			2			1	4	12	10		40	28	2.80	1.75	4.67
Joshua Knight	1	2	1				2-70							75	20	2.00	1.25	3.33
Hale Knight	1		1		1							30	Stud 2	131	19	1.90	1.18	3.16
Wid. Mary Kimball			1		3	2			½	4	7	5			14	1.40	.87	2.33
John Kent	1		1				1					10	½		17	1.70	1.06	2.83
James Kimball	1		1			3			½	5	9		1	20	22½	2.25	1.40	3.75
Capt. Paul Libbey	1	2	2	2		2			2	6	16	20		82	42½	4.25	2.65	7.08
David Langley	1	4	3		1		1		2	6	8	5		94	46	4.60	2.87	7.67
Clement Libbey	1			1	1									24	11	1.10	.68	1.83
Joshua Lane	1						1								12	1.20	.75	2.00
Jos. Libbey Lebanon													4		4	.40		
Joseph Lamston Lebanon													2		2	.20		
Col. T. McDuffee	1	4	5	1	4	3	2		3	25	32	40	6	306	106	10.60	6.62	17.67
Col. Wm. McDuffee	1	2	3	2	3	2	7	½	1	8	20	20		45	34½	5.45	3.40	9.08
Capt. Wm. McDuffee	1	2	4		6	4	1	1½	8	12	20	30	2	107	72	7.20	4.50	12.00
Capt. D. McDuffee	1	2	5	1	3	4	1	1	8	18	40	35		134	88½	8.85	5.53	14.75
Jno. McDuffee	1														8	.80	.50	1.33
Sam. McDuffee	1														8	.80	.50	1.33
Jacob McDuffee	1		2	2	3	1			1½	4	16	10		71	34	3.40	2.12	5.67
Ja. McDuffee Jr.	1	2	3			3	1		2	4	12	10		44	41	4.10	2.56	6.83
David McDuffee	1														8	.80	.50	1.33
T. McDuffee Jr.	1	2							1	3	8				21	2.10	1.31	3.50
Benja. Meder	1		2	1	5	1	1	⅔	1½	5	12	15		42	38	3.80		6.33
Natl. Meder	2		4		5	1	1 aged	½	1½	6	12	10		19	50½	5.5		8.41
Joseph Meder	1	2	3	1	1	1	1		2	6	12	15		110	44	4.40		7.33
Jona. Meder	1	2	2	1	3	1	1		1½	6	12	10		20	41	4.10		6.83
Francis Meder	1		4			1	1		1	5	12	20		20	34	3.40		5.67
Lim. Meder	1		2						1	2		10		24	16½	1.65		2.75
Josiah Main	1		1	3	3	1	2	½	1	3	10				34½	3.45	2.15	5.75
Amos Main	1		1			2									11	1.10	.68	1.83
Jos. Main Jr.	1														8	.80	.50	1.33
Wm. McNeal	1	2	4	1		2	1	½	1	5	8	10	1½	88	42½	4.25	2.65	7.08
Wid. Sarah Morrison			2	3	1	3	1		1	4	8				23	2.30		3.83
John Miller Lebanon													2		2	.20		
James Meder	1															.80		1.33
Richd. Nutter				2	1		1	½	½	2	8	10		18	15	1.50	.93	2.50
Capt. Saml. Nute	1														8	.80	.50	1.33
Wm. Nutter	1		2			1			1	2					18½	1.85	.96	2.58
Richd. Nutter Jr.	1		1												10	1.00	.62	1.67
John Nutter	1		1												10	1.00	.62	1.67
Joshua Nutter	1	2	1		1	1			½	1				25	19	1.90	1.18	3.16
Moses L. Neal Jr.	1					1	1					30			16	1.60	1.00	2.67
Steph. Nutter	1														8	.80	.50	1.33
John Osborne	1		1				1					20	Stud ½		20	2.00	1.25	3.33
Joseph Richards	1	2	1		2	3	1		1½	6	14	10		32	39	3.90	2.43	6.50
John Richards	1														8			1.33

Names of Inhabitants	Entries					Total Tax
Col. Thos. Shannon	1 1 2½ 2 · 1 · 13 9 3 40	140 92	41	4.10	2.56	6.93
Saml. Nay	1 2 4 1 3 2 1 ½ 2 6 16 10	99	50	5.00	3.12	8.33
Abm. Smith	1 1 · 10 2		13	1.30	.81	2.11
Saml. Horey	Stock 30 · 4 4 30 7		47	4.70		7.83
Jos. Sherburne	1		8	80	.50	1.33
Daylen Haspale (?) Dover	1 5 8 10	32	12	1.20		2.00
Thomas Tebbets Esq.	1 2 3 4 4 5 2 2 2½ 17 32 30 2	270	88	8.80	5.50	14.67
Geo. Tebbets	2 · 3 6 3 3 2 1 1½ 10 24 30	200	73	7.30		12.16
Elijah Tebbets	1 2 3 · 2 · 1 · 2 7 12 20		42	4.20		7.00
David Tebbets	1 · 3 1 2 · · 1½ 3 4 8 10	50	30½	3.05		5.8
Robert Tebbets	1 4 4 · · 1 ½ 3 4 10 15	50	44	4.40		7.33
Wid. Ruth Tebbets	· · 2 3 2 · 1 · 1 4 8		23	2.30		3.83
Elias Tebbets	2 2 · 1 · 5	24	12	1.20		2.00
John Tebbets	1 · · 1 1 2 · · 1 2 · 10	107	19	1.90	1.18	3.16
Ebenr. Tebbets	1 · 2 2 1 3 1 1 11 8 20	42	47	4.70	2.93	7.83
James Tebbets	1 · · 1 · · 1 · 4	25	18	1.80	1.12	3.00
Lynah (?) Tebbets	1 · 1	60	11	1.15		1.91
David Tebbets Jr.	1 2		14	1.40		2.33
James Tebbets Jr.	1		8	.80		1.33
Tobias Twombly	1 · 1 · 2 · 6		15½	1.55		2.58
Isaac Twombly	1 · 2 1 1 2 · 1 1 4 10		20	2.00		3.33
Wm. Twombly	1 · 2		10	1.00	62	1.67
Fred. Twombly Jr.	1 2 2 1 · 1 4	10	22	2.20	1.37	3.67
Stephn. Twombly	1		8	.80	.50	1.33
David Twombly	1		8	.80	.50	1.33
Wid. Twombly	2 1 1 · · 1 14 9 20 15	30	34	3.40	2.12	5.67
Wm. Trickey	1 2 1 1 1 2 1 2½ 12 20 20	185	56	5.60	3.50	9.33
John Trickey Jr.	1 2 1 1		19½	1.95	1.21	3.24
John Trickey	1 4 2 1 2 1 1 3 1 7 16 10	40	49	4.90	3.06	8.16
Jos. Tucker	· 2 5 · 1		15½	1.55	.93	2.56
Benjn. Tuttle	1		8	80		1.33
Nicholas Tebbets	1		8	80		1.33
Jos. Tebbets Jr.	1		8	80		1.33
Benja. Tebbets	1		8	80		1.33
Jedediah Tebbets Berwick	8 16	30	15	1.50		2.50
Saml. Tuttle Somersworth	5 16	48	14	1.40		2.33
Moses Varney	1 · 2 · 3 · 1 4 8		26	2.60		4.33
Elijah Varney	1 · 2 · 1 ½ 1 3 8 20 6	8	32	3.20		5.33
Benjn. Varney	1 2 · 1 1 1 1 1 2 5 8	10	33	3.30		5.33
Benja. Varney Jr.	1 · 2 · 2	81	16	1.60		2.67
Thos. Varney	1 · 3 4 3 · ½ 2 4 8		19	1.90		3.16
Joseph (?) Varney	1		8	.80		1.33
Tobias Varney	1 2 4 2 · 1 · 2 8 12 15	20	[illegible]	[illegible]		[illegible]

Names of Inhabitants	Entries					Total Tax
Saml. Willingford (?)	1 2 2 · 2 1 · ½ 1 3 12 10	30	32	3.20	2.00	5.33
Jos. Whitehouse	1 · 2 · 1 · · · 1 · 5	18	15	1.50		2.50
Jethro Whitehouse	1 · 2 · · · 1 · 1 2 4 · 2		22½	2.25	1.40	3.75
Stephn. Whitehouse	1 · 2 2 · 3 · · 2 1 8		23	2.30	1.43	3.83
Thos. Whitehouse	1 · 2 · · · · · · · 5	7	13	1.30	.81	2.16
Benjn. Whitehouse	1 · 1		10	1.00	.62	1.67
Israel Whitehouse	1		8	.80	.50	1.33
Wm. Warren	1		8	.80	.50	1.33
Saml. Kelsen (?)	1 · · · 1		9	.90	.56	1.50
James Waldron	1 · 2 2 2 2 1 · 1 4 16 10	25	40	4.00	2.50	6.67
Capt. Wm. Wentworth 3	1 2 3 1 2 · 1 ½ 2 8 12 20		46	4.60	2.85	7.00
Elijah Witham	1 · 3 · · 2 · · ½ 1 4 5	19	19	1.90		3.16
Jos. Waldron	1 · 1 3 3 2 1 ½ 1 7 10 10	78	38	3.80	2.37	6.33
John Witherell	1 · · 2		11	1.10	.68	1.83
Isaac Watson	1		8	.80	.50	1.33
Francis Wentworth Somersworth	5	180	11	1.10		1.83
Daniel Waldron Dover		30	5½	.55		.95
Moses Young	1 · 1 4 4 1 · ½ 3 8 16 10	63	42	4.20	2.62	7.00

Doomages agreed on & entered in the foregoing List

Stock in Trade	
Joseph Hanson	10
John Kindge	9
David Barker	9
Capt. Saml. Horey	30
Stephen Perkins	4½
Hatevil Knight	2
Tradesmen	
Jabez Dame Esq. Tanner	2
John Odiorne Sadler	3
John Hesit (?) Sadler	2
Josiah Wentworth Blksmith	1
James Tebbets Blacksmith	4
John Smith Blacksmith	2
Caleb Jackson Tanner	2
Anthony Whitehouse Do.	2
Simon Torr Esq. Do.	2
[illegible]	2

Mills	Income
Col. John McDuffee & Jabez Dame Esq. falling mill	8
upper Sawmill at Norway Plains	24
Squamanagonic upper Sawmill	18
Ditto upper Cornmill	6
Do. Lower Cornmill	6
Garlins Sawmill	18
Cushings Sawmill	

Abatements made August 30th 1800 [illegible]
Stephen Twombly [illegible] 0.90 - 0.50
Josiah Main [illegible] 0.90 - 0.50
Wentworth [illegible] 0.80 - 0.50
[illegible] 1.70 - 0.91
William [illegible]

See page (50)

State of Newhampshire } To Richd Dame Collector of
Strafford ss } Taxes for the Town of Rochester for the
Year 1798 Greeting

Pursuant to Laws of the State aforesaid directing Selectmen to
assess the Estates of Nonresidents their proportion of State &
County Taxes & for repairing highways & for collecting the same
You are therefore in the name of the State of Newhampshire
directed and Impowered to collect of all persons appearing
to pay the same, the several sums in Dollars & cents set to the
names of the Original Rights mentioned in the within list
and pay the same to the Selectmen in office by the Twentieth
Day of March next, and if any [illegible] right or parcel of a
Lot being not paid and the owner or owners do neglect to
make payment or any person in their behalf you are
to take the steps of the Law in that case made and provided
and for your Lawful proceedings this shall be your sufficient
warrant. Given under our Hands & Seals Rochester this 28th
Day of May AD. 1798

Jonas C. March } Selectmen
Beard Plumer }

Abatements

Morris Tauler & others	3d Div	19c	Charge 40 -	59c
Joseph Hunt	4 Div			10
John Hall & others	2 Div	60	Charge 40	1.00
				1.69

allowd March 21. 1799

Warrant for Collecting Parish Tax. See page 135. & [illegible]

State of Newhampshire } To Sebastian Cowen Jr appointed Collector
Strafford ss } of Taxes for the first Parish in Rochester
for the year 1798 Greeting

Pursuant to a Vote of the Inhabitants of the first
Parish in Rochester for raising money for hiring
preaching in sd parish and other parish Expences and
for raising and Collecting the same.

You are hereby required in the name of sd State
to levy and Collect of all persons named in the foregoing
list the sums set to their names in Dollars & Cents
and pay Joseph Haven Two hundred Sixty seven (?)
and the remainder to the Selectmen in office or
else pay the whole to the Selectmen by the Twentieth
Day of March next and if any person or persons shall
neglect or refuse to pay after Legal warning or notice
you are to take the same by Destraint and sale as
Law Directs and for your Lawful proceedings this shall
be your sufficient warrant. Given under our hands
and Seals in Rochester this eighth Day of May AD. 179[illegible]

Jonas C. March } Selectmen
Beard Plumer }

~~Abatements Do~~
~~Benj Roberts [illegible] 1.56~~

Septr 10th

Then Richard Dame appearing Made affirmation that he would
faithfully & impartially Discharge and
perform the office of Collector of Nonresident taxes for the year 1798 as the
[law] Directs before me
John Plumer Justice

Isaac Hanson	1	2
Moses Hodgden	1	2
Ichabod Hayes Jr	1	2
Daniel Hayes 3d	1	2
Samuel Hodsdon	1	2

1798 — 140

Inhabitants Names	Polls	Oxen	Cows	3 Year Olds	2 Year Olds	1 Year Olds	Horses	Orchard	Tillage	Mowing	Pasture	Buildings	Mills	Amount of money at interest	Total	Town Tax	Parish Tax	Road Tax
James C. March	1	-	1	-	-	-	140	-	-	-	+	20	8	-	21	2-10	0-53	3-50
John Murray	1	2	2	1	1	3	1	-	-	4	8	5	-	46	35	3-50		5-83
Elijah Meder	1	-	3	2	2	4	340	½	2	8	20	10	-	39	45½	4-55		7-58
William Moore	.	.	.	.	.	.	.	.	.	.	.	.	.	-	-			1-33
Abraham Nute	1	-	1	-	-	1	-	.	.	.	.	.	.	46	11½	1-15		1-91
James Nutter	1	2	2	1	1	4	140	-	1	3	8	.	-	32	36	3-20	0-80	5-33
Ichabod Pearl	1	4	5	4	2	3	1	½	2	12	30	15	-	74	75	7-50	1-87	12-50
John Pearl	1	-	2	3	-	3	1	-	1	6	12	10	-	52	36½	3-65	0-90	6-28
Lt. Anthony Peavey	1	2	2	-	5	2	1	-	1	2	-	10	3	94	38	3-80		6-33
Daniel Peavey	2	2	3	2	-	2	240	-	1	5	8	-	-	49	44	4-40	1-10	7-33
Lt. Ephm. Perkins	1	2	1	-	2	2	1	-	1	4	8	10	-	34/2	33½	3-35	0-85	5-58
Amos Place	1	2	3	-	3	-	1	-	1	4	6	-	-	41	35½	3-55	0-87	5-91
Saml. Parkhurst	1	-	-	-	-	-	1	-	-	-	-	-	-	-	12	1-20		2-00
Joseph Plummer Jr.	1	1	1½	1	2	-	-	-	1½	3	-	-	-	-	22	2-20	0-55	3-67
Eleazer Pearl	1	.	.	.	.	.	.	.	.	.	.	.	-	-	8	0-80	0-20	1-33
Lem. Richardson	1	2	3	1	1	1	240/1	½	½	4	8	15	Stock 3	44	44	4-40	1-10	7-33
James Roberts	1	2	5	-	2	4	[illegible]/1	½	2	10	16	25	-	55/[illegible]	72½	7-[illegible]		12-08
David Roberts	1	-	3	1	4	3	1	-	1½	7	12	10	-	98	48½	4-85		7-08
John Roberts	1	-	2	-	-	1	1	-	-	-	-	10	-	48	18½	1-85	0-46	3-08
James Rummals	1	-	2	2	5	2	-	-	1	4	-	5	-	75	28½	2-85		4-75
Joseph Roberts	1	4	2	1	1	1	-	-	1	2	-	10	-	82	33	3-30		5-50
Ezekiel Ricker	1	2	4	4	1	5	1	-	1½	13	16	10	-	58/3	60½	6-05	1-51	10-08
John Rand	1	2	-	-	-	1	-	-	-	-	-	-	-	-	14½	1-45	0-36	2-41
Samuel Rand	1	-	-	-	1	-	1	-	-	-	-	-	-	-	13	1-30	0-33	2-16
Nathl. Rand	1	-	-	-	-	-	350	-	-	-	-	-	-	-	38	3-80	0-95	6-33
Joseph Rummals	1	-	1	1	-	2	-	-	1	2	-	-	-	24	16½	1-65	0-41	2-75
Benjn. Rummals	1	-	-	1	-	-	1	-	-	-	-	-	-	-	13½	1-35	0-33	2-24
Benjn. Reed	1	-	1	-	2	1	-	-	1	2	4	-	-	26	18	1-80	0-45	3-00
Richd. Rundlet	1	-	1	1	2	-	240	-	½	2	4	-	-	28	20½	2-05	0-51	3-41
John Robinson	1	-	.	.	.	-	-	-	-	-	-	-	-	60	9½	0-95	0-23	1-58
John Rummals	1	-	.	.	.	-	-	.	.	.	.	-	-	-	8	0-80		1-33
Capt. Thos. Shannon																		
Timothy Stevens	1	-	1	-	5	-	-	-	½	2	8	-	-	18/[illegible]	22	2-20	0-55	4-67
Jonathn. Swanton	1	2	1	-	1	-	-	-	1	2	4	-	-	50	23	2-30		
John Twombly of M[illegible]	1	4	-	1	1	2	-	-	-	5	8	-	-	104/4	28	2-80	.	4-67
Lem. Twombly	1	-	1	-	-	-	-	-	-	-	-	-	-	-	10	1-00		1-67
James Twombly Esq.	1	-	3	4	5	3	1	1	2	15	20	20	-	104/2	63	6-30	1-57	10-50
Jo. Thompson Jr.	1	-	1	-	3	2	-	-	-	2	-	-	-	20	16½	1-65		2-75
James Tasfitturn																		
Edward Varney	1	-	1	2	2	1	-	-	1	6	8	5	-	93/[illegible]	29	2-90	0-79	4-83
Stephen Varney	1	2	2	1	-	3	-	-	1½	5	12	5	-	73/[illegible]	36½	3-65		6-08
Mordecai Varney	2	-	3	4	2	4	2[illegible]/2	-	2	8	14	10	-	126/[illegible]	59	5-90		9-83
Caleb Varney	1	2	4	1	1	2	1	½	2	12	24	15	-	23/[illegible]	58½	5-85		9-75
Moses Varney Jr.	1	2	2	-	-	-	-	-	-	-	-	-	-	100	20½	2-05		3-41
Daniel Varney	1	-	3	1	4	-	1	-	1½	6	18	10	-	102	42	4-20		7-00
Saml. Varney	1	-	1	-	-		1	-	-	-	-	-	-	20	11	1-10		1-83
Mason Wingate Esq.	2	4	4	3	3	3	[illegible]/1	-	2½	15	32	15	-	72/[illegible]	87	8-70	2-17	14-50
John Walker	1	-	1	6	1	3	340	-	1	6	8	5	-	20	35½	3-55	0-88	5-91
David Watson	2	-	3	4	3	-	340	-	2	8	12	10	-	46	51	5-10	1-27	8-50
Nathl. Watson	1	-	4	2	1	5	250/1	-	2	10	16	10	-	100/32	51	5-10	1-27	8-50

1798 — 141

Inhabitants Names	Polls	Oxen	Cows	3 Year Olds	2 Year Olds	1 Year Olds	Horses	Orchard	Tillage	Mowing	Pasture	Buildings	Mills	Amount of money at interest	Total	Town Tax	Parish Tax	Road Tax
Edmund Wingate	1	2	1	2	-	1	-	-	1	4	8	5	-	64	29½	2-95	0-73	4-91
Jonath. Wentworth	1	-	2	1	4	2	330/140	-	1½	6	10	10	-	16/[illegible]	35½	3-55	0-88	5-91
Jonath. Wentworth Jr.	1	-	2	4	2	2	1	-	1	6	12	10	-	22/[illegible]	39	3-90	0-97	6-50
Robt. Watson Jr.	1	.	.	.	.	.	.	-	.	.	-	.	.	-	8	0-80	0-20	1-33
John Wingate	1	2	2	1	-	1	1	-	1	6	8	10	-	49/[illegible]	37	3-70		6-16
Lt. Jno. Waldron		-	-	2	6	1		-	1	8	24	-	9	stock	64	6-40		10-67
Wm. Whitehouse	1	-	3	2	3	2	[illegible]/7	½	1½	8	16	10	-	2[illegible]	44½	4-45		7-41
Stephen Wiggin	1	.	.	.	.	.	.	.	.	.	.	.	.	-	8	0-80	0-20	1-33
Elias Wadleigh	1	.	.	.	.	.	.	.	.	.	.	.	.	-	8	0-80	0-20	1-33
Joseph Young	1	-	-	-	-	4	-	-	-	-	-	-	-	140	13½	1-35	0	2-24

State of New Hampshire }
Strafford ss } To Lieut. Ephraim Perkins Jr. appointed Collector of Taxes for the Second parish in

(155) Rochester for the year 1798 Greeting

By virtue of sundry laws of sd State directing & impowering Selectmen to raise money for the support of schools and other necessary expenses and in pursuance of a precept from the State Treasurer to raise money for said State You are hereby required in the name of said State to levy & collect of all the persons mentioned in the foregoing list herewith committed you to collect the several sums set to their names in Dollars & Cents which sums you are to collect in Silver & Gold or orders drawn on you by the Selectmen of said Rochester for the time being and you are hereby directed to pay the State Treasurer of said State the sum of one hundred & fifty five Dollars by the first day of March next and One hundred and fifty Dollars to the Selectmen by the first day of December next and the whole of the remaining sum to the Selectmen by the twentieth day of March next and if any person or persons shall neglect or refuse to pay their sd taxes after legal notice or warning you are to take the same by destraint & sale as the law directs and for your lawful proceedings this shall be your sufficient warrant

Given under our hands & Seals in Rochester this eighth day of May AD 1798

Beza Plumer }
Richd Dame } Select Men of Rochester
Jonas C. March }

State of New Hampshire }
Strafford ss } To Lieut Ephraim Perkins Jr appointed Collector of Parish Taxes for the second parish

(15[illegible]) in Rochester for the year 1798 Greeting

Pursuant to sundry votes of the inhabitants of said Rochester for raising money for the support of the Gospel & other Parish expences and for raising and collecting the same You are hereby required in the name of said State to levy and collect of all the persons named in the foregoing list the sums set to their names in Dollars and Cents & pay the same to the Selectmen in office in Silver or Gold or orders drawn by the Selectmen on or before the first day of March next and if any person or persons shall neglect to pay his or their taxes after legal notice or warning you are to take the same by distraint & sale as the law directs and for your lawful proceedings this shall be your sufficient warrant

Given under our hands and seals in Rochester this eighth day of May AD 1798

Jonas C. March }
Mead Plumer } Select-men of Rochester

Abatements in foregoing list

	Town tax	Parish
Tristram Garland pole tax	0-80	0-20
David Leighton pole tax	80	20
Nathl. Rand sd Horse	2-70	68
Lt. Anthy. Peavey overrated	0-77	
Robert Evans under age	0-80	
Samuel Beck paid	5-87	50
[illegible]		85
[illegible]		90
[illegible]		92

	State
Robert Berry	80
	5-87
	6-67

Rochester April 29th 1799 Recd Six Dollars & Sixty [illegible] Cents abatement of Town Tax & Seven Dollars & [illegible]

24	-	19	1:90	47	3:16
31	-	14½	1:45	33	2:41
25	-	13	1:36	30	2:16
18	-	12½	1:25	-	2:8
-	-	8	0:80	-	1:33
97	16	56	5:60	127	9:16

Wm Hard	1	·	·	1	2	·	2	·	4	8	23	·	28	2:20	55	3:67
Caleb Wingate	1	1	·	·	·	·	·	·	·	·	·	·	12	1:20	30	· ·
Ichabod Libby	1	·	2	3	·	1	5	1	6	16	36	10	39	3:90	90	6:50
Abel Hart	1	·	·	1	·	·	·	·	·	·	·	·	10	1:00	·	1:67
[illegible] Perry	1	·	·	1	·	·	2	·	·	·	·	·	11	1:10	·	· ·
Stephen Watson	Wakefield with 8							·	·	·	80	10	11	1:10	· ·	1:83

State of Newhampshire
Strafford ss

To Benjamin [illegible] appointed Collector of taxes for the Northeast parish in Rochester for the year 1778

Greeting

By virtue of Sundry Laws of sd State directing Selectmen & Impowering them to Raise money for the Support of Schools and other necessary Expences and in pursuant of a warrant from the State Treasurer to Raise money for sd State Treasury and Collect of all persons Named in the foregoing list I have committed you to Collect the Several Sums Set to their names in dollars & Cents which sums you are to Collect in Silver or gold or order drawn on you by the [illegible]

Town Accounts for 1798

In Collector Paul Hartfords hands for 1787	85	10
In Coll.r Lt Richard Place's hands 1794	61	52
In Coll.r Elijah Varneys hands 1796	24	08
In Coll.r Ichabod Corson Jr hands 1797 —	360	88
In Coll.r Joseph Holmes hands 1797 —	214	18
In Coll.r Anthony Peavey's nonresd list 1797	13	45
Due from Lt Anthy Peavey for Collg sd list —	5	55
Due on Moses Canney Esqrs Exor ———	109	40
Raisd in Ichabod Corsons list for 1798 —	910	25
Raisd in Lt Ephm Perkins list for 1798	531	90
Raisd in Benjamin Seates list for 1798	343	20
Raisd in Richd Dames nonresidt list for 1798	32	66
paid by Richd Dame for collecting sd list —	014	00
Recd for sale of Town lands this year —	130	00
Recd for rent for Town lots ———	3	00
Returnd in Selectmens hands in Notes & Indents	271	94
Notes given by the Selectmen to fulfill contracts	168	00
	3276	11

The way said Money has been laid out

Paid the State Treasurer in part for 1798	247	25
Paid Committe for laying out a road from the Dock to the blue hills ———	9	00
pd Richard Cross for cleaning the Courthouse	2	00
pd Josiah Main for his service as Town Clerk for 97	15	00
pd Benjamin Rollings for neglect in not paying him seasonably his bill on the Court house	6	46
pd Paul Demerit for plank for Norwayplain bridge	2	33
pd Moses Chamberlin to redeem a piece of land Illegally Assessd ———	42	00
pd the expence of a rule of court in sd case ———	2	60
pd the sum deducted from Howard Hendersons note being allowed by a rule of Court ———	32	44
pd the Cost & expence of said rule of court &c	16	60
pd for Money expended on the Road by David Roberts	12	00
pd Daniel Dame as Assessor for 97 ———	1	50
pd Ichabod Corson Jr for repairing the pound	3	00
pd Widow Witherill for a road at S E end of her land	7	64
pd Enoch Varney towards a Road through his land	3	43
pd Samuel Pinkham for Timber for the bridge Near Place's mill ———	8	95
pd Edward Knight for timber for Dock bridge in part	15	8
pd Capt Samuel Furber for newheading his drum	1	75
pd Joseph Holmes for collecting Town Tax in full for the year 1797 ———	17	75
pd Ichabod Corson Jr for collecting Town Tax in full for the year 1797 ———	23	12
pd the Selectmen for running a road by Ichd Wentworths	3	00
pd Selectmen for running a road by Jon.a Pottles —	3	00
pd Selectmen for running a road by Enoch Wentworths	3	00
pd Selectmen for attending court to prevent presentment	1	00
pd Selectmen for taking care of the poor ———	2	00
pd Benjamin Seates in full for collecting town tax for 98 —	15	00
pd for labor & timber for bridge at the No 2 pond ———	48	10

School Account for 1798

pd Corl David Places dist in full for 1797 —	20	43
pd Norway Plain dist in full for 97 ———	25	71
pd Israel Ham's dist in full for 97 ———	4	00
pd Capt Daniel McDuffee's dist in full for 97 —	20	19
pd Ensn Corson's dist the ballance for 95 - 96 & pt 97 —	20	00
pd Corl Roberts's dist the ballance 95 & part 96 —	18	00
pd Jabez Dame Esqr dist in full for 96 - 97 & 98 —	71	67
pd Corl McDuffee's dist in full for 97 & part for 98 —	60	45
pd Edmund Tebbetts dist in full for 97 & 98 —	29	98
pd Joseph Jones dist in full for 97 & 98 —	28	16
pd Lt James Place's dist in full for 96 & part 97 —	20	06
pd Samuel Gray's dist in full for 97 ———	6	87
pd John Ham's dist in full for 97 & 98 ———	27	70
pd Ichabod Hayes's dist in part for 96 ———	12	25
pd Joseph Holmes dist in full for 1797 ———	07	10
pd Paul Demerits dist in full for 1797 ———	18	10
pd Enoch Wingates dist in full for 97 ———	13	05
pd Thos Ham's dist in full for 95 - 96 & 97 ———	15	29
pd Gilbert French's dist in part for 97 & 98 —	06	00
pd Paul Jewetts dist in part for 97 —	07	50
pd Benja Meder's dist the ballance of 96 & part 97 —	15	50
pd Simon Torr's dist in full for 97 —	21	16
pd Joshua Hartford's dist in part for 97 ———	4	00
pd James Berry's dist in full for 95 —	14	22
pd Capt Plumers dist the ballance for 97 & in full for 98	32	73
pd Capt Daniel Hayes dist in full for 98 ———	15	07
pd William Jennings dist ball 95 & in full for 97 & 98 —	26	91
pd Capt Jno Brewsters dist in full for 97 & 98	11	05
pd Capt Daniel McDuffee's dist the ballance due for 96	1	00
pd Corl Places dist in full for 98 ———	20	77
	600	98

pd Corl John Waldron to redeem a piece of land In Hatevil Knights Nonres list 95 Illegally assesd	1	66
~~pd Enoch Varney for a road through his land~~	3	43
Allowed Abatements in Ichabod Corson's list for 97 —	8	76
Allowed Abatements in Joseph Holmes list for 97 —	3	90
Allowed Abatements in James C Hayes list for 97 —	1	00
Allowed Abatements in Benja Seates list for 98 —	4	20
pd Josiah Main in part for services as Town Clerk 98 —	1	52
pd Selectmen for taking the Inventory for 1798 and making a return to the General Court ———	20	00
pd Selectmen for making rate lists & Counterparts —	10	00
pd Do for making surveyors lists & districting Do ———	8	50
pd Do for making school lists & districting schools —	10	00
pd the Assessors in full for 98 ———	3	00
pd the Selectmen for appointing Collectors & writing bonds	4	00
pd the Selectmen for making and giving out Nonrd list —	3	00
pd the Selectmen for writing & exchanging 7 deeds & [illegible]	1	75
pd for writing paper through the year ———	1	50
pd the Selectmen for recording Inventory & Counterpart	5	00
Selectmens services through the year ———	20	00
pd the ballance due the Selectmen for 97 ———	380	73
Allowd Abatement of Wentworth Rowells tax in Lt Places list 95	1	00
Allowed Abatements in Richd Dames Nonresd list 98 —	1	69
pd the ballance of the poor bill for 97 & part 98 —	213	81
pd towards Notes of hand given last year ———	200	72
pd a ballance towards the Court House not allowed last year	29	79
pd Interest money for sums hired & neglect of payment the year past ———	27	52
pd Selectmen for settling about School Houses 1 Day at Capt Shannons time & expences	4	42
pd the Auditors in full for 98 —	10	00
	979	3.
	600	0.

1798 148

Outstanding in Collectors lists &c

In Collector Paul Hartfords hands for '81	85	10
Remains in Ichabod Corson Jr list for 98	645	89
Remains in Lt Ephraim Perkins's list 98	145	80
Due on Moses Canney's Exr Exon	89	40
In Selectmens hands in Notes & Debt Indents	180	70
	1148	89
The sum that has been paid out	2127	16
The whole Amount Recd by the Selectmen	3274	05
	3276	11
which leaves a ballance due from Selectmen	2	06

A true Statement of the Town Accounts ~~both~~ debt & credit through the year as kept by us Rochester March 23d 1799

Richd Dame
Jonas C. March } Select men
Beard Plumer

In Auditing the Town Accounts for the year 1798 we find them well Vouched accurate & to our appearance honest true & just as exhibited to us by the Selectmen this 23 March 1799

Jabez Dame
Richd Furber Jr } Auditors
William Palmer

149

South West parish Accounts 1798

In Collector Joseph Holmes's list for 96	53	87
In Coll. Joseph Holmes list for 97	77	32
Returned A note of hand of Anthony Peavey	30	62
Raised in Lt Ephraim Perkins list for 98	74	37
	236	18
Bal. of the Selectmen for 97	9	46
	245	64

The way said Money has been laid out

Paid the Revd Benja Green in part for preaching	98	74
pd David Watson & Committee's order	1	00
pd Selectmen for making parish list &c	2	00
	101	74

Outstanding in Collectors hands &c

Remains in Joseph Holmes's list for 96	53	87
in Do for 97	77	32
Remains in Lt Ephraim Perkins list for 98	6	62
The ballance due on a note signd by L. Peavey	10	62
	148	43
	101	74
The whole amt paid & outstanding	250	17
The whole amount Recd by Selectmen	245	64
which leaves a ballance due to the Selectmen	4	53

Lower Parish Accounts for 1798

In Collector Ichabod Corson's hands for 97	325	30
Raised in Collector Ich. Corsons list for 98	436	82
	762	12

The way said Money has been laid out

Paid Revd Joseph Haven in full his salary 97	266	67
Paid Revd Joseph Haven in part for 98	82	53
Paid for building the parsonage barn in full	138	00
Paid Committee bill for letting out & settling for Do		
Paid for sweeping & taking care of Meeting house 97 & 98	14	00
Paid Ich. Corson for Collecting parish list in full 97	8	12
Allowd abatements in Ich. Corson's list for 97	3	38
Paid Selectmen for making parish lists &c 98	2	50
Paid Revd Mr Havens bill for articles to repair the Parsonage House in 95	4	85
Paid the Selectmen the balance due to them in 97	4	99
	465	04

Outstanding in Collectors hands &c

Remains in Ichabod Corsons hands for 98	346	36
Paid out & outstanding by the Selectmen is	811	40
the whole Amount received is	762	12
which leaves a ballance due the Selectmen	49	28

North East Parish Accounts 1798

In James C Hayes list for 95	18	02
in Ditto for 97	58	89
Returned from first parish money lent them	30	00
Raised in Benja Seates list 98	62	62
~~Recd a note of James C Hayes~~		
	169	53

The way said Money has been laid out

pd the Revd Elihu Whitcomb in full for preaching	30	00
pd Revd John B Perkins in full for preaching	30	00
pd the Expence for boarding Ministers in full	22	50
pd James C Hayes for Collecting 95 tax in full	4	00
Allowed abatements in Do for 95	0	51
Do for 97	3	34
pd Selectmen for making parish lists &c	2	00
pd Aaron Wingate Esq for money pd Revd Mr Kimball	7	00
pd James C Hayes a mistake in cast of his list 95	0	96
pd Aaron Wingate Esq the ballance due for paying Mr Kimball	1	50
	101	81

Outstanding in Collectors hands &c

Remains in Benja Seates's list for 98	62	62
Remains a note of hand signd by James C Hayes	5	85
whole amt paid & outstanding	170	28
whole amt Recd by Selectmen	169	53
Which leaves a ballance due the Selectmen		75

A true Statement of the parish matters for 1798 as kept by the Selectmen Rochester March 23d 1799

Jonas C. March } Select men
Beard Plumer

In auditing the foregoing several parish matters we find them well [illegible]

March 23d 1799

Sum paid for Support of the Poor for the year 1798

Paid Dr James Howe's acct for Service in full 5.00
pd Zebulon Dame towards keepg Thos Cook a poor 34.65
pd Stephen Harford towards keepg Ephm Alley 60.00
pd James Coleman in full for keepg Wm in 97 55.00
pd Do in part for keepg his Mother Wm in 98 18.13
pd Nathl Meder in part for keepg Dol Robinson Child 13.00
pd Solomon Drown in full for keepg Hannah Chesle 12.00
pd for pair Shoes for Wm Ham which is in full 1.34
pd for Sunday bills & keepg Wido Waymouth in pt 98 14.69
Whole Sum paid the year 1798 213.81

Sums paid towards Notes of hand given 1797
pd Benjamin Chesle in part his note 11.65
pd Paul Demerit in part Do 3.00
pd Lieut John McDuffee in full of his notes 20.00
pd Benjn Rollins in full of his Note 76.71
pd John Brown his Note in full 25.61
pd John Plumer Jr Esq in part his large Note 33.64
pd Do one Small note in full 3.55
pd Capt Samuel Storer in part of his Note 26.56
Whole Sum paid this year 1798 200.72

Notes of hand given by Selectmen or on their behalf for 1798 — $
one to Simon Torr for Money hired 100.00
× one to Capt Beard Plumer Do 30.00
× one to Enoch Hoyt Jr for Do × 35.00
Sum Credited to the Town in 98 acct 165.00

Abatements made in Ichabod Corson's list for 1798 see page 135 brot forward for want of Room

	$ Town	Parish
Stephen Wentworth 3d overrated	0.33	0.00
Benjamin Roberts Parish	0.00	1.56
James Tebbets a horse lost	0.40	0.25
George Hill a cow too much	0.20	0.12
Caleb Jackson a horse lost	0.40	0.00
David Barker a Colt lost	0.14	0
Col Thomas Roberts Decd poll tax	0.80	0.50
Capt Moses Roberts a horse lost	0.40	0.25
Wentworth Twombly Decd poor	1.00	0.62
Jonathan Meder Sunday Cattle lost	0.64	0.00
Stephen Twombly Decd poor	0.80	0.50
Josiah Main Jr not 21 years old when taxed	0.80	0.50
Wentworth Cook not 21 years old when taxed	0.80	0.50
William Connor gone away from the Town last made August 20th 1800	1.30	0.81
Lemuel B. Horce gone away ~~part paid~~	38	0.35
David Heard overrated	49	0.00
Isaac Watson gone away out of Town	80	0.50
Elisha Pike gone out of Town poor	3.80	
allowed and Receipt for by Corson town part	13.40	

October 20th 1800 Ichabod Corson Jr

pr Benjamin Heard	1.93
William Henderson	2.06
Ensn Moses Hayes not legally taxed	1.75
Joseph Perkins Jr	0.87
	13.42

Recd the above parish list of abatements this 6th of March 1801
Ichabod Corson Jr

Settlements with Collectors in 1799

April 27th 1799 Recd of Ichabod Corson Cash
pd Stephen Whitehouse for Wood for Widow Waymouth
pd Joseph Tucker for Do
pd Capt Daniel McDuffee for Geo Mellen & Jn Hayes
pd Do for 97 acct charged that year
× pd Benja Rollins in pt Norway plain Dist 1798
pd Daniel Page a note given 97. 7 Dolls
pd Israel Ham Dist in full 98
Cash Recd Some time past
and gave a Rect for 98 list in part 2

Do Settled with Lt Ephm Perkins for Collect 98 list
Abatement of Town list in full
pd Jn Hayes School District for 97 & 98 in pt
pd Nat Watson in pt of Jn Hayes Dist 95
pd Saml Drown District in full for 1798
pd Aaron Wingate Esq
pd John Down for Richd Walker Dist in full 98
pd David Watson for Supporting Thos Ramy in pt
pd Col Richd Furber School District in full 98
pd James Leighton District School in full for 98
pd Jonathan Wentworth Dist School in full 98
pd for Collecting parish Tax in full 98
Abatements of parish Tax 98
Being the Whole of Town list 145.80
& whole balance of parish list 6.62
Receipted in full 98 lists 152.42

August 26th 1799 Settled with Ichabod Corson Jr
pd Josiah Main for Services as Town Clerk for 1798
pd Edward Cole towards Postgundar
pd Alexr Whitehouse for Wood for Wido Waymouth
× and Abatement of Jn Whitehouse parish Tax 1798
pd Jn Ricker Jr for keepg Abner Hodgdon Dist 1798
pd Capt Brewster for Service as Constable in Rose Case
pd Cash for Richd Dame to pay Moses Bickford for ...
and gave a Receipt for 1798 Tax for

6 Do Recd Joseph Havens Receipt for 1798 Salary
also another

× And gave a Rect for Parish Tax for 1798 list

October 28th Recd of Ichabod Corson Jr Cash
pd Edward Cole towards Postgundar
× pd David Heard for wood for Widow Waymouth
and gave a Receipt for 1798 list for

× Also Recd Joseph Havens Receipt for 1798

6 Do Recd of Moses Bickford Jr as Cash
pd Edward Cole towards Postgundar
pd Dr Saml Plumer in pt his district 1798
pd Ebenr Ham for Bridge plank 5.45 John Hayes
pd Stephen Harford towards keepg Ephm Alley
and gave a Receipt in pt 1799 list for

6 Decemr 30th Recd of Ichabod Corson Jr as Cash
pd Nat Meder towards keepg Dol Robertson Child
× pd Peter Cushing towards Norway plains Jn Hayes
and gave a Receipt for 1798 list for

[illegible]	2	[illegible]	140	10	20	94
Capt. John Downing	3	58	140	4	8	37
Richard Wibird Esqr.	2	90	160	5	10	46
Thomas Packer Esq.	3	73	140	5	10	46
Henry Tebbets & John Tebbets	3	43	111	4	8	37
Nicholas Hayford & John Kenny	3	17	95	1½	3	14
Philip Chesle Jos. Chesle Jona. Chesle	3	26	94	3½	7	32
[illegible] Chesle Saml. Chesle Jona. Williams	3	29	46	2	4	18
Richd. Hussey Job Hussey Jos. Jenkins	3	91	110	3	6	28
Clement Hall Jno. Nutter Jno. Nutter	2	9	68	2	4	18
Edwd. Evans Jos. Evans Benja. Evans	2	28	58	2	4	18
Benja. Mason Wm. Dame Jno. Leighton	2	89	70	3	6	28
Nathl. Randal Saml. Randal Wm.	3	36	140	5	10	46
Randal Ditto	4	113	10	1	2	9
John Ham Jno. Burnham Jno. Ham Jr.	1	88	14	2	4	18
Do. formerly Improvd by Robt. Evans	2	8	53	3	30	28
Do. owned by Ichabod Tebbets	2	8	15	1½	3	14
Ditto	3	46	40	1½	3	14
Ditto	4	92	10	1	2	9
[illegible] Willey Jno. Norway Edwd. Whitehouse	3	24	140	5	10	46
[illegible] Robinson Saml. Corson Jno. Rollins	2	24	40	3	30	28
John Drew John Cook Benja. [illegible]	3	14	55	2	4	18
[illegible] Horn Wm. Horn Wm. Horn Jr.	3	10	85	3	6	28
[illegible] Ricker Geo. Ricker Jos. Rollins	3	37	82	2½	5	22
[illegible] Trickey Thos. Trickey Hatevil Nutter	2	91	84	3	6	28
[illegible] Daniel Jos. Daniel Jr. Jethro Bickford	1	112	20	2	4	18
Moses Davis Jr. Thos. Willey Wm. Jackson	2	17	60	3	6	28
Ditto	4	87	10	1	2	9
Gershom Wentworth Esq. Improver [illegible]	2	87	58	4	40	37
Richard Waldron Jr.	3	111	56	2	4	18
John Gray Abner Thurston Thos. [illegible] James [illegible]	3	50	70	2	4	18

State of Newhampshire } To [illegible] Knight Collector of [illegible] for
Strafford ss } the Town of Rochester for 1799 Greeting
Pursuant to Laws of the State aforesaid Directing Selectmen to assess the Estates of Non-residents their proportion of [illegible] for repairing highways and for Collecting the same, you are therefore in the name of the State aforesaid Directed and Impowered to collect of all persons appearing to pay the same the several sums in Dollars and Cents set to each Division of the original Rights mentioned in the foregoing and pay the same to the Selectmen in office by the [illegible] day of March 1800, and if any Right Lot or Parcel of a Right or Lot being not paid and the owner or owners do neglect to make payment or any person in their behalf, you are to take the steps of the Law in that case made and provided for collecting the same and for your Lawfull proceeding this shall be your sufficient Warrant. Given under our hands and seals in Rochester this 25th day of May 1799.

Richd. Dame }
Jeshua Allen } Selectmen
[illegible] Plumer }

[illegible]	98.40
Feb. 24th 1800 Recd. of Moses Bickford Cash	6.30
pd Capt. Saml. Stevens part his note	5.40
pd John Hanson for bridge plank 1.80 [illegible] Whitehouse for [illegible]	11.00
pd Richd. Nutter for [illegible] for widow Alley	6.52
pd Jacob Hanson in part of Road thro his land	10.98
pd Jotham Nute in part his Dest. for 1797	138.60
and Gave a receipt for 1799 list in part	
Do. Recd. of Ichabod Corson Jr. pd James Coleman	6.33
pd Isaac Brown for work on Wid. Waymouth's house	1.50
pd James Chesle 3.33 pd Joshua [illegible] for Norway plains	12.80
pd Wid. Morrison for keep[illegible] in full	2.55
And Gave a receipt for 1798 list for	23.18
March 18th 1800 Settled with Benjamin Hales Recd. Cash & note	9.31
pd John Twombly in pt. for Road 1.60 Oliver [illegible] Do. 1.40	3.00
pd Benja. Corsons Tax for 98 & 99 Discounted by Sundrys	1.67
pd Lt. Elijah Horns school list 99 28.83 Cr. Treas. 99 33.52	62.35
pd Capt. John [illegible] Dest. 98 13.32 Paul Jewett 98 20.30	33.62
pd Paul Jewett bal. 93 4.80 pt. 99 5.78	10.58
pd Samuel Ricker Dest. 98 4.73 Enoch Wingate 98 15.00	19.73
pd Capt. Danl. McDuffee Dest. 98 20.06 [illegible]	20.06
pd Esq. Palmer & Jos. Hoyt for N. L. pond bridge in full	27.00
pd James Berry Jr. for Road 20 James Berry Do. 33 in full	53.00
pd John Remick for a Road 49.00 in full	49.00
pd for Labour on bridge by John Twombly	22.53
pd Saml. Twombly Dest. 99 5.70 Jotham Nute Do. part 5	10.70
pd John & James Varney for work for Aaron Wentworth	4.00
pd for Collecting 99 Tax 17.00 Abatements Do. 4.90	21.90
March 17th 1800 Recd. of Moses Bickford Cash	28.35
pd Dr. John McDuffee the balance of a Note given 1797	36.88
pd Elihu Wentworth for work on bridge by John Twombly	1.19
pd David Langley bal. his school 98 2.22 pd [illegible]	12.22
pd Danl. Dame for Norway plains Dest. 99 pt. 98	31.50
pd Enoch Hoyt for wood for Norway plains Dest. 99	7.00
pd Jos. Tucker for wood for Wid. Waymouth	3.33
pd Zebulon Dame for poor 4.27 pd Richd. [illegible] for wid. Alley [illegible]	11.51
pd Edw. Cole the balance for [illegible]	1.65
pd Saml. Allen for Coleman 1 Doll. Do. for his father [illegible] Tax 90 1.67	2.67
pd Micah Allen toward school in Capt. Corson Dest. 98	3.25
and gave a Receipt in part of 1799 town list for	136.55
also Recd. Joseph Haven Rect. for 1799 [illegible] Cash 21 Doll.	[illegible]
pd Richd. [illegible] Dearborn Jewett for taking care of [illegible] 1800	[illegible]
and gave a Rect. in part of parish Tax for 1799	2[illegible]
March 22d 1800 Recd. of Ichabod Corson Jr. Joseph Haven Rect. 98 [illegible]	84.[illegible]
pd [illegible] Rollins for service as Com. [illegible] letting out land Do. 2	11.[illegible]
pd Col. [illegible] for [illegible] Do. 4 Zebulon Dame for poor 5.20	9.[illegible]
pd Maj. Allen school list 98 17.29 James [illegible]	21.[illegible]
pd Isaac [illegible] for wood 3 Doll. [illegible]	[illegible]

154:

March 22^d 1800

	Dolls. cts
Rec^d of Moses Bickford Cash	87.15
p^d James Place for paying Matthew Welch	00.75
p^d Ens^n Corson District in p^t 1799	4.60
p^d Wm Jennes District in full 1799	11.50
p^d Jon^a Heard Esq. [illegible] order 187	2.37
p^d Capt Moses Robert viewing Bridges &c	3.00
p^d James Place District in part 1798 & 99	16.00
p^d James Robertson forword 3.75 [illegible] D^o 1.40	5.15
p^d Jonah Main for services as Town Clerk 1799	16.00
p^d Israel Ham District in full 99. C^t places D^o 99	35.75
p^d Col^o McDuffee District in full 99. 32.20 abatement 8.18	40.38
p^d for Collecting Town list in full 27.95 p^d D^o Ham 3.75	31.70
gave his note for balance of 99 town list	36.61
More abatement allowed	47
and gave a Receipt in full for 1799 Town list	291.43

155.

School accounts for 1799

No. 1 Jacob Hanson £10.83	March 6. 1802 paid Mary Young by Director order p^d Comm^ee for paying the [illegible] 1803	3.14 7.69 10.83
No. 2 Jabez Dame Esq. 22.71	April 1800 p^d Joseph Ham J^r by Director order	22.71
N° 3 Col^o John McDuffee 32.20	March 24^d p^d the whole to W^m [illegible] & Joseph Bickford by Director order	32.20
N° 4 William Jennes 11.50	p^d March 1800 by Director order	11.50
N° 5 Israel Ham 15.75	March 21st paid the Directors for paying their Schoolmaster	15.75
N° 6 Ens^n Ichabod Corson 17.38	March 26^d p^d the Director for paying their school March 6. 1804 p^d by Committees order	4.60 12.78 17.38
N° 7 Maj^r Joshua Allen 19.71	March 6th 1802 paid [illegible] by the Directors order March 11th 1803 p^d Moses Roberts by Directors order	14.00 5.71 19.71
N° 8 Norway plains	March 3 1800 Gave Samuel Dame an order for the whole by Director order [illegible]	24.15

We the Subscribers appointed a Committee to settle all Accounts [and demands] of every Discription between Rochester and Farmington having met viewed the Towns accounts and Considered the Premises, and After mature Deliberation have agreed that the Said Towns of Rochester and Farmington Continue to enjoy all priviledges & properties within their Own lines Respectively. And that the Town of Rochester Discharge all demands that have arisen against them and receive all monies now due and that a full discharge of all Demands prior to settling the Towns [accounts] March 26th 1799 against each other Cease. Reserving to the Town of Farmington their proportion of what monies the County of Strafford Shall refund towards building the Courthouse if any agreeably to what they paid -

Rochester August 30th 1799

Aaron Wingate
Richd Furber
Jonas C. March
} Committee for Farmington

Jabez Dame
William Palmer
Richd Dame
Beard Plumer
Joshua Allen
} Committee for Rochester

Norway plains Continued 1797

	Dol	cents
Capt Thos Shannon	3	23
John Smith	2	21
Capt Saml Stover	8	16
Joseph Sherburne	1	70
Wm Shannon		68
James Tebbets	2	38
Enoch Tebbets	3	91
David Twombly	1	36
Elijah Tebbets Jr	1	53
Thomas Varney Jr	5	44
Ste Wentworth	1	44
Isaac Wentworth	7	31
Josiah Wentworth	4	59
Daniel Watson	1	53
Isaac Watson	1	36
David Wiggins		68
Nathaniel Adams Esq	2	38
Dudley Palmer	2	21
Ephraim Perkins	5	44
Ephm Perkins Jr	2	63
Joseph Palmer	2	04
Stephen Perkins	2	72
Joseph Richards	6	80
Andrew Pierce	1	36
Stephen Pinkham	1	87
William Perkins	2	29
James Rann	1	70
Col Thos Roberts Estate	3	91
Capt Moses Roberts	5	35
Lieut Thos Richards	1	70
Lt Edward Rollins	6	63
Lieu Tim° Roberts	4	93
John Rendall	5	61
John Rendall Jr	5	27
Benja Rollins	1	36
Jonathan Richards	1	70
Daniel Rogers	2	29
Benja Roberts	4	59
John Roberts Jr	4	59
John Raynall	1	36
John Richards	1	36
Ezra Roberts	1	70
Levi Robinson	1	36
Tim° Richardson	2	04
John Richardson	7	14

A Record of the assessments made for Building Bridges and repairing Roads in Rochester 1799 as the Same was Destributed off by the Selectmen

Norway plains Bridge

Capt John Brewster	6	63
John Baker	6	63
Otis Baker	5	27
John Bickford Jr	6	29
Stephen Brewster	2	21
David Barker	3	57
Joseph Ballard	1	53
John Brown	3	23
Tristram Copps	1	70
Abraham Cook	4	35
Dr Samuel Chamberlin	4	76
Saml Chamberlin Jr	3	48
Peter Cushing	5	61
Joseph Clark Esq	4	35
James Chesle	8	92
Daniel Calf	2	72
Richard Cross	1	70
Edward Cole	1	87
William Connor	1	36
Wentworth Cook	3	40
Moses Canne Esq	1	70
Jabez Dame Esq	13	77
Levi Dearborn Esq	4	93
Joseph Dame	1	36
Aaron Downs	8	67
Moses Downs	7	14
Gershom Downs	5	95
Gershom Downs Jr	7	14
Richard Dame Jr	7	65
Paul Dame Jr	8	41
Caleb Dame	3	23
Daniel Dame	1	36
Silas Dame	8	33
Silas Dame Jr	1	36
Paul Dame	1	53
Paul Downs	1	36
Ensn Richard Furber	3	31
Daniel Garland	5	86
Dudley Garland	3	31
Dr James Howe	4	35
Joseph Heard	5	52
Stephen Harford	5	69
Jacob Hanson	7	39
Nathaniel Horn	1	53
Nathaniel Heard	6	29
Paul Harford	1	36
Enoch Hoyt	3	82
Moses Horn	10	20
Tristram Heard	4	76
Abraham Heard	9	18
Joseph Heard Jr	4	93
William Henderson	6	63
Reuben Hampshire	1	70
Ebenezer Horn	1	78
Joshua Hayes	1	36
John Hanson Jr	1	70
Enoch Hoyt Jr	1	53
Temple Hoyt	1	36
Abraham Hull	1	36
Thomas Hanscomb	1	70
Joseph Heard 3d	4	59
Joseph Hanson	4	93
Mark Hurtress	4	35
Benja Hoyt	4	93
Benja Harford	1	36
George Hull Jr	1	36
Shadrach Heard	1	36
Dennis Hoyt	1	36
Samuel Hayes	3	06
Abner Hodgdon	6	20
~~Josiah Jenkins~~		
Caleb Jackson	4	76
Dearborn Jewett	1	70
Joseph Knight	4	84
Hatevil Knight	3	40
Joshua Knight	3	23
John Knott	3	23
Dr Paul Libbey	6	20
Capt Wm McDuffee	9	69
Capt Danl McDuffee	11	65
Samuel McDuffee	1	36
James McDuffee Jr	5	78
David McDuffee Jr	8	33
Josiah Main	6	80
Amos Main	1	87
Josiah Main Jr	1	36
Richard Matthews	1	36
Moses L Neal Esq	3	00
Richd Nutter Jr	1	70
Richd Nutter 3d	1	36
Jotham Nutter	3	48
Stephen Nutter	1	36
John Odiorne	3	74
Barnabas Palmer	2	72
Lt Richd Place	5	95
Paul Place	4	76
James Pickering	7	82
Levi Pickering	2	55
Daniel Page	11	05
Benjamin Page	2	21
Majr Solomon Perkins	3	40
Dr Samuel Pray	2	04
Benja Palmer	2	72

Turn to left han[illegible]

Thomas Brown	3	82
Joseph Bickford	11	05
Isaac Brown	1	78
Moses Bickford	1	53
Ichabod Bickford Newf	1	44
Benjamin Dame	9	01
Lt Samuel Downing	6	46
Zebulon Dame	5	04
Richard Dame	15	64
Jonathan Downing	1	36
Capt Alexander Hodgdon	10	28
John Hammel	1	95
Moses Hammet	4	16
Jonathan Heard	6	71
Joseph Hodgdon	1	36
Benjamin Hayes Jr	6	80
Moses Hayes Jr	7	48
William Jennes	6	29
William Jennes Jr	4	16
Col John McDuffee	18	02
Lt John McDuffee 2d	1	36
Richard Nutter	2	89
John Nutter	1	78
John Plumer Jr Esq	17	17
John Mt Place	4	42
Ebenezer Pearl	8	16
Moses Young	7	99
Tobias Twombly	1	42
Isaac Twombly	3	57
Benjamin Tuttle	1	36
Ebenezer Tebbets	8	67
Moses Varney	3	57
Ebenezer Varney	5	86
Benjamin Varney Jr	3	40
Thomas Varney	6	80
Jeremiah Varney	1	36
Thomas Varney 3d		85
Moses Varney Jr	1	53
Amos Varney		68
Elijah Varney Jr	2	38
Benja Whitehouse	1	78
Jacob Wallingford	3	40

Joseph Page's Road

Joseph Page	9	01
Daniel Page Jr	7	05
David Jennes	6	37
James Horn of Dover	2	04
	24	47

Isaac Bickford	5	52
Dependance Bickford	10	20
John Bickford 3d	2	4
Solomon Drown	4	42
Ensn Henry Drown	1	36
Jonathan Hayes	1	78
Samuel Davis Foss	5	44
Ephraim Foss Harvey	1	70
Aaron Ham	7	48
Israel Ham	17	17
Stephen Ham	4	93
William Ham	4	59
Richard Hayes	5	75
Nathaniel Ham	3	57
Joseph Hayes	12	34
Samuel Ham	3	06
Nathl Ham Jr	1	53
Thomas How	5	10
Lt Joshua Holmes	2	89
Joshua Holmes Jr		76
Jacob Hanson Meder	3	00
Eleazer Ham	2	97
Benjamin Heard	4	93
Joseph Giles	7	31
Ephraim Garland	1	36
James Garland	3	23
Daniel Jennes	6	12
Paul Jennes	6	97
Isaiah Jenkins	6	80
Jonathan Jennes	4	42
Aaron Jennes	3	14
Moses Jennes	2	59
Nathanl Hayes Jr	4	42
Ensn James McDuffee	11	05
Benja Meder	6	97
Nathaniel Meder	8	84
Francis Meder	5	69
Lemuel Meder	3	57
William McNeal	5	69
Wido Sarah Morrison	4	08
David McDuffee	1	36
John McDuffee Jr	1	36
Jacob McDuffee	7	14
Jonathan Meder	7	31
Joseph Meder	1	02
Lt James Place	11	22
Jonathan Place	1	87
Diamond Pearl	4	08
Abraham Pearl	1	87
Samuel Robertson	3	74
James Robertson	2	63
Samuel Leavy	8	84
Tobias Varney	7	48
Turner Whitehouse	2	38
Anthony Whitehouse	3	82
Stephen Whitehouse	4	42
Alexander Whitehouse	2	62
Israel Whitehouse	1	36
Moses Waldron	6	97
Elijah Whitham	3	48
Wido Martha Pike	1	87
Daniel Jennes Jr	3	06
Winthrop Nutter	1	62

274.63

Benja Evans Jr
Reuben Heard Jr
Jonathan Heard Jr
Daniel Hussey
Howard Henderson
Ephraim Ham
Richmond Henderson
Jonathan Hodgdon
Daniel Ham
William Heard
Ephraim Hammet
Jonathan Henderson
Col David Place
Stephen Place
Joseph Tucker
Duglas Starpole
Elijah Varney
Nicholas Varney
Silas Varney

Little Falls Brid[ge]

John Bickford
Tristram Bickford
John Cloutman
Jeremiah Folsom
Wido Mary Kimball
James Kimball
David Langley
James Langley
Dr Saml Plumer
Ebenezer Plumer
Joseph Perkins
John Plummer 3d
Thomas Plummer
Daniel Plumer
Joshua Rollins
Simon Torr Esq
John Tebbets
William Trickey
John Trickey Jr
George Willand
Enoch Willand
Stephen Wentworth 3
William Warren

Samuel Jennes's R[oad]

Benjamin Evans
Benja Hanson Evans
William Evans
Lt Joshua Holmes
Joshua Holmes Jr
Jacob Hanson
Moses Jennes
Aaron Jennes
Samuel Jennes
Joseph Meder
Winthrop Nutter
Ephraim Kimball

Ephraim Twombly Jr.

	D	C
Hezekiel Clastman	4	76
Elihue Wentworth	5	61
George I Hayes	5	44
Esq John Hagen	1	36
Joshua Canon	1	80
Esq John Hirsh	3	74
Thomas Hurber	1	36
Clement Hayes	3	74
Theodore Ham	2	46
Nicholas Hartford	1	53
Jotham Ham	4	·8
William Hatch	2	55
Pelliah Hanson	1	06
Ebenezer Jones	5	20
Esq William Jones	2	65
Levi Jones	1	53
Gilman Jewett	2	80
Richd Monson	4	56
Theodore Monson	1	36
Daniel Monson	1	06
Capt Samuel Nute	1	36
Thomas Pinkham	4	59
Jonathan Pinkham	2	72
Joseph Perkins	2	89
Nathaniel Pinkham	2	38
Samuel Palmer	6	29
Jedediah Ricker	1	19
Samuel Ricker	4	·8
John Ricker	2	72
Ebenezer Ricker	4	93
Timothy Ricker	2	27
Timothy Roberts	4	42
Samuel Twombly	5	61
Ebenezer Twombly	2	4
Ephm Twombly Jr	6	80
John Twombly	3	·6
Richd Walker	7	31
James Wentworth	4	93
Saml Wentworth	5	27
John Wentworth	4	93
Stephen Wentworth	5	44
Isaac Worster	2	89
William W Lord	4	59
John [illegible]	3	40
Wentworth Dore	1	87

John Varney

	D	C
Dudley Burnham	5	95
Ebenezer Canon	2	4
Jeremiah Cook	3	14
James Goodwin	2	38
Jesse Hanson	2	80
Capt Daniel Hayes	11	70
Ezekiel Hayes	6	27
Ichabod Hayes	3	·6
Stephen Jenkins	9	·9
Stephen Jenkins Jr	7	14
Ebenezer Jenkins	1	97
Roberts Mathes	3	63
William Mathes	3	23
Samuel Nute	11	13
Lieut Jotham Nute	6	88
Francis Nute	3	82
Samuel Nute Jr	3	74
Josiah Nute	—	68
Jonathan Pottle	2	89
Otis Pinkham	3	40
Ephraim Plumer	8	23
Olaver Perry	2	38
Hubbel Roberts	1	61
Tobias Ricker	1	53
William Tuttle	4	42
John Twombly Jr	2	42
Enoch Varney	3	40
James Varney	9	·1
John Varney	6	80
Benjamin Varney	3	57
Samuel Varney	2	72
Aaron Varney	5	95
Jacob Varney	1	02
Caleb Wakeham	11	22
Enoch Wingate	4	35
Ephraim Wentworth	4	59
Ichabod Wentworth	6	29
Samuel Wentworth Jr	3	57

Joseph Plumer

	D	C
William Adams	2	55
Simon Brown	1	36
Moses Chamberlain	5	27
David Canon	2	29
Benj Canon	1	76
Joseph Copp	1	70
Fredrick Cate	1	95
Ephraim Door	1	36
Jonathan Door	2	72
Daniel Door	2	118
Miles Davis	2	38
John Fifield	3	40
Esq James C Hayes	9	18
John Hanson	3	57
Joseph Hight	6	88
Lieut Elijah Horne	8	24
Richard Horne	4	16
Elisha Jennes	2	97
Stephen Jenness	2	4
Beard Plumer	17	51
Joseph Plumer	13	39
William Palmer Esq	11	39
John Palmer	3	16
Col Jos Palmer	7	69
John Remick	2	38
Benjamin Teates	9	18
John Teates	1	70
Jedediah Teates	5	95
Ephraim Twombly	6	80
David Wallingford	5	35
Caleb Wingate	7	48
Mr Griffiths	2	..
Edmon Whitcham	1	36

Paul Jewett

	D	C
Thomas Applebee	2	66
William Applebee	1	61
James Berry	5	36
James Berry Jr	8	50
William Berry	1	36
Francis Berry	1	36
Isaac Brant	5	50
Samuel Chapman	2	04
Micah Door	2	21
James Door	1	70
Nathaniel Durbin	9	52
Jeremiah Goodwin	9	52
Samuel Goodwin	1	36
Daniel Grant	1	36
Zebulon Gilman	3	23
Paul Jewett	17	05
Reubin Jones	4	50
James Merrow	2	12
Benjamin Miller	3	2[illegible]
Nichl Miller	5	10
Richard Miller	4	[illegible]
Mark Miller	3	[illegible]
Keith Miller	1	3[illegible]
Henry Miller	1	3[illegible]
John Remick Jr	7	3[illegible]
John Smith	7	3[illegible]
Gershom Wentworth	4	4[illegible]
Otis Wentworth	2	
Amos Whitcham	4	[illegible]
John Whitcham	4	[illegible]
Obadiah Whitcham	3	
Josiah Whitcham	3	
John McDuffee	1	

90	·65
80	[illegible]
60	·50
40	20

Doomages agreed on & entered in the foregoing list

Stock in trade	Ratable	Mills	Ratable
Joseph Hanson	9	Col. McDuffee & Dames fulling mill	8
David Barker	9		
Capt. Saml Storer	20		
Nath[l] Adams Esq.	12	Upper Sawmill at Norway plains	24
Joseph Ballard	1		
Jabez Dame Esq.	2	Cushings Sawmill	8
Simon Torr Esq.	2		
Anthony Whitehouse	2	Upper Sawmill at Squamanagonnic	18
John Osborne	2	Lower Sawmill D[o]	12
John Hunt	2	Upper Gristmill D[o]	6
Stephen Hanson	6	Lower Gristmill D[o]	6
Josiah Wentworth	1		
John Smith	2	Garlins mill	18
James Tebbets	2		

Warrants

State of New Hampsh[r] }
Strafford ss } To Moses Bickford appointed Collector of Taxes for the first parish in the Town of Rochester for 1799 Greeting

By Virtue of Sundry laws of said State directing Selectmen to raise money for the Support of Schools & other necessary expences & in pursuance of a precept from the County Treasurer to raise money for s[d] County: You are hereby required in the name of said State to Levy & collect of all persons named in the foregoing list herewith committed you to collect in Silver or gold or orders drawn on you by the Selectmen of Rochester for the time being. and you are hereby directed to pay the County treasurer the Sum of Eighty Dollars by the first day of December next and three hundred Dollars more you are to pay the Selectmen by the first Day of January next and the whole of the remainder of said list you are to pay the Selectmen in office by the tenth day of March next and if any person or persons shall neglect or refuse to pay their said Taxes after legal warning or notice you are to take the same by Destraint and Sale as the Law directs and for your Lawful proceedings this shall be your sufficient Warrant. Given under our hands & Seals the 28th day of May 1799

Rich[d] Dame }
Ichabod Plumer } Selectmen of Rochester
Joshua Allen

Abatement made in the foregoing list for 1799 –

	Town	Parish
Jonathan Stead overrated	65	0.33
Benj[n] Dame a cow lost	0.20	—
Jos. Meder for his Cattle died &c	2.00	—
Benj[n] Waldron a cow lost	0.20	10
Nehemiah Chritman's parish Tax		1.40
Lemuel Meder parish Tax		1.05
Winthrop Nutter an ox lost	0.30	—
Benj[n] Roberts overrated	0.10	—
Stephen Twombly a Soldier	1.00	50
Joshua Hayes D[o]	80	40
Joseph Palmer D[o]	1.20	60
Samuel Lock D[o]	1.40	—
Nath[l] Hayes overrated [illegible]	33	—
William Perkins	80	85
Benja Wentworth Crazy		40
	8.98	

Rochester March 22[d] 1800
Rec[d] Eight Dollars & ninety eight cents for the above abatement in Town list – Moses Bickford

Moses Hayes not legally taxed		1.50
William Connor gone away	0.80	0.40
Ephraim Garland D[o]	0.80	0.40
Richard Nutter 3[d] D[o]	0.80	0.40
Isaac Watson D[o]	0.80	0.40
Benjamin Little gone D[o] to sea	0.80	
George Hull J[r] very poor	0.80	—
Abraham Hull		40
	4.80	9.13

March 4th 1801 Rec[d] the above
Moses Bickford

Rec[d] March 4th 1801 nine dollars and thirteen cents for the above abatements in parish column Moses Bickford

Abatement in Benj[n] Scates list for 1799

	Town	Parish
James Garland gone out of Town	0.80	0.20
James Goodwin a cow lost	0.20	0.00
Ebenezer Twombly lame	0.80	0.20
Frederick Caile unable to work	0.80	0.20
Gershom Wentworth an ox lost	0.30	0.8
Joseph Hoyt a cow lost	0.20	[illegible]
David Wallingford a cow lost	0.20	0.5
Thomas Furber for a sick child	0.80	0.20
Benj[n] Corson Parish Tax		0.25
[illegible] Goodwin in bad health	0.80	0.20
Ebenezer Corson parish Tax		30
Joshua Corson parish Tax		27
	4.90	

March 18th 1800 Rec[d] four Doll ninety cents in full for the above town abatement –

Benjamin Scates

.	41	.	16½	1
.	28	.	14	1
.	35	.	13	1
8	197	1	56	5

State of Newham { To Benjamin Scales appointed Collector of
shire Strafford ss { taxes for the Northeast Parish in Rochester
for 1799
By virtue of sundry laws of sd State directing Selectmen and impowering [illegible]
=wering them to Rais money for the Suport of Schools & other necessary
Expences and in pursuant of a precept from the County treasurer
(L.S.) To rais money for the County of Strafford you are hereby required
In the Name of sd State to Levi and Collect of all persons named
In the foregoing List herewith Committed you to Collect the
Several Sums set to there Names in dollars and Cents which Sums
You are to Collect in Silver or gold or orders drawn on you by
The Selectmen of Rochester for the time being and you are [illegible]
Quested to pay the County treasurer of sd County thirty three dollars
And 52 Cents By the first Day of December Next and one hundred and
Forty dollars to the Selectmen of Rochester by the first day of December
Next and the whole of the Remain [illegible] to sd Selectmen By the tenth day
Of march Next and if any person or persons shall neglect or Refuse
To pay his or their tax after Legal warning or Notice you are to
Take the Same by Distraint and Sail as the Law directs and for
your Lawfull proceedings this shall be your suffisient warrant
Given under our hands and seal this 28 day of may 1799
Beard Plumer
Richd Dame { Select
Joshua Allen { men

State of Newham { To Benjamin Scales appointed Collector of the
shire Strafford ss { for the town of Rochester for the year 1799
Greeting
Pursuant to Sundry votes of sd town of Rochester for Raising
Money for the Suport of the gospel and other parish Expences
(L.S.) And for raising and Collecting the Same you are hereby Requi[red]
In the Name of sd State to Levi and Collect of all persons
In the foregoing List the Sums set to there names in dollars
& Cents and pay the whole Sum in dollars and Cents in Silver
Gold or Selectmens order to the Selectmen for the time being
By the first day of march Next and if any person or per[sons]
Shall Neglect or Refuse to pay after Legal warning as [illegible]
You are to take the Same by Distraint and Sail as the Law
Directs and for your Lawfull proceedings this shall be yo[ur]
Suffisent warrant given under our hands and Seal in Roch[ester]
This twentyeighth Day of may in the year of our Lord 17[99]
Beard Plumer
Joshua Allen { Se[lect]
{ men

1799 174

Town accounts for 1799 Credit

	Doll	Cents
In Collector Paul Harford's hands for 1781	85	10
In Collector Ichabod Corson Jr. hands for 1798	645	89
In Lieut. Ephm. Perkins hands for 1798	145	80
Raised in Moses Bickford's list for 1799	917	35
Raised in Benjamin States list for 1799	363	45
Received for Timber sold on School Lott 3d Dc.	303	90
Due on an Execution against Moses Canney Esq.	89	40
Returned in Notes and indents by Selectmen 98	180	70
Received the sum due from Selectmen 1798	2	06
Raised in Nathaniel Knight's Nonresident list 1799	14	62
Recd fines of Wm. Palmer Esq.		83
	2749	10

The way said money has been laid out

	Doll	Cents
Paid the County Treasurer for 1799 in full	113	52
pd for Plank & timber for Norway plains bridge	23	69
pd for Plank & timber for Squamanagonnic bridge	2	09
pd Comm. settling with Farmington in full	7	50
pd Balance of Poor Acct for 98 & part of 1799	219	44
pd Selectmen Running & settling road by James Berry	4	00
pd Selectmen running & settling road by Ichabod Wentworth	3	00
pd Isaac Wentworth, Ebenr. Corson, James Goodwin, Oliver Berry & John Twom[illegible] for a Road thro' their land	28	25
pd Comm. [reviewing &] appraising Bridges & thro the Town	10	00
pd towards Notes given by former Selectmen	224	98
pd Edwd. Knight the balance for timber for Dock bridge	4	05
paid Edward Cole in full for Painting Postguides	29	34
pd Richd. Dame for [expences] carrying on Capt. Stone's cause with David Wiggin as allowed by arbitrators	49	68
pd Peter Cushing some abatement on Norway plains Schoolhouse he being a Creditor thereon	24	59
pd Josiah Main the balance for service T. Clerk 1798	13	48
pd Lt. Ephm. Perkins for Collecting 1798 Tax in full	19	00
pd Ditto abatements in Sd list in full 1798	6	67
pd abatement of Benj. Hanson Jr. Tax in Jo. Holmes list 1797	1	00
pd for a Lock for Courthouse 2.42 putting on .25	2	67
pd Shubael Roberts for a Road thro' his land & deed	10	25
pd Samuel Bragg for bindg Town Book		75
pd Selectmen Running road and opening by Natl. Hayes	2	00
pd Selectmen Runng & openg road by Saml. Jenness	4	00
pd Selectmen endeavouring to procure a road by Richd. Monson to Middleton Road	5	00
pd Selectmen Runng & settling road from David Corson to Thomas Appleby's 3	5	00
pd Selectmen Runng Roads by Timo. Roberts Jr. & Jotham Knight	3	00
pd for assisting to run & open a Road by Benj. Dame	1	00
[illegible]	2	[illegible]

1799 [illegible]

Settlement of School accounts 1799

	Doll	Cents
	20	52
pd Col. Furber's District in full for 1798 in [illegible]	17	88
pd Jonathan Wentworth District in full 1798	6	33
pd Daniel Canney's District in full 1798	8	37
pd Joseph Emerson's District in full 1798	9	78
pd John Murray's District in full 1798	6	73
pd the balance of Gilbert French's Dist. 1797 & 1798	18	95
pd balance of Wentworth Hayes Dist. 1797 & in full 1798	45	24
pd Ichabod Hayes Dist. ye balance for 1796 & in full 97 & 98	44	44
pd Simon Torrey's Dest. in full 1798 and 1799	9	02
pd Ephraim Hodgdon's Dist. in full 1798	31	63
pd Israel Hanson's District in full 1798 and 1799	33	46
pd Richard Walker's District in full 1797 & 1798	15	67
pd Benj. Meder's Dist. the balance of 1797 in full 1798	47	26
pd Norway plains Dist. in full 1798 and 1799	32	50
pd Lieut. James Place's Dist. bal. 1797 in pt. 98 & 99	36	40
pd Col. John McDuffee's Dist. the balance 1798 & part of 1799	15	00
pd Capt. Thomas Roberts District in full 1797 [illegible]	20	00
pd Squamanagonnic District in full for 1799	30	88
pd Paul Jewett's Dist. bal. of 1793 (4?) in full 98 & part 99	28	83
pd Lieut. Elijah Morrow's District in full 1799	10	43
pd Samuel Rickers District in full 1798 & 1799	31	05
pd Enoch Wingate's Dist. in full 1798 & 1799	15	98
pd Capt. Daniel Hayes District in full 1799	30	32
pd Ensn. John Fish Dist. the bal. of 1797 in full 98 & 99	21	06
pd Capt. Daniel McDuffee's dist. in full 1798	11	50
pd Willm. Jenness District in full 1799	7	85
pd Ensn. Corson District in part 1798	17	29
pd Maj. Jotham Allen District in full 1798		
	624	87

	Doll	Cents
Paid Jacob Hanson in full for a Road thro' his land at the Hamhills as appraised by committee	25	00
pd the Assessors in full for 1799	2	00
pd Selectmen Settling with Collectors, Services as Treasurer arranging Town accounts in full	18	00
	3	56
paid the Southwest Parish the balance due on Settlement	6	00
pd Selectmen & appraisers selling timber on School lott 3d	1	67
pd abatement of Capt. Wm. Allen's Tax in P. Cushing's list 1798	49	
pd John Hamick Jr. in full for a Road thro' his land	93	
pd James Berry in full for a Road thro his land	20	
pd James Berry Jr. & Wm. Berry in full for a Road		80
pd abatement Jona. Goodwin poll tax in States list 1798	17	00
pd Benja. States for Collecting Town list 1799	4	90
pd Abatements in Benj. States list 1799		
pd Wm. K. Atkinson a demand he had against Selectmen for 1793 respecting Howard Henderson's case	2	00
pd Willm. Appleby his full for a Road thro his land	10	00
pd Henry Rines & Henry Millar for a Road	4	00
pd John McDuffee Jr. for a Road thro his land	1	00
pd Selectmen viewing & running Road by [illegible]	2	00
paid Interest money for notes & their payment	40	78
pd Howard Henderson the five pounds voted him for a Road he purchased of Ensn. James McDuffee in 1796 & Interest	20	41
pd Josiah Main in full of his service Town Clerk 1799	16	00
pd Auditors in full for service this year	6	[illegible]
	283	12

First Parish account 1799

	Dollars	cents
Returnd in Ichabod Corsons hands 1798	346	36
Raisd in Moses Bickfords list for 1799	341	78
	688	14
The way said money has been laid out		
Paid Joseph Havens Salary the balance for 1798	244	13
Paid Joseph Havens Salary for 1799 in full	266	67
Paid Comm[tee] bill hiring & building Parsonage barn	7	17
Paid Rich[d] Cross in full taking care of meeting house 1798	5	00
Paid Selectmen the balance due them 1798	49	28
Paid Selectmen making parish list &c 1799	2	50
pd Comm[ee] selling old meeting house [illegible]	22	00
Paid out by Selectmen in 1799	596	75
Remain in Ichabod Corsons list for 1798	49	70
Remain in Moses Bickfords list for 1799	48	72
paid out and outstanding	695	17
Rec[d]	688	14
which leaves a balance due to Selectmen of	7	03

South west Parish account 1799

Remains in Joseph Holmes list for 1796	53	87
Remains in Joseph Holmes list for 1797	77	32
Remains in Ephraim Perkins list for 1798	6	62
Do the balance of a Note of hand from L[t] Rays	10	62
	148	43
The way said money has been laid out		
Paid Farmington Committee as p[r] receipt	32	94
P[d] Farmington Selectmen as p[r] receipt	37	00
P[d] Joseph Holmes for collecting 1796 & 1797 taxes	6	00
P[d] abatement in Joseph Holmes list for 1796	4	50
P[d] abatement in Jo Holmes list in 1797	6	15
P[d] Jo Holmes to release nine persons he took prisoners their Taxes, Keepers bill &c [illegible]	30	66
P[d] said nine persons for wrong imprisonment	9	60
P[d] Lieut Eph[m] Perkins for collecting 98 parish list	2	60
Paid D[o] Abatement made in 98 list in full	7	42
P[d] Selectmen of Farmington Lieut Rays note	10	62
P[d] the balance due the Selectmen on Settlem[t] 1798	4	50
whole sum paid out in 1799	151	99
Rec[d]	148	43
Due to Selectmen of Rochester which is given up to Farmington by agreement	3	56

North east Parish account

Returnd in Benjamin Scales list for 1798	62	62
Returnd a Note of hand of James C Hayes	5	85
Raisd in Benj[a] Scales List for 1799	68	05
The way s[d] Money has been laid out	136	52
Paid Rev[d] Daniel Weston in full for preaching	40	00
P[d] expence boarding Ministers in full	16	00
P[d] Rev Tho[s] Russel in full for preaching	4	00
p[d] Benj[a] Scales for collect[g] 98 tax in full	3	00
p[d] Abatement in Scales 98 list	2	35
p[d] Selectmen for Making list for parish in 1799	2	00
p[d] Selectmen the balance due last year		75
p[d] by Selectmen the year past	68	10
Returnd in Benj[a] Scales hands in 1799	68	5
	136	15
which leaves a balance due from Selectmen of	136	52
		37

The foregoing is a true acc[t] of parish matters as before this 22[d] of March 1800 — Paul Plumer, Joshua Allen, Selectmen

Sums p[d] towards poor & Notes of hand in

Pd Will[m] Ham J[r] Note in full
pd Daniel Pages Note in full
p[d] Cap[t] Beard Plumers note in full
pd Enoch Hoyt J[r] Note in full
pd Balance of Benj[a] Cheslei's note in full
pd Balance of Paul Demerits Note in full
pd Lieut John M[c]Duffee's note in full
pd Balance of John Plumer J[r] Esq[r] note in full
pd Balance of Capt. Sam[l] Torrens note in part
[illegible] in full as Charged in Town acc[t] 1799

Sums paid for Support of poor in 1799

Paid James Coleman in full for his brother W[m]
P[d] Nat[l] Meder the balance of 98 & [illegible] for 1799 for Dolly Robinson Child
P[d] Stephen Hanford in full for Eph[m] Allen funeral
pd for Supplies for Wid[o] Waymouth in full
pd Some Assistance for Aaron Wentworth
pd David Watson for keep[g] the [illegible] Mary Ray in part
P[d] Some assistance grante Matthias Welch in 98
pd the balance in full for Hannah Chesle
pd for building Wid[o] Alleys house in full [illegible]
pd Zebulon Dame in part for Thom. Cook
the full sum charged in 1799 acc[t]

May 12th 1800 Then agreed with Ichabod to collect the Town and Parish Tax first Parish in said Town and appointed to said Office which he accepted and bond to collect and pay the same in his warrant. At the same time appointed John Odiorne to collect nonresident Tax for said year which accepted and gave bond accord[ingly]

Rich[d] Dame
Joshua Allen

Report of the Committee for viewing Bridges &c

Pursuant to appointment we the subscribers have proceeded to view the roads and bridges in the Town of Rochester and hereby report as follows

First – That Norway plains bridge be rebuilt; that it be Twenty shafts wide, to be covered with whitepine four inch plank. That there be one double pier and five single piers, of four rows of posts each and seven Stringes of fourteen inches Square. the piers to be well braced and the whole to be of white Oak, or such as the Committee will accept. – That there be two hundred Dollars laid out in building Abutments on the east shore of Rocks and that for the whole expense of said bridge there be appropriated Seven hundred Dollars in labour at forty two cents per day including extra for hire of Workmen and Overseers &c and for railing the same —

Secondly: That Squamanagonnic Bridge be rebuilt and Two hundred and fifty Dollars be allowed at forty two cents per Day for rebuilding the same; in common form with white Oak piers to be well filled with Rocks and railed —

Thirdly That Three hundred Dollars be laid out at forty two cents per day in rebuilding and repairing Binghams Bridge with White Oak piers and common covering five Stringes fourteen Inches Square and railing —

Fourthly: That Eighty Dollars be allowed for repairing Walkers Bridge in the best manner Sd Sum can be laid out at 42 cents per Day

Fifthly: That Eighty Dollars be laid out for rebuilding Little falls Bridge with wooden abutments and one White Oak pier & common covering as the district shall chose. —

Sixthly That twenty eight Dollars be laid out in building a Causeway between Benjn Evans and Samuel Jones at forty two cents per Day —

Seventhly That Joseph Page, Daniel Page Junr and David Jennes be allowed Twenty four Dollars to repair their Road & bridge from Sd Jennes to James Chesley at forty two cents per Day —

Eighthly That the Two Districts on Salmon falls Road be allowed One hundred Dollars to repair their main Road at forty two cents per day, and the remainder of their Taxes to be laid out rebuilding Norway plains bridge —

Ninthly That the Inhabitants of the North East parish be assessed their equal proportion with the first parish to be laid out in Labour on the roads and bridges at forty two cents per Day the Quarter on and adjoining Middleton Road to be directed to repair said Middleton Road except Seventy Days work which are to be laid out Clearing and making the Cross road from Capt Daniel Hayes to Samuel S. Wentworths —

Tenthly. That a District be formed from Hezekiah Cloutmans to Samuel Twomblys inclusive to repair Wakefield road from said Cloutman to Palmers mills —

Eleventhly. That the remainder of Wakefield road be repaired by the Inhabitants on and adjoining Sd road including the bridge at the branch —

Twelfthly. That the remainder of said Northeast parish be included in a District to rebuild the bridge at Zebulon Gilmans, meaning the half that is on Rochester side, to be built in common form of Good timber, and the remainder of their Labour to be laid out on the road from David Corsons to Paul Jewetts — Allowing the Selectmen to relieve such of the Inhabitants as they shall Judge proper who live remote from any public or placed road that can be made passable by releasing a part or whole of their Taxes for making their own Roads provided the same be laid out in a Limited time

Rochester November 18th 1799.

Hedgd Plumer
Joshua Allen
} Committee

To the Selectmen of Rochester

Settlements with Collectors 1800.

	Dollars
October 20th Received of Jeth. Corson Jur Cash & sundries as cash	22.83
pd Peter Cushing Esqr Clerk order for bridge & horse for School house	6.09
pd State Treasurer the balance for 1798	106.00
+ Abatements in Town list for 1798	13.40
and gave a Receipt for 1798 list in part	148.32
Received of Jeth. Corson Jur Cash	7.00
1801 Jany 21. cash pd by Capt Plumer [illegible] cash pd at Sundry times 16 Doll	34.00
× pd Wm James Place for his School District 1799	7.13
and gave a Rect towards 1800 list	48.13
March 4th Settled with Benjamin Seates Recd cash	142.24
pd State Treasurer his part in full 1800	95.21
pd County Treasurer his part in full 1800	33.52
pd Caleb Wakeham School District 1800	19.00
pd Moses Chamberlains Do 17	34.00
Ensn Jotham Nutes Do 17. Saml Twomblys Do 6	29.50
Paul Jewetts Do 23.50. Richd Walkers Do 10	29.50
Esqr Wm Palmers Do 19.50	2.00
pd Saml Wentworth Jr for a Road thro his land	6.00
pd Richard Moulton for expense on Road	5.32
pd Ephm Wentworth for a Road thro his land	20.00
pd for Collecting town tax in full 1800	12.63
pd abatements in town list in full	3.05
pd Dr John Smith in '88 & '89. & Simon Brown in 89	17.00
pd Ensn John Fish School District in full 1800	40
gave two notes for 20 Dollars each	487.97
gave a Receipt in full for 1800 town list	
Do — Settled with Moses Bickford recd cash & as cash	10.61
pd towards Schooling in Col McDuffees dist 1800	12.50
pd Geo Hayes for work on Twomblys bridge	1.80
pd Capt Moses Roberts for work on pound	1.50
pd on Capt Saml Rogers Note	5.40
Abatements made this day in 1800 town list	4.80
which was in full for 2 notes held against him	36.61
Do Settled Moses Bickfords parish list 1799	
Recd Cash 30.84. for Collecting parish in full 8.75	39.59
Abatements in 1799 parish list in full	9.13
and gave a receipt in full for parish list 1799	48.52
March 5th 1801 Recd of Jehabod Corson Jr as Cash	44.70
pd Lieut Timo Roberts for keeping Widw Morrow in pt	15.00
pd Esqr Dames School list 1800 24 Doll. Maj Allens Do 20	44.00
pd Col D Place & Dand Hayes for work on Walkers bridge	14.84
pd County Tax for 1800 80 Doll. John Brown on Cond[illegible] 1.12	81.12
pd Esqr Corsons Dist 1799. 15.40 Taxes for R. Dame 14.14	29.54
pd Zebulon Dame Tax for keeping Thomas Cook a poor	4.73
pd Benjn Whitehouse for Wid. Waymoths shoes	1.50
pd John Odiorne for a Road 4.20 Tax for Maj Allen 10.92	15.12
pd for Timber for bridges in Lt Timo Roberts dist	1.00
pd Dr James Howe for visiting paupers	4.90
pd Saml Kimball for Capt D. McDuffees dist 1799	15.00
pd An Abatemt Benj Heards parish Tax 1799	1.93
pd Israel Hams School list 1800 18 Doll. for R Dame 4.15	22.15
pd Isaac Pearl for wood for Wid. Waymoth	2.75
pd as cash 18.20. Collecting parish Tax 1798 9.33	27.53
pd John Brown for work on parsonage House	3.70
pd Richd Cross for Taking care of Meeting House 1800	6.00
pd Abatements of parish Tax 1798	11.14
	346.68

× and Recd in full balance of 1798 list 209.13
+ and Parish list balance 1798. 49.70
× and in part of 1800 list 87.85
346.68

Abner Hodgdon 10 dollars	in 1804 acct pd Thos [illegible] pr order	[illegible]
No 14 Medcborough district 20 dollars	March 21. 1801 gave Simon Otis an order on J. Conner by Comtee order [illegible] [illegible] 30th 1802 gave David [illegible] an order on Ichabod Corsor for 12 Dolls —	8.0 12.0 20.

School Account in the upper Parish 1800

No 1 Richard Walker 10. dolls	Paid March 4th 1801 to Beny Stiles [illegible] pay the Committee —	10.00
No 2 Jotham Nute 17. dollars	Paid March 4th 1801 Do	
William Palmer 19.50	Paid March 4th 1801 Do by Commit order —	
[illegible] Chamberlin 17 dollars	Paid March 4th 1801 Do	
Caleb Wakeham 19 dollars	Paid March 4th 1801	

3	1	1	2	1	1	1	5	12	(mill 2)		48	6.00	2.40	6.00
1	1	2				1½	3	8	·	50	34	4.25	1.70	4.25
1	·	·	·	·	·	·	·	·	·	·	10	1.25	.50	1.25
[illegible]			[illegible]			1	·	3	·		53	6.63	2.65	6.63
·	·	·	2 yr			·	·	mill 1c			11½	1.44	--	1.44
						1	·	4	·	45 [illegible]	4	.50	· ·	50
				1		([illegible] 2)		1	·		15	1.88	.75	1.88
[illegible]	·						1	12	·	60	7½	.94	--	.94
·	1	1				1	2	4	·	·	13½	1.69	·	1.69
·	·	·	·	·	·	·	·	·	·	·	8	1.00	--	1.00
	·	·	·	·	·	·	·	·	·	·	8	1.00	.40	1.00
·	·	·	·	·	·	·	·	·	·	·	8	1.00	--	1.00
·	·	·	·	1	·	·	·	·	·	·	12	1.50	.60	1.50
3	·	4	2	1	½	½	3	10	2	83	28	3.50	1.40	3.50
1	2	2	1	1	¼	1	4	10	2	20	32	4.00	1.60	4.00
1	·		·	·		½	1	·	2	·	13½	1.69	.67	1.69
1	·	·	·	1		1	·	12	8	100	37½	4.69	1.40	4.69
3	3	·	1	1	·	2	6	16	2	50	77½	9.69	3.87	9.69
1	·	·	1	1	·	3	6	16	1	34	51	6.38	2.55	6.38
1	·	·	·	1	·	1	2	12	4	4	26	3.25	1.30	3.25
2	·	1	·	1	·	1	2	12	1	40	33	4.13	--	4.13
3	·	·	·	·	·	½	1	8	1	72	28	3.50	--	3.50
1	3	1	3	·	1	1½	5	20	1	38	45½	5.69	2.27	5.69
1		·	·	1	·	1½	1	4	1	50	32	4.00	1.60	4.00
1	1	1	·		·	1	·	·	·		13½	1.69	0.67	1.69
1		·	·		·	1			·		11	1.38	.55	1.38
1					·	1	·	·	1	·	12	1.50	.60	1.50

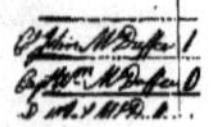

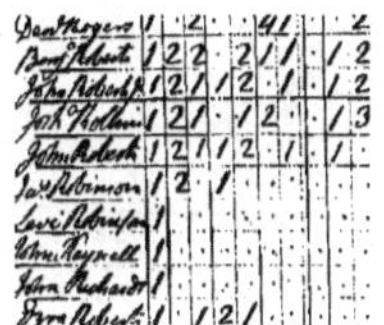

Danl Rogers	1		2			4	1			2
Benj Roberts	1	2	2		2	1	1		1	2
John Roberts Jr	1	2	1	1	2		1		1	2
Josh Rollins	1	2	1		1	2			1	3
John Roberts	1	2	1	1	2		1		1	
Jas Robinson	1	2		1						
Levi Robinson	1									
Wm Rayswell	1									
John Richards	1									
Ezra Roberts	1		1	2	1					

Strafford ss   [illegible] Taxes for the first Parish in the Town of Rochester for 1800   Greeting

By virtue of Sundry Laws of said State directing the Selectmen to raise money for the support of Schools and other necessary Expences and in pursuance of precepts from the State & County Treasurers to raise money for State & county purposes

You are hereby directed in the name of said State to levy and Collect of all persons named in the foregoing list the Sums Set to their names in Dollars and Cents and pay the County Treasurer of said County Eighty Dollars by the first day of December next and you are hereby directed to pay the Treasurer of said State Two hundred and forty five Dollars by the first day of December next and five hundred Dollars more you are to pay the Selectmen or their order by the first day of January next and the whole of the remainder of said list you are to pay the Selectmen in office for said Town by the Twentieth day of March next and if any person or persons shall neglect or refuse to pay his or their said Taxes after legal notice or warning you are to take the same by distraint & sale as the Law directs and for your Lawful proceedings this Shall be your Sufficient Warrant. Given under our hands and seals in Rochester this third day of May AD 1800

Richd Dame — } Select
Beard Plumer } men of
Joshua Allen } Rochester

State of Newhampshire Strafford ss

To Ichabod Corson Junr - appointed collector of parish Taxes for the Town of Rochester for 1800   Greeting

Pursuant to Sundry votes of the Inhabitants of Rochester impowering the Selectmen to raise money to hire preaching and for collecting the same — you are hereby impowered and directed in the name of said State to collect of all persons named in the foregoing list the several sums set to their names in Dollars and cents and pay Joseph Haven Two hundred and Sixty six Dollars and sixty six cents by the Twentieth day of March next and the remainder to the Selectmen by said time. Or pay the Selectmen for the time being or their order the whole of said list by said time and if any person or persons shall neglect or refuse to pay the same after legal warning or notice you are to take the Same by distraint and sale as the Law directs and for your lawful proceedings this shall be your sufficient warrant Given under our hands and seals in Rochester this third day of May Anno Dom. 1800   Beard Plumer } Select

[illegible]

1800 Nonresident List for 1800 –

Proprietors Names	Div.	No.	Qty	Value	State Tax	County Tax	Rep. Tax
[illegible] Thomas Westbrook	1	131	140	4	.12	.5	.50
[illegible] Burgin	1	88	30	3	.10	.3	.38
[illegible]	3	34	35	2	.6	.2	.25
[illegible] Joseph Jones	3	92	140	5	.16	.6	.63
[illegible] Mc[illegible]	2	19	300	8	.25	10	1.00
[illegible]	4	116	10	1	.3	.1	.13
[illegible] Thomas [illegible]	2	119	100	4	.12	.5	.50
William [illegible]	2	3	140	10	.32	.12	1.25
[illegible] John [illegible]	3	58	140	4	.12	.5	.50
Richard Wibird Esq.	2	90	160	5	.16	.6	.63
[illegible] Ricker Esq.	3	73	140	5	.16	.6	.63
[illegible] & John Kenney	3	17	35	1½	.5	2	.19
[illegible] Joseph [illegible]	3	91	40	2	6	2	.25
Edward [illegible] Joseph Evans and Benjamin Evans	2	28	58	2	.6	.2	.25
[illegible] Wm. Dame [illegible] Leighton	2	89	70	3	.10	.3	.38
[illegible] Randal [illegible] Randal and William Randal	4	113	10	1	.3	.1	.13
John Sias James Burnham	1	88	14	2	.6	.2	.25
& John Sias Jun.	2	8	15	1½	.5	.2	.19
Saml Wille John Norway & Edward Whitehouse	3	24	140	5	.16	.6	.63
Timo. Robinson Saml Corson and John Rollins	2	24	40	3	.10	.3	.38
Joseph Ricker Geo. Ricker and Jeremy Rollins	3	37	82	2½	.8	.3	.31
John Trickey Thos. Trickey and Hatevil Nutter	2	91	84	4	.12	.5	.50
Joseph Daniel Jos. Daniel Jr. and Jethro Bickford	1	112	20	2	.6	.2	.25
Moses Davis Jr. Thos. Willey	2	17	60	3	.10	.3	.38
and William Jackson	4	87	10	1	3	1	13
Joseph Stephenson John York & John Ambler	2	15	80	3	.10	.3	.38
John Gray Abner Thurston Thos. Waistcoat & James Nock	3	50	70	4	.12	.5	.50
Morris Fowler John Hoyt Thos. Holmes Benja. [illegible]	2	11	4	1	3	1	13

State of New Hampshire } To John [illegible] appointed Collector of the [illegible]
Strafford ss – } nonresidents for the [illegible] for 1800

Pursuant to [illegible] Laws of the State aforesaid directing [illegible] to assess the Estates of Nonresidents their proportion of State County Taxes for repairing highways and for collecting the same. You are therefore in the name of the State aforesaid [illegible] and Impowered to collect of all persons appearing to pay the shares the several sums in Dollars and cents set to each Owner of the original right mentioned in the foregoing list and pay the same to the Selectmen in office by the first day of [illegible] next and if any Right Lot or parcel of a Lot or right being not paid and the owner or owners do neglect to [illegible] or any person in their behalf you are to take the steps of the Law for collecting the same and for your lawful proceeding this shall be your sufficient warrant. Given under our hands and Seals in [illegible] the [illegible] Day of May 1800

Richd Dame } Select
[illegible] Plumer }
[illegible] Allen } men

191

1800 Abatements made this year – –

In Ichabod Corson Jr. List

	Town	Parish
Daniel Page deceased	1.00	0.40
Capt. Thomas Shannon deceased	1.00	0.40
Solomon Drown disabled by lameness	1.00	
Moses Horn disabled by Sickness	1.00	0.40
Benja. Whitehouse over rated	00.17	
Temple Hoyt one Cow over rated	0.25	0.10
Enoch Hoyt Jr. over rated	.16	0.7
Elijah [illegible]	1.00	
Daniel Calf Deceased	1.69	0.67
Joseph Haven Jr. gone out of town	1.00	0.40
Nathaniel Haven Jr. gone out of town	1.00	0.40
Richard Mathes gone out of town	1.00	0.40
[illegible] Hanson not 21	1.00	.40
Jonathan [illegible] a Cow lost too much	13	5
Isaac Morton gone out of town	1.00	—
Isaac McDuffee not 21 when taxed	1.00	—
Stephen Perkins over rated	.37	15
Ezra Roberts over rated	.30	
Abraham Hall poor	1.00	—
George Hall Jr. gone away	1.00	
Paul Roberts a pub[illegible] to his father 1797	80	40
	16.87	
Credited to Corson on Extending him		.40
August 8th 1803 Daniel Rogers [illegible]	2.50	1.00
John Richards poor	1.00	
John Rowell poor	1.00	40
Ebenezer Horn Jun. poor	1.00	40
David McDuffee poor gone	3.00	1.20
Samuel Richards Deceased	1.13	45
William Perkins Drug [illegible]	1.88	75
Solomon Berry poor gone	1.00	
	$29.38	8.87

Recd the above March 10th 1804 being twenty [illegible] Dollars Dudley Palmer Town [illegible]

Ichabod Corson

March 4th 1806 Recd the above — Ichabod Corson

Abatements in Benja. Seates list

	Town	Parish
Moses Davis gone out of Town	1.38	.00
Miles Davis Cow lost	.25	
John Smith poor	1.00	
Joshua Corson		25
Ebenr Corson a Cow lost	25	32
Benja. Corson		25
William Adams gone out	1.69	—
Wm. Furber gone out of town	1.00	
Thomas Furber poor	1.00	
Elisha Jenness Deceased	1.00	20
William Griffith poor	56	
Joseph Perkins gone out of town	1.00	
Francis Nute a Steer lost	25	
Simon Brown		
Caleb Wingate a Dead horse	3.25	0.75
Jonathan Pinkham poor		20
Thomas Pinkham poor		32
	12.63	
John Smith for 1798 & 1799	2.05	
Simon Brown for 1799	1.00	
	15.68	

Recd the above of the Selectmen Being the Town tax abatements March 4th 1801 fifteen D. & 68 Cents

Paul Ellis – 20
Gershom Ward – 40

Benjamin Seates Col

"In the name of Sd State to levie and Collect of all persons
Named in the foregoing List the Sums set to their names in dol
and Cents and pay the County treasurer of Sd County thirty three dollars &
Fifty five Cents by the first day of December Next and you are hereby dir
To pay the treasurer of Sd State Ninety five dollars and twenty one Cen
By the first day of December next and one hundred & Sixty dollars
More you are to pay the Selectmen or there order by the first day of
January next and the whol of the Remainder of Sd List you are
To pay the Selectmen in office for Said town by the twentieth day
of march next and if any person or persons Shall neglect or
Refuse to pay his or their Said taxes after Legal warning or
Notice you are to take the Same by distraint and Sail as the
Law directs and for your Lawfull proceedings this Shall be your
Sufficient warrant given under our hands and Seal in Rochester
This first day of may 1800

Benjd Plumer } Select
Richd Dame
Joshua Allen (men

State of Newhampshire Strafford ss to Benjamin Bates your
Collector of taxes for the town of Rochester for the year 1800 Greeting
Pursuant to Sundary votes of Sd town for raising money for the
Suport of the gospil and other parrish Expences and for Raising
and Collecting the Same you are hereby Required in the name of
Sd State to live and Collect of all persons named in the foregoi
List the Sums set to their Names in dollars and Cents and pay the
whol Sum in dollars & Cents or Silver or gold or Selectmens or
To the Selectmen for the time being by the first day of march
Next and if any person or persons Shall Neglect or Refuse to pay
after Legal warning or notice you are to take the Same by
Destraint and Sail as the Law directs and for your Lawfull
Proceedings this Shall be your Sufficient warrant given
Under our hands and Seal in Rochester this Second Day
of may in the year of our Lord 1800

Benjd Plumer } Selec
Joshua Allen (men

Name	Dolls	Cents
Samuel Adams	1	36
Capt John Brewster	2	20
John Baker	1	99
Otis Baker	1	62
John Bickford Jr	2	25
Daniel Barker	2	77
Joseph Ballard	–	78
John Brown	1	10
Moses Brown	–	42
Tristram Coffin		72
Abraham Cook	1	47
Dr Saml Chamberlain	1	68
Samuel Chamberlain	1	20
Peter Cushing	1	95
Joseph Clark Esq	1	36
James Chesley	2	38
Daniel Colf	–	70
Richard Coffin	–	57
Edward Cole	–	63
Wentworth Cook	–	63
Moses Canne Esq	–	26
Joshua Chamberlain		
Jabez Dame Esq	4	25
Levi Dearborn Esq	1	47
Joseph Dame	–	42
Aaron Downs	2	89
Moses Downs	1	99
Gershom Downs	1	68
Gersh Downs Jun	1	99
Richd Dame Jun	2	36
Silas Dame Jun	2	72
Caleb Dame	1	05
Daniel Dame	–	42
Silas Dame	2	77
Paul Downs	–	42
Capt Richard Furber	1	20
Daniel Garland	1	99
Dudley Garland	–	99
Dr James How	1	47
Joseph Heard	1	73
Stephen Hanford	2	20
Jacob Hanson	2	62
Nathaniel Horn	–	52
Nathaniel Heard	1	70
Paul Hanford	–	50
Enoch Hoyt	1	20
Moses Horn	2	46
Tristram Heard	1	36
Abraham Heard	2	83
Joseph Heard Jun	1	70
William H[illegible]	1	96

Warrant Dated Augst 27th 1800 to [illegible] Collr

Name	Dolls	Cents
Reuben Hannaford	–	57
Ebenezer Horn	–	52
John Hanson Jun	–	52
Enoch Hoyt Jun	–	89
Temple Hoyt	–	52
Abraham Hull	–	42
Thomas Hancomb	–	52
Joseph Hanson	1	87
Mark Hunking	1	41
Benjamin Hoyt	1	62
Benja Hanford	–	42
George Hull Jun	–	42
Simeon Hoyt	–	42
Abner Hodgdon	1	57
Ebenezer Horn Jr	–	42
Caleb Jackson	1	83
Joseph Knight	1	52
Hatevil Knight	1	10
John Hunt	–	98
Dr Paul Libbey	1	89
Capt Wm McDuffee	2	46
Capt Danl McDuffee	3	64
Saml McDuffee	–	42
James McDuffee Jr	2	01
David McDuffee Jr	1	26
Josiah Main	1	83
Amos Main	–	63
Josiah Main Jr	–	42
Richd Matthews	–	42
Moses Neal Esq	–	78
Richd Nutter Jr	–	63
Jotham Nutter	–	99
Stephen Nutter	–	42
John Odiorne	1	26
Barnabas Palmer	–	84
Lt Richd Place	1	62
Paul Place	1	62
James Pickering	2	36
Levi Pickering	–	99
Daniel Pages Estate	2	94
Benja Page	–	68
Majr Solomon Perkins	–	89
Dr Saml Pray	–	63
Benja Palmer	–	47
Dudley Palmer	–	73
Ephm Perkins	1	36
Ephm Perkins Jr	–	94
Stephen Perkins	1	31
Andw Rines	–	42
Stephen Pinkham	–	44
William Perkins		
Joseph Richards	2	25
James Rann	–	42
Col Thos Roberts Estate	1	10
Capt Moses Roberts	1	41
Lt Saml Richards	–	47
Lt Edward Rollins	1	94
Lt Timo Roberts	1	57
John Randall	1	46

Norway Plains Continued	Dolls	Cents
John Randall Jr	1	43
Benja Rollins	–	68
Jona Richards	–	47
Daniel Rogers	1	05
Benja Roberts	1	47
John Roberts Jr	1	47
John Raynall	–	42
John Roberts	1	47
Ezra Roberts	–	73
Levi Robinson	–	42
Thos Shannon Esq Estate	–	89
John Smith	–	73
Capt Saml Stoner	4	30
Joseph Sherburne	–	52
William Shannon	–	63
James Tebbets	–	94
Enoch Tebbets	1	20
David Twombly	–	42
Elijah Tebbets Jr	–	52
Thos Varney Jr	2	20
Stephen Wentworth	–	23
Isaac Wentworth	1	90
Josiah Wentworth	1	52
Daniel Watson	–	63
James Waldron	2	36
Thomas Wentworth	–	73
175.25		
Samuel Allen	2	62
Micah Allen	2	10
Lt Timo Corson	2	67
William Ellis	–	57
Clement Libbey	–	75
Heard Roberts	3	25
Joseph Tebbets	9	78
Elijah Tebbets	1	65
Robert Tebbets	2	41
David Tebbets	1	62
Wdo Ruth Tebbets	1	15
Silas Tebbets	–	78
Benja Tebbets	–	94
James Tebbets Jr	–	42
Jedediah Tebbets	–	78
Ensn John Trickey	2	31
Wm R Witherell	–	84
John Witherell	–	76
Joseph Tebbets Jr	–	52
30.65		

Warrant to Saml Allen dated September 3d 1800

Half to work on Roads and half on Norway plains bridge if necessary or the whole on the Roads in his own district if not needed on Norway plain Bridge — Saml Allen Col.

Gingles Bridge	Dolls	Cents
Isaac Bickford	1	94
Dependance Bickford	2	52
John Bickford 3d	–	68
Solomon Drown	1	10
Experience Drown	–	42
Jonathan Flagg	–	63
Ephm Foss Bennington	–	57
Aaron Ham	2	25
Israel Ham	4	98
Stephen Ham	1	83
Richard Hayes	1	62
Joseph Hayes	3	93
Samuel Ham	1	05
Stephen Ham Jr	–	42
Thomas How	1	60
Eleazer Ham	–	94
Benjamin Heard	1	05
Nathl Hayes Jun	1	31
Daniel Jenness	1	73
William Jenness	1	20
William Jenness Jr	1	62
Daniel Jenness Jr	–	84
Paul Jenness	2	10
Jond Jenness	1	10
James McDuffees Estate	3	36
David McDuffee	–	63
John McDuffee 4th	–	63
Jacob McDuffee	1	94
Wm McNeal	2	10
Wdo Morrison	1	05
Thomas Place	3	25
Diamond Paul	1	41
Abraham Paul	–	63
Samuel Robinson	1	20
James Robinson	–	80
Samuel Seavy	2	99
James Whitehouse	–	78
Anthony Whitehouse	1	20
Israel Whitehouse	–	42
Stephen Whitehouse	1	26
Alexr Whitehouse	–	73
Moses Waldron	2	15
Elijah Whitham	1	15
Joseph Giles	2	15
James Garland	1	20
68.46		

Warrant dated Aug 26th 1800 to Jos Hay

[illegible] District	Doll	Cts
Simon Torr Esq.	4	35
John Bickford	1	78
Tristram Bickford	—	52
John Coutman	1	73
Widow M. Kimball	—	73
David Langley	2	10
James Langley	—	42
Ephraim Langley	—	63
Dr. Saml. Plumer	3	09
~~[illegible]~~ Plumer	1	36
Thomas Plumer	—	42
Daniel Plumer	—	42
John Plumer 3d.	—	84
Joseph Perkins	—	94
~~William Perkins~~	—	—
Joshua Rollins	1	31
Fran. Richardson	—	73
John Tebbets	1	20
Willm. Trickey	2	88
John Tucker Jr.	1	10
Geo. Willand	1	26
Enoch Willand	—	73
Stephen Wentworth 3d.	2	41
William Warren	—	42
Warrant dated August 26th 1800	37	37

Col. D. Places Bridge		
Col. David Place	3	57
Stephen Place	—	84
Benja. Evans Jun.	1	10
Reuben Heard Jr.	1	41
Jona. Heard Jun.	1	34
William Heard	—	89
Daniel Hayes	1	89
Howard Henderson	3	00
Richmond Henderson	1	60
Jona. Henderson	—	68
Ephraim Ham	2	46
Daniel Ham	—	84
Ephraim Hammet	—	57
Jona. Hodgdon Jr.	1	62
Joseph Tucker	—	84
Duglas Hayes	—	78
Elijah Varney	1	57
Nicholas Varney	—	84
Silas Varney	—	52
Warrant Dated Aug. 26 1800	26	36

Benja. Meder	2	06
Nathl. Meder	2	59
2 Francis Meder	1	92
1 Lemuel Meder	—	78
1 Tobias Varney	2	27
2 Josiah Jenkins	2	01
1 Jona. Meder	1	96
2 Samuel D. Foss	1	68
1 Wallace Foss	—	42
1 Samuel [illegible]	—	42

Squamanagonnic		
Joseph Bickford	3	12
Thomas Brown	1	15
Isaac Brown	—	47
Moses Bickford	—	63
Ichabod Bickford	—	36
Henry Bickford	—	42
Benjamin Dame	3	20
Lt. Saml. Downing	1	78
Zebulon Dame	1	41
Richard Dame	4	46
Capt. Alex. Hodgdon	2	20
John Hammet	—	52
Moses Hammet	1	31
Jonathan Heard	1	94
Joseph Hodgdon	—	42
Benja. Hayes Jr.	2	15
Moses Hayes Jr.	2	67
Col. John McDuffee	5	36
Lt. John McDuffee 3	—	42
Richd. Nutter	1	05
John Nutter	—	52
John Plumer Jr. Esq.	5	46
John Mc. Place	1	41
Ebenezer Read	2	67
Tobias Twombly	—	42
Isaac Twombly	1	20
Ebenezer Tebbets	2	94
Ebenezer Varney	1	83
Benja. Varney Jr.	1	05
Moses Varney	1	15
Thomas Varney	1	52
Jeremiah Varney	—	42
Elijah Varney Jr.	—	94
Moses Varney Jr.	—	52
Amos Varney	—	18
Shubael Varney	—	10
Thomas Varney 3	—	42
Jacob Wallingford	1	78
Benja. Whitehouse	—	68
Moses Young	2	77
		63.20

Benja. Evans	1	31
B. Hanson Evans	—	68
Wm. Evans	—	63
Joshua Holmes Jr.	—	63
Jacob Hanson	1	73
Moses Jennes	—	86

Evans [illegible] 1800

Major Joshua Allen	2	52
Benja. Adams	1	10
Ichabod Corson Jr.	4	06
Abijah Clark	1	68
John Clark	—	42
Jacob Ellis	1	62
Capt. Nathaniel Hayes	1	47
Isaac Horn Dover	—	99
Col. John Goodwin	2	04
Moses Roberts Jr.	2	25
Tobias Twombly Jr.	3	01
Stephen Heard	1	47
Capt. Saml. Langton	—	57
Samuel Wingate	1	68
David Wingate	2	67
Benja. Wingate	—	68
Benja. Wentworth	—	94

Warrant to Joshua Allen dated Septr. 3d 1800 to work half on the Road in his district and half on Norway plain Bridge if needed or if not then all on his own Road

Town accounts for 1800 — Cr

	Doll	cts
Remains in Paul Harfords hands for 1781	85	10
In Ichabod Corsons Jr. hand for 1798	342	56
Raised in Ichabod Corson Jr. Town list for 1800	1161	68
Raised in Benjamin Scates list for 1800	486	76
Due on Moses Canney Esq. Execution	89	40
Returnd in Notes of hand by Selectmen 1800	161	27
Raised in John Odiorne Nonresident list 1800	15	61
Recd of Committee for Selling Town lands	18	50
Recd Sum due from Selectmen 1799	41	89
Remains in Hatevil Knights Nonresident list	14	62
	2417	39

The way said money hath been laid out

	Doll	cts
Paid the State treasurer in full the balance 1798	100	oo
pd State Treasurer in part for 1800	95	21
pd County Treasurer in full for 1800	113	52
pd for hire of Workmen and Rum on Walker bridge	20	78
pd for timber for Norway plains bridge	15	36
pd Samuel Wentworth Jr. in full for a Road	2	oo
pd Richd Monson some expence on a Road thro his land	6	oo
pd Moses Bickford for Collecting 1799 town tax	27	98
pd Abatements in said Bickfords Town list 1799	13	78
pd Benja Scates for Collecting Town Tax 1800	20	oo
pd Abatements in Benja Scates Town list 1800	12	63
pd Dr. John Smith & Simon Brawn's Tax 1798 & 1799	3	05
pd Abatements in Ichd Corson Jr. Town list 1798	13	40
pd for some repairs on the pound	1	53
pd George Hayes for work on Twomblys Bridge	1	80
pd towards notes of hand given by former Selectmen	95	70
pd Ephraim Wentworth for a Road thro his land	5	32
pd balance of poor's Acct 1799 and part 1800	71	95
pd Selectmen running line between Roch. & Wakefield	6	oo
pd Selectmen running Cross line by Dudly Burnham	4	50
pd for taking the Inventory in 1800	7	oo
pd for Making Ratelist and Counterpart	8	oo
pd for Making Surveyors lists	7	oo
pd for making School lists & districting schools	7	oo
pd for making second Bridg tax	7	oo
pd for Running Road by Samuel Jennes & return	3	oo
pd Selectmen running Road by Littlefalls & return	2	oo
pd Do. writing Deeds and 2 Indentures for poor	1	33
pd for writing paper thro the year	1	50
pd for some abatements and other expences in finally settling all acct on Norway plains School house	17	30
pd for Running Road by Richard Monson & return	3	oo
pd Some extra for Master workman on Lying last bridge	4	30
pd Interest money more than we received	32	49
pd time and expence procuring Collectors & bonds	3	33
pd for repairing windows [illegible]	3	30

paid 2d Jotham Nutes School District in full 1800	17	oo
pd Jabez Dame Esq. Do. in full 1799 & 1800	40	71
pd Capt. Daniel McDuffee Do. 1799	23	16
pd Lt. James Places Do. 1799	15	22
pd Benja Meder Do. 1799 & part of 1798	22	oo
pd part Col. J. McDuffees Do. 1800	12	50
pd Ensn John Fish's District 1800	17	oo
pd Paul Jewets District 1800	23	50
pd Caleb Wakehams Do. 1800	19	oo
pd Samuel Twomblys Do. 1800	6	oo
pd William Palmer Esq. Do. 1800	19	50
pd Moses Chamberlins Do. 1800	17	oo
pd Richard Walkers Do. 1800	10	oo
pd Major Allens School Do. 1800	20	oo
pd Ensn Corsons Do. 1799	15	40
pd Israel Hams Do. 1800	18	oo
pd Abner Hodgdon Do. in part 1797	7	oo
Paid the Committee Account for selling town lands	2	84
pd John Odiorne in part for a Road thro his land	4	20
pd for Timber for Bridges in Lt. Richd Roberts District	1	oo
pd Simon Torr Esq. for a Road thro his land in full	2	oo
pd the Assessors in full for 1800	2	oo
pd a Note against John Roe given up outlawed	10	oo
and two Dollars Indents which will not be rec'd	6	oo
pd the Auditors for their service 1800 in full		
paid Interest on Joseph Hansons note renewed	21	54
	358	5[illegible]

Outstanding in Collectors hands

In Paul Harfords hands for 1781	85	1[illegible]
In Ichabod Corsons hands for 1800	1025	7[illegible]
In John Odiornes Nonresident list 1800	15	6[illegible]
Due on Moses Canneys Execution	89	4[illegible]
Returnd in notes of hand	149	1[illegible]
	1564	9[illegible]
	766	2[illegible]
	358	5[illegible]
	$2489	6[illegible]
	2417	39
which leaves a balance due to selectmen of	72	2[illegible]

The foregoing is a true statement of the Towns account for the year 1800 as kept by us and rendered to the Commissioners this 7th Day of March 1801

Richd Dame
Beard Plumer
Joshua Allen
} Selectmen

In auditing the foregoing account for the year 1800 we find them well cast accurate just [illegible] true as exhibited to us by the Selectmen this 7th Day of March 1801

Jacob Hanson
Simon Torr
} Auditors

Returnd in Ichabod Corson Jr. hands for 1798	49	70
Returnd in Moses Bickfords hand for 1799	48	72
Raisd in Ichabod Corson Jr. List for 1800	345	06
	443	48

The way said money has been laid out

Paid the Selectmen the balance due 1799	7	03
pd Moses Bickford for Collecting Parish tax 1799	8	75
pd Abatement in parish List for 1799 Bickford	9	13
pd Selectmen Making Parish Tax for 1800	2	50
pd Richd Cross taking care of Meetinghouse	6	00
pd Abatement in Jehd Corson Jr. List 1798	13	07
pd Jehd Corson Jr for Collecting 1798 tax	9	33
pd John Brown for work on parsonage house	3	70
pd John Plumer Jr. &c. for boards for parsonage house	—	80
	60	31

Remains in Ichabod Corsons hands 1800	345	06
Cash in Selectmens hands	38	11
	443	48

Returnd in Benja Scales List for 1799	68	05
Raised in Benj Scales Parish List 1800	68	67
paid for making parish Tax 1800	2	00
	138	72

Remains in Benj Scales hands for 1799	68	5
Remains in Benj Scales hands for 1800	68	67
Recd of Selectmen 1799		37
	137	09
Which leaves a balance due to Selectmen of	1	63
	138	72

The foregoing is a true Statement of parish accounts for the year 1800 as kept by the Selectmen and rendered this 7th Day of March 1801

Richd Plumer, Joshua Allen — Selectmen

We have cast the Counterparts examined the foregoing parish accounts for the year 1800 as presented to us by the Selectmen which appear to us to be fair and Just. March 7th 1801

Jacob Hanson, Simon Torr — Auditors

Sums paid for Support of the poor in 1800	$
Paid Nathaniel Meder the balance in full for 1799 for poor	8.75
pd for Support of Widow Waymoth bal. for 1799 & pt. 1800	21.67
pd Sol. Perkins in full for Hepzibah Nute & Daughter to 1801	8.00
pd Lt. Roberts in part for Widow Merrow	15.00
pd Zebulon Dame in full for Thos Cook	4.73
pd Some Supplies for Aaron Wentworth	1.80
pd Dr. James Hows Bill for visiting paupers in full	8.00
pd Selectmen taking care of poor	4.00
which is the Sum Charged in 1800 acct	71.95

Sums paid on Notes of Hand given by former Selectmen

	Doll.
pd Capt Saml Hows Note in full the balance	95.70

March 31st 1801. Nathaniel Meder took the Widow Rebecca Merrow (from Lt Timothy Roberts) of the Selectmen for 50 cents pr Week for one year exclusive of Clothing

April 17th Joshua Holmes Jr took Doll Robinson Child (from Nathaniel Meder's) of Selectmen for Seventeen Dollars for one year Including Clothing and all expenses except some extra to be allowd for care in her learning

May 18th 1801 Then we the Subscribers agreed with and appointed Moses Bickford to Collect the Town and Parish Taxes in the first Parish in Rochester for said year who accepted said trust and gave bonds to Collect the same and pay the same agreeably to his Warrants. Also appointed Stephen Perkins Collector of Nonresident Taxes for said year who accepted said Trust and gave bonds to collect and pay the same

Richd Dame, Joshua Allen — Selectmen

204

1801 Settlement with Collector 1801

	Dolls
March 9th. 1801 Rec^d of Ich^d Corson J^r. Cash	94.00
x Jacob McDuffee School list for 1800 paid	12.00
and gave a Rec^t towards 1800 list	106.00
June 1st Rec^d of Ichabod Corson J^r. Cash 173.92	173.92
pd Nathaniel Meder in full for Doll Robinson Children	18.50
pd Simon Torr Esqr District in full 1800	24.00
pd Benj^a Meder District in part 1800	8.00
x pd [illegible] Plummer in full for a Road	1.00
pd [illegible] Allens District in part 1800	10.00
pd abatement [illegible] James Tax 1800	.09
and gave a Rec^t in part of 1800 town list for	235.51
February 20th 1802 Rec^d of Moses Beckford in Cash p^r this day	18.00
pd Benj^a Meder District in part 1801	7.00
pd Nathaniel Meder in part keeping Wid^o Merrow	15.10
pd Danl Hussey, Nathl Hayes J^r & Ja^s Garlin for Col^o Place bridge	16.66
pd Dr Timothy Roberts in full for Wid^o Merrow 1800	13.00
pd Enoch Willand towards bridge timber	5.60
pd Lt James Place Dist. for 1800. 1801 & part 1795	37.83
pd Cash and orders some time since now allowed	40.33
pd County treasurer his part in full	75.00
pd Henry Beckford 4.50 & Isaac Peak 1.80 for wood widow	6.30
pd Sundry taxes discounted for Maj^r Allen as Cash	10.07
pd Sundry taxes [illegible] Richd Dame as Cash	10.70
pd Wentworth Cooks tax illegally assessed in 1799	1.20
pd Richard Cross taking care of [illegible] Place in full	6.00
	262.79
March 6th	
paid Jacob McDuffee District in full 1801	12.00
Enoch Willand for bridge timber in full	5.07
pd John Plummer J^r Esqr for Supplies Wid^o Waymoth	15.55
pd D^o a Note for 36 Doll. & 9.36 Interest	45.36
pd Edwd Cole towards post guides	2.25
pd Joseph Hayes bill Compleating Singlass bridge	25.60
	4.41
pd James Place for wood 1.50 Benj^a Hayes D^o 3	4.50
pd Sundries bill for Col^o Place Bridge	15.29
Cash 7.16 pd Jabez Dame Esq School list 1801 24 Doll	31.16
and gave a Rec^t 1801 list for	424.00
March 6th 1802 Rec^d Benj^a [illegible] in Cash	5.28
Danl Monsons order for Aaron Wentworth	4.00
Mellar's & Rollins order for a Road	45.00
County Treasurer 33.52 R^d Walker School 1799 8.25	41.77
Esqr Palmer School 1801 18.70 . Paul Jewill 1801 24.50	43.20
Eph^m Twombly 1801 15.80 Jo^s Walker bridge order 2.80	18.63
John Twombly Tax abated for a Road thro his land	2.37
Capt Plummers Tax 1801	11.75
and gave a receipt for 1801 list Town	172.00
Rec^d of Ichabod Corson March 6 in Cash	10.00
Levi Jones Order Ich^d Corsons Dist 1799	14.00
Edwd Coles ord^r Norway plains Dist 1800	30.00
David Twomblys ord^r on Benj Meder Dist 1801	15.00
	3.00
John Odiorne for a Road in part	16.61
pd Capt Daniel McDuffee District in part 1800	16.00
pd Josiah Main service as Town Clerk 1800	10.53
pd Ich^d [illegible] 3.33 Benj^a Hayes 3^d [illegible] 4.20 for wood	7.43
pd Maj^r Allen balance of acc^t for selectman 1801	
And gave a receipt in part 1800 town list for	122.87

Sums paid towards Support of the poor 1801

pd Some Supplies in full for Aaron Wentworth	5	75
pd Nathl Meder in full for Dol Robinson Child 1800	18	50
pd Sol. Perkins in full for his mother [illegible] burial	6	10
pd Supplies for Wid^o Waymoth in full 1800 [illegible]	29	45
pd Supplies for Wid^o Merrow 1800	13	00
pd the balance for Wid^o Merrow 1801	15	00
pd Nathl Meder in part for Matthias Welch		50
pd Some Supplies for Matthias Welch	2	—
pd Selectmen taking care of poor in full	90	30
which was the sum charged in 1801 acc^t		
Some Supplies for Wid^o Waymoth for 1800 for wood brot in after the above was entered and charged	7	20

See March 6th 1802 —

Jacob Main Acc^t for keeping school in [illegible]

1802 April To 7 m^o & 6 Days at 24 doll p^r m^o	$174	00
March 1st 1803 To 5 m^o p^d Ditto	120	00
To two months board at $1.00 p^r week	8	
	302	00
March 10th 1804 Interest for Delay	7	11
	309	11

the way the same has been paid

March 2^d 1802 by p^d by Hatevil Knight as p^r order Charged in 1801 account	25	00
	5	00
October 6th 1802 by p^d by Ich^d Corson as p^r receipt	2	50
Feby 26. 1803 by p^d by John Odiorne as p^r rec^t	109	88
March 7 D^o by p^d by Selectmen as p^r receipt	23	36
these three last charged in 1802 accounts		
March 16 1803 by p^d by Benj^a Hayes as p^r rec^t	10	00
D^o 24 D^o by p^d by [illegible] Dame as p^r receipt	21	47
March 29 D^o took up an order he gave Nathl Upham	80	00
October 15th 1803 p^d by Selectmen as p^r receipt	11	90
March 26th 1803 p^d by Benj^a Hayes	20	00
Decr 5th 1803 p^d by Benj^a Hayes Cash		
	309	11

The way said sums have been Charged

In 1801 acc^t p^d Norway plains District for	1801	25	00
In 1802 acc^t p^d Col McDuffee Dist for	1800	22	50
	1801	35	00
D^o	1802	36	00
D^o	1801	13	00
p^d Jacob Hansons Dist	1801	14	00
p^d Squamanagonnic		11	00
To be Charged in 1803 acc^t bal. of Norway plain acc^t	1801	36	00
Norway plain Dist	1802	8	00
Squamanagonnic balance	1801	108	61
Charged in Town account for 1803 from town stock		309	11

			10
35	1½	2	15
40	2	2	20
58	2	2	20
70	3	3	30
10	1	1	10
14	2	2	20
15	1½	2	15
140	6	6	60
82	3	3	30
84	4	4	40
20	2	2	20
30	3	3	30
0	4	4	40

No. 4
William Jen
12 Dolls.

No. 5
Joseph Hayes
18 Dolls

No. 6
Joseph Tebbets
19 Dolls

No. 7
Major Joshua A
20 Dolls

No. 8
Norway Plains
36 Dolls

No. 9.

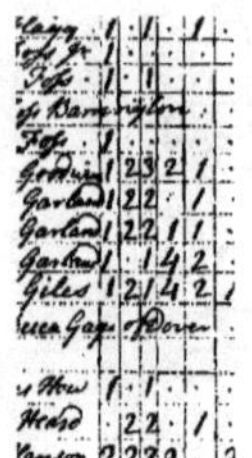

…ah Hanson	1 1 1 1 1 4 3 20 40	42	4.25	1.91	3.97
…mas How	1 2 1 4 6/90 2 2 4 1 17	30	3.00	. .	3.00
…h Huntress	1 3 1 1 2y.0 ½ 1 3 8 7	24	240	108	225
…y Hoyt	1 3 2 1 3 8	22	220	99	206
…ah Hodgdon	1	8	80	36	75
…mis Hoyt	1	8	80	36	75
…Henderson	1 2 1	16	160	72	150
…Hammett	1 1	10	100	45	95
…ner Horn	1 4 ½ 1 20 1 1 64	27	270	121	253
…iel Ham	1 2 1	16	160	72	150
… Heard	1 2 1	16	160	72	150
…Hodgdon Jr.	1 2 2 1 1 3 2 1 20	31	310	139	290
…chek Heard	1 2	14	140	63	132
…n Horn Jr.	1	8	80	36	75
…hen Ham Jr.	1	8	80	36	75

Name			
Jon^a Meder	1	.	2
Francis Meder	1	2	2
Simuel Meder	1	.	3
Josiah Main	1	2	2 1
Amos Main	1	.	1 1
Josiah Main Jr.	1		
Wm McNeal	1	2	3
Wd Sarah Morrison	.	2	2
John McGillis	[illegible]		
Henry Mellen Esq.	Do		
Capt Isaac Morton	1		
John Mills	1		
Maj. Jotham Morrow	1		
John Nutter	1	2	2

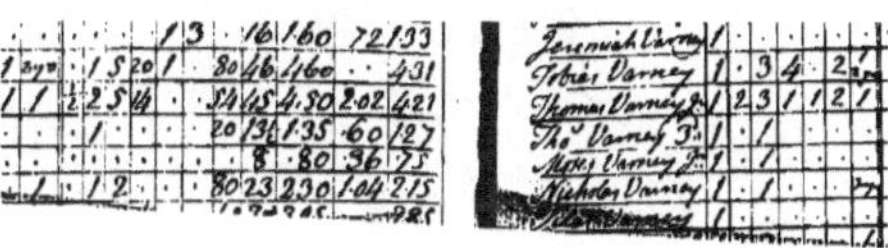

CORRECTION

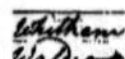

Doomages agreed on by the Selectmen & Assessors entered in the foregoing Inventory

	Dollars		Dollars
Joseph Haven Stock in Trade	20	John Odiorne Sadler	2
Samuel Adams D°	20	John Hunt D°	2
Joseph Sherburne D°	12	Joseph Ballard Hatter	2
Levi Dearborn Esq. D°	3	McDuffee & Dame's fulling mill	8
Jabez Dame Esq. Tanner	2	Norway plain upper Saw mill	24
Simon Torr Esq. D°	2	Cushings Sawmill	12
Anthony Whitehouse D°	2	Squamanagonnic upper Sawmill	18
Caleb Jackson D°	1	D° Lower Sawmill	12
Benj^a Tebbets D°	1	D° upper gristmill	6
James Tebbets Blacksmith	3	D° Lower gristmill	6
John Smith D°	2	Garlins Sawmill	18
Nicholas Varney D°	1½	Lower Cornmill Norway plain	6

State of Newhampshire }
Strafford ss. } To Moses Bickford, appointed Collector of Taxes for the town of Rochester, for the year 1801 Greeting.

(L.S.)

By virtue of sundry laws of said state, directing selectmen to raise money for the support of schools and other necessary expenses; and pursuant to a precept from the Treasurer of said County.

You are hereby required in the name of said state to levy and collect of all persons named in the foregoing List herewith committed you: to collect the same set to their names in Dollars and cents and pay or cause to be paid to the Treasurer of said County, for the time being seventy five Dollars by the first day of December next and pay the selectmen three hundred Dollars by the first day of said December and the whole of the remainder of said List by the first day of March next and if any person ~~and if any person~~ shall neglect or refuse to pay his said Taxes, after legal notice, you are to take the same by destraint and sale as the Law directs; and for your lawful proceedings this shall be your sufficient warrant. Given under our hands and seals in Rochester the fourth day of May 1801.

Richd Dame }
Beard Plumer } Select-
Joshua Allen } men

State of Newhampshire }
Strafford ss. } To Moses Bickford, appointed Collector of parish Taxes, for the town of Rochester for 1801. Greeting.

(L.S.)

Pursuant to sundry votes of the town of Rochester impowered the selectmen to raise money to hire preaching, and for collecting the same. You are hereby directed to collect of all persons named in the foregoing List, the sums set to their names in Dollars and cents, and pay Joseph Haven two hundred and sixty six Dollars by the first day of March next, and the remainder to the selectmen or their order by said first day of March next, or pay the whole to the selectmen by the first day of March next, or to their order; and if any person shall neglect or refuse to pay the money after legal warning or notice, you are to take the same by destraint and sale as the Law directs, and for your lawful proceedings this shall be your sufficient warrant. Given under our hands and seals this [illegible] day of May 1801.

Joshua Allen } Select-
Beard Plumer } men

Abatements in 1801 List in Moses Bickford's List

	Town	Parish
Wallace Ross removed	1.00	0.45
Israel Henderson D°	.80	.36
Isaac Morton D°	80	36
Elijah Otis not legall	80	—
Benj^a Palmer removed	90	.40
Lt Samuel Richards D°	80	36
John Richards	80	—
David Stone	80	36
Enos Varney	80	0.0
Daniel Jennes		
John Clark removed	80	36
	8.30	

rec^d the above Town abatements March 7th 1803 -

	Town	Parish
Jon^a Heard a yoke of oxen too much	40	18
Ebenezer Horn poor	1.00	45
Johnson Bryant poor	80	36
Ebenezer Horn Jr.	80	36
John Mills removed	80	36
Adam Perkins	80	—
John Roberts	2.70	1.21
Levi Robinson		36	5.93
	7 30	

Rec^d Rochester Aug^st 29th 1803 of the Selectmen fifteen Dollars Sixty cents for the above Town List abatements and five Dollars and Ninety three cents for the parish abatements for the year 1801. Also Thirty Dollars in full for Collecting — Moses Bickford

Abatements in Benjamin Scates List 1801

	Town	Parish
Timothy Ricker	1.45	0.36
Jeshua Wentworth	1.60	0.40
Amos Whitham		0.18
Miles Davis after List	20	
Samuel Braydon		0 75
Dodavah Copp	1.10	
Paul Ellis a poor	1.00	
Jonathan Corson	0.80	
~~Thomas Turtwelt~~	80	20
Pelatiah Hanscomb	80	20
Otis Wentworth	80	
Samuel Chapman Lt.	1.15	50
Robert Hait Dec^d	1.00	20
John Twombly lame	80	
	11.50	

	Town	Parish
Also John Varney Tax for work on Roads 1800	4.94	
Dodavah Copp poor 1800	1.38	27
Thos Pinkham 1799. 1800 and 57 cents for 1798	4.96	10
Robert Hait 1800		
James Marsh pd 1798	25	
Tobias Ricker pt. 1800	1.25	
	24.28	
also 50 cents more in R Walkins List for 1801 than we allowed	50	
and a overcast of his List for 1801	55	
	25.33	

March 7th 1802 received the above abatements of Town taxes for 1801 being twenty five Dollars and 33 cents and twenty Dollars more for Collecting said Town tax in full

Benjamin Scates Colle

State of Newhampshire } To Benjamin Yeates apointed Collector
Strafford ss { Of taxes for the second parish in the
(L.S.) Town of Rochester for the
year 1801 Greeting

By Virtue of Sundry Laws of s^d State directing Selectmen
To Rais money for the Suport of Schools and other Necessary
Expenses and in persuant of a precept from the County treasurer
To rais money for the use of s^d County you are hereby directed
In the Name of s^d State to Levie and Collect of all persons named
In the foregoing List the Sums Set to there Names in dollars
And Cents and pay the County treasurer of s^d County thirty three
dollars & fifty two Cents by the first day of December next
And one hundred and fifty dollars more you are to pay the
Selectmen or their orders by the first day of January next and
the whol of the Remaining Sum of s^d List you are to pay
the Selectmen in office by the tenth day of march next and if any
person or persons Shall neglect or refuse to pay his or there taxes
After Legal warning or notice you are to take the Same by
Destraint and Sail as the Law directs and for your Lawfull proceeding
this Shall be your Suffisent warrent Given under our hands and Seal
In Rochester this forth day of may 1801 Beard Plumer } Select
Richd Dame } Men
Joshua Allen

State of Newhampshire } to Benjamin Yeates apointed Collector
Strafford ss { of taxes for the town of Rochester for
(L.S.) the year 1801 Greeting

Persuant to Sundry votes of the town of Rochester raising
Money for the Suport of the gospel and other parish Expences
And for Raising and Collecting the Same you are hereby Required in
the Name of s^d State to Levie and Collect of all persons Named
In the foregoing List the Sums Set to there names in Dollars
And Cents and pay the whol Sum in dollars & Cents or Silver
Or gold or Selectmens orders to the Selectmen for the time being
By the first day of march next and if any person or persons
Shall neglect or Refuse to pay after Legal warning or
Notice you are to take the Same by destraint and Sail as the
Law directs and for your Lawfull proceedings this Shall be your Suffisent
Worrent given under our hands and Seals in Rochester this forth
Day of may in the year of our Lord 1801
Beard Plumer } Select
Joshua Allen } Men

Town accounts for 1801 — Credit

	Doll	cts
Remains in Paul Harfords hands for 1781	85	10
Remains in Ichabod Corsons hands for 1800	1025	70
Rais'd in Moses Bickfords list for 1801	907	28
Rais'd in Benjamin Scates list for 1801	377	45
Returnd in John Odiorne's nonresident list 1800	15	61
Rais'd in Stephen Perkins nonresident list 1801	10	24
Due on Moses Canney Esqr. execution	89	40
Returnd in notes of hand by Selectmen of 1800	149	10
	2659	88

The way said money has been laid out

	Doll	cts
Paid the State treasurer the balance in full 1800	245	00
pd County treasurer in full 1801	112	52
pd Dependance Bickford in full for a Road laid out by the Towns committee in 1794	10	00
pd Selectmen new running & settling for sd road	1	00
pd Wm. K. Atkinson Esqr. a note given by Selectmen 1789	5	35
pd Doct. Saml. Hanner in full for a road thro' his land	1	00
pd Poors bill in full 1800 and part 1801	90	30
pd Selectmen running line between Rochester & Barrington	5	00
pd Do. running line between Rochester and Dover	3	00
pd Do. running & establishing line by Somersworth	3	00
pd Do. runng road by Wm. McLords land Lemuel Ricker's	3	00
pd Do. laying out a Road by Wm. Jennes and Deeds	1	67
pd sundrys bills finishing Col. Places bridge	32	70
pd Selectmen taking Inventory	7	00
pd Do. Making Ratelist & counterparts	8	00
pd Do. making Surveyors list & destrict Surveyors	7	00
pd Do Destricting Schools & giving out lists	7	00
pd Do making nonresident list & appointg Collector	3	00
pd Do. Recording Ratelist & Town account in full	5	00
pd Do. appointing Collectors & writing Bonds	3	67
pd Enoch Willand in full his account for bridge timber	10	67
pd Abatement Wentworth Cooks poll tax 1799	1	20
pd abatements in Stephen Perkins nonresident list 1801	1	97
pd Selectmen attending Court on account of Roads	2	00
pd for writing paper thro' the year	1	50
pd Edward Cole for painting post guides	9	33
pd Some expences on behalf of the Town in Dr Howe's and Lieut Edward Rollins case		
pd Hatevil Knight for boarding Town Schoolmaster 1801	16	00
pd Benjamin Meder Dest. in full 1800 & pt. 1801 & 1797	36	33
pd Jacob McDuffee's Destrict in full 1800 & 1801	24	10
pd Norway Plains Destrict in full 800 and 1801 in pt.	55	—
pd St. James Places Dest. the balance 1795 in full 1800 1801	37	83
pd Joseph Tebbets Dest. in part 1800	10	—
pd Simon Torr Esqr. Dest. in full 1800	24	
pd Joseph Pages Destrict in pt. 1799 & 1800 & balance 1797	17	33
pd Samuel Adams for repairing the pound	—	92
[illegible]		

1801 Town account Continued

	Doll	cts
Paid an error in miscast of notes last year	1	17
Paid the Assessors in full for 1801	1	00
paid Major Allens Destrict in part of 1799	14	00
pd John Odiorne in part for a road thro' his land	3	—
pd Jabez Dame Esqr. Destrict in full 1801	24	00
pd Selectmens services thro' the year	15	00
pd Selectmen taking care of the School lot	1	25
pd Selectmen the balance due last year	72	27
pd Interest money more than we received	32	27
pd the Auditors in full for 1801	6	—
pd John Odiorne to redeem a piece of Land Illegally assessed in Hatevil Knights list 1797	4	50
pd Josiah Main his service as town Clerk 1800	16	00
pd Capt. Daniel McDuffees Destrict in part for 1800	16	61
pd Some Supplies for wid. Waymouth for 1800 omitted	7	20
	214	27

Outstanding in Collectors hands

	Doll	cts
Remains in Paul Harfords hands for 1781	85	10
Remains in Ichabod Corsons hand for 1800	561	62
Remains in Moses Bickford hand for 1801	483	28
Remains in Benja. Scates list for 1801	205	45
Remains in John Odiornes nonresident list 1800	15	61
Remains in Stephen Perkins nonresident list 1801	10	24
Due on Moses Canne Esqr. Execution	89	40
Returned in notes of hand	56	80
	1507	50
	214	27
	1003	36
	2725	13
which leave a balance due Selectmen of	65	25
	2659	88

Rochester March 8th 1802 The above is a true Statement of the Town account as kept by us and presented to the Auditors for the year 1801

Richd. Dame
Beard Plumer
Joshua Allen
} Selectmen

The foregoing account as rendered to us by the Selectmen appear to be well Cast Accurate and well vouched this 8th of March 1802

John Odiorne
William Palmer
} Auditors

1801 Parish accounts for 1801 -

Remains in Ichabod Corsons hands for 1800	345	06
Cash recieved of Selectmen of 1800 —	38	11
Raised in Moses Bickfords list 1801 —	301	07
	684	24

The way said money has been expended -		
Paid Joseph Havens Salary		
Pd Richard Cross taking care of meeting house	6	00
Pd Selectmen making Parish list —	2	50
Returned in Ichabod Corsons hands for 1800 -	345	06
Returned in Moses Bickfords hands for 1801 -	301	07
Due from the Selectmen to the Parish --	29	61
	684	24

The upper Parish accounts 1801 —		
Remain in Benjamin Scates hands for 1799	68	05
Remain in Benjamin Scates hands for 1800	68	67
Raised in Benjamin Scates list. for 1801 -	63	38
	200	10

Paid Benjamin Green for Preaching in 1800	46	67
Paid Isaac Hersey for Preaching	3	00
Paid Lt Elijah Horn for house room for meeting	6	00
Paid Selectmen for making Parish list -	2	00
Pd Abatement in 1799 list	4	92
Pd Benj Scates for Collecting 1799 tax in full	3	00
Pd a Balance due Selectmen of 1800	1	63
Remains in Benjamin Scates hands for 1800 -	68	67
Remain in Benj Scates hands for 1801 —	63	38
Due from the Selectmen		83
	200	10

Rochester March 6th 1802 The foregoing is a true account of parish matters as kept by us and rendered to the Commissioners for said year 1801 —

Joshua Allen } Select
Beard Plumer } men

We have cast the list and examined the foregoing parish accounts as exhibited by the Selectmen and find them accurate and well vouched
March 6th 1802.

John Odiorne } Auditors
William Palmer

1802 April agreed with Nathaniel Meder to take the widow Rebecca Merrow one year for fifty cents pr week exclusive of Clothing for which he is to make out his bill —

Agreed with Joshua Holmes Jr to take Dolly Robinsons child one year for eighteen Dollars including clothing and all expences —

May 28th 1802 Then agreed with Benjamin Hayes to Collect the Town and Parish Tax for the year 1802 in the first parish who accepted the appointment of Collector as aforesaid and gave bonds for the performance thereof. also agreed with and appointed Benjamin Scates to Collect the Town & Parish Tax in the North east parish who accepted said trust.

Richd Dame } Select
John Odiorne } men
Joshua Allen

[illegible]	70.00
pd Jacob Hains 20 & 8.50 & Ben Meden Dist in part 1801 6.	34.50
pd Joshua Knight repairing pound in p	2.50
pd J. P. Hale Esq 5doll. Simon Foss bridge list in full 9.83	14.83
pd Josiah Main in full his Services 1801 16 Doll	16.00
pd Jacob Wallingford on J Hanson School house act	5.67
pd George Hayes Col Palmer bill viewing Road	33.67
pd Wm McNeal for supplying Saml Bickford a poor	3.00
pd Nathl Meden in pt for keeping poor 1801 —	16.00
pd Joshua Holmes Jr poor bill in full 1801 —	19.00
pd John Hickey for work on road 4 doll. as cash 1.64	5.64
and gave a Rect in part his Town Tax 1801 for	220.21
December 1st 1802 Recd of Benja Scales as Cash —	15.85
John Fish School list 1801 17.50 : D. Burnham, Do 18.50	36.00
Jotham Nute Do 18.50 Richd Walker Do 10	28.50
for Collecting 20 doll Abatement 1801	31.01
Selectmen receipt for Part of Sum Due Milton	130.00
	241.36
and gave a Rect in full 1801 206.00	
and part 1802 for — 35.36	
241.36	
March 7 1803 Recd of Benj Hayes Cash & [illegible]	52.20
pd Jacob Hains 30 : Richd Dame Jr for wood for school 3 -	33.00
Thomas Varney 3d for bridge 2.34 : Rd Cross for meeting house 6.	8.34
County Treasurer 100 : Jon Hearl for poor Child 33.50	133.50
John Roberts Jr on N. P. bridge 17.07 Cap Brewster Do 1.50	18.57
Col Plase for his bridge 8.35 : James Garland Do 2.00	10.35
John McPlase for Wd Weymouth 3.48 Benj Hayes Do 11.67	15.15
Joseph Sherburne for Stone for bridges	3.94
Jacob Wallingford for John Roberts School house	6.93
Isaac Bickford School 1802 16 Doll Jacob Hanson Do 1802 10	26.00
Maj Perkins boarding School master	12.71
James Tebbets for pound 1.67 : Eqn Clark for services 5.36	7.03
Jona Hearl Jr for bridge 1.25 Cap Danl McDuffe for bridge 9.12	10.37
and gave a Rect in part of 1802 list for town	338.09
Do Settled with Moses Bickford recd Cash & Taxs	20.80
pd Thos Varney 3d towards Squamanagonic bridge —	1.00
Danl Rogers towards Norway plain bridge —	3.38
John Brown for Do 4 Do Richd Nutter Jr 1.59	5.59
John Richardson Maj Perkins order boarding Schoolmaster	3.00
Silas Dame Jr towards Road 1800 : Abatement 8.30	23.30
[illegible] 1801 Town tax for	57.07

Do recd of Moses Bickford in cash —	12.80
pd Joseph Bickford for bridge plank due [illegible]	1.00
and gave a rect in part of 1801 town list —	13.80

1802 A list of Taxes assessed agreeably to a vote of the Town past May 31st 1802 for building and finishing Schoolhouses in said Town

Name	$	cts
Major Joshua Allen	13	00
Samuel Allen	12	25
Micah Allen	10	12
Samuel Adams	8	75
Benjamin Adams	8	25
Capt John Brewster	10	62
Thomas Brown	4	87
Joseph Bickford	12	00
Isaac Brown	2	75
John Brown	5	00
John Baker	10	25
Otis Baker	6	00
David Barker	14	75
Isaac Bickford	9	50
John Bickford Jr	12	50
Dependance Bickford	10	12
John Bickford	5	50
Tristram Bickford	3	25
Moses Bickford	4	62
Joseph Ballard	4	50
John Bickford 3d	5	00
Stephen Brewster	2	25
William Blake	4	12
Moses Brown	2	00
Henry Bickford	3	50
Abraham Cook	7	12
Dr Samuel Chamberlin	8	50
Tristram Copp	3	37
Joseph Clark Esquire	9	25
Peter Cushing	11	25
John Cloutman	7	25
Hezekiah Cloutman	7	00
Ichabod Corson	22	50
Lt Timothy Corson	11	25
James Chesle	9	62
Abijah Clark	8	75
Richard Copp	3	25
Edward Cole	10	00
Samuel Chamberlin Jun	8	00
Thomas Chesle	2	00
William Cook	2	00
Jabez Dame Esquire	17	62
Levi Dearborn Esq Estate	4	00
Benjamin Dame	10	25
Zebulon Dame	7	75
Lt Samuel Downing	9	50
Joseph Dame	2	00
Aaron Downs	12	37
Moses Downs	9	50
Gershom Downs	2	00
Gershom Downs Jr	10	00
Gershom Downs 3d	9	75
Richard Dame	24	25
Richard Dame Jr	10	50
Silas Dame	15	37
Silas Dame Jun	10	00
Solomon Downs	7	25
Ensign Henry Drown	2	00
Caleb Dame	5	00
Daniel Dame	2	00
Paul Downs	4	62
Jonathan Downing	2	00
Samuel D[illegible]	[illegible]	[illegible]

Name	$	cts
John H. Dearborn	1	00
Benjamin Evans		
Benj Hanson Evans		
Benjn Evans Jun	5	00
David Evans	2	00
Jacob Ellis	9	12
Ensn Richard Furber	6	37
Samuel D Foss	9	25
Wallace Foss	3	25
Samuel Foss Jun	2	00
Jonathan Flagg	2	00
David Foss	2	00
Capt John Goodwin	9	00
Daniel Garlin	9	12
Dudley Garlin	5	75
James Garlin	6	75
Joseph Giles	10	50
Paul Giles	2	00
Dr James How	8	37
Joseph Heard	7	25
Jacob Hanson	12	25
Stephen Harford	9	62
Ensn Nathaniel Hayes	8	75
Capt Alexander Hodgdon	14	75
John Hammett	2	12
Joseph Hanson	13	12
Benjamin Hayes	11	00
Lt Joshua Holmes	6	62
Aaron Ham	11	25
Wid Mehitabel Ham	17	75
Stephen Ham	9	25
Paul Harford	3	00
Enoch Hoyt	5	50
Wid Alice Horn	10	00
Nathaniel Heard	11	25
Tristram Heard	7	75
Benjamin Heard	6	12
Joshua Holmes Jr	3	37
Abraham Heard	14	25
Nathaniel Hayes Jr	9	12
Richard Hayes	9	75
Abner Hodgdon	10	12
Daniel Hussey	12	12
Jacob Hanson med	9	25
Joseph Heard Jun	6	50
Nathaniel Ham	5	87
Howard Henderson	12	25
Moses Hayes Jun	13	00
Ephraim Ham	11	25
Joseph Hayes	18	75
William Henderson	12	12
Moses Hammett	5	25
Eleazer Ham	4	75
Jonathan Heard	8	50
Jonathan Heard Jr	6	00
Richmond Henderson	9	50
George S. Hayes	8	50
Reuben Hannaford	2	81
Samuel Ham	5	50
John Hanson Jr	3	00
Enoch Hoyt Jr	2	75
Temple Hoyt	3	50
Thomas Hanscomb	3	50
Stephen Heard	6	37
Thomas Ham	6	87

1802 Schoolhouse tax

Name	$	cts
Mark Hunking	6	62
Benjamin Hoyt	6	58
Joseph Hodgdon	2	00
Dennis Hoyt	2	00
Jonathan Henderson	2	00
Ephraim Hammett	2	75
James Horn	6	87
Daniel Ham	4	00
Jonathan Hodgdon Jr	7	75
Stephen Ham Jr	2	00
John P Hale Esq	3	25
Paul Ham	2	00
Joshua Hayes	2	00
Benjamin Harford	2	75
John Haven	2	50
John Heard	2	00
John Hoyt	2	00
Daniel Hayes Jr	2	00
Ephraim Ham Jr	2	00
Joseph Heard 3d	2	37
Meshech Heard	2	00
Paul Jenness	10	00
William Jenness	9	75
Daniel Jenness	7	75
Moses Jenness	7	62
Aaron Jenness	9	25
David Jenness	9	75
Isaiah Jenkins	10	50
Caleb Jackson	8	87
Jonathan Jenness	6	50
Samuel Jenness	7	00
Daniel Jenness Jr	5	00
William Jenness Jr	6	00
Jeremiah Jenness	2	50
Jonathan Jenness Jr	2	50
Joseph Knight	7	50
Joshua Knight	5	62
Hatevil Knight	7	75
John Kent	6	25
Paul Kimball	.	.
Paul Libbey	11	25
David Langley	8	00
Clement Libbey	3	50
Capt Saml Langton	3	25
James Langley	2	00
Ephraim Langley	2	75
Col John McDuffee	27	50
Capt William McDuffee	11	75
Capt Daniel McDuffee	16	12
Lt John McDuffee 3d	8	87
Samuel McDuffee	2	00
Jacob McDuffee	10	75
James McDuffee	10	50
David McDuffee	9	50
John McDuffee 4th	9	50
Benjamin Meder	10	50
Nathaniel Meder	13	37
Jonathan Meder	11	87
Joseph Meder	3	00
Francis Meder	7	00
Josiah Main	10	50

Name	$	cts
Amos Main	3	12
Josiah Main Jr	2	00
William McNeal	9	50
Wid Sarah Morrison	6	00
Samuel Meder	6	25
Micah Meder	3	75
Jacob Main	2	00
Edward S. Moulton	2	75
Moses L. Neal Esq	4	25
John Nutter	5	75
Jotham ~~Nutter~~	5	25
Richard Nutter Jr	2	50
John Odiorne	6	25
Elijah Otis	2	50
Jethro Otis	3	50
John Plumer Jr Esq	25	00
Dr Samuel Plumer	14	75
Col David Place	15	00
Barnabas Palmer	3	50
Lt James Place	17	37
Lt Richard Place	9	00
John Mc Place	6	00
Paul Place	7	50
James Pickering	11	00
Levi Pickering	4	87
Joseph Page	14	62
Benjamin Page	17	12
Daniel Page	10	25
Major Solomon Perkins	4	75
Stephen Place	5	75
Dr Samuel Pray	3	00
Ebenezer Pearl	9	75
Ephraim Perkins	6	00
Diamond Pearl	5	37
William Perkins	4	50
Wid Martha Pike	2	75
Joseph Perkins	4	00
Abraham Pearl	4	00
Isaac Pearl	4	50
Stephen Pinkham	2	50
John Plumer 3d	2	50
Ebenezer Plumer	4	12
Stephen Perkins	4	00
Andrew Pierce	2	00
William Pickering	3	00
Thomas Pinkham	3	00
Adam Perkins	2	00
Joseph Palmer	2	00
Col Thomas Roberts Estate	[illegible]	00
Lt Samuel Richards	2	00
Lt Edward Rollins	8	37
Lt Timothy Roberts	9	12
Samuel Robinson	2	00
John Rendall	7	12
John Rendall Jun	9	00
Heard Roberts	18	00
Benjamin Rollins	5	00
Moses Roberts	12	50
John Richardson	11	50
Timothy Richardson	4	50
Jonathan Richards	2	00
Daniel Rogers	6	00

School house tax continued

	Dolls	Cents		Dolls	Cents
Benjamin Roberts	7	75	Moses Varney	5	75
John Roberts	6	12	Elijah Varney	7	25
John Roberts Jun	8	00	Benjamin Varney Jr	11	50
James Robinson	6	50	Thomas Varney	6	75
John Richards	2	75	Jeremiah Varney	2	00
Joseph Richards	7	25	Tobias Varney	12	00
Ezra Roberts	6	75	Thomas Varney Jr	8	50
Joshua Rollins	4	50	Thomas Varney 3d	4	00
Ichabod Richards	3	00	Moses Varney Jun	2	50
John Raynall	2	00	Nicholas Varney	4	37
Samuel Richards Jr	2	00	Silas Varney	2	50
Levi Robinson	2	00	Elijah Varney	3	50
Wid Lillis Shannon	2	75	Enos Varney	2	00
Samuel Seavy	11	50	Stephen Wentworth	2	00
John Smith	4	75	James Wentworth	10	50
Joseph Sherburne	6	50	Josiah Wentworth	8	12
David Stone			Ebenr Wentworth	10	25
Simon Torr Esqr	21	25	Samuel Wingate	8	50
Joseph Tebbets	18	75	David Wingate	15	25
Elijah Tebbets	7	50	Benja Wingate	4	25
David Tebbets	7	75	George Willand	6	00
Robert Tebbets	9	50	Enoch Willand	9	75
Wid Ruth Tebbets	6	50	Jacob Wallingford	9	25
Silas Tebbets	4	75	Turner Whitehouse	3	50
John Tebbets	7	00	Anthony Whitehouse	5	87
Ebenezer Tebbets	15	00	Benj Whitehouse	3	25
James Tebbets	6	50	Alexander Whitehouse	4	25
Enoch Tebbets	9	50	Israel Whitehouse	2	25
David Tebbets Jr	4	12	Daniel Watson	2	25
Joseph Tebbets Jr	2	37	James Waldron	12	00
Benjamin Tebbets	7	25	Stephen Wentworth 3d	11	37
James Tebbets Jr	2	00	Elijah Whitham	5	00
Jedediah Tebbets	12	00	Moses Waldron	12	50
Nicholas Tebbets	2	37	John Wetherell	8	75
Tobias Twombly	1	25	Benja Wentworth	5	25
Isaac Twombly	6	50	Thomas Wentworth	3	50
Tobias Twombly Jr	13	25	James Woodhouse	2	00
David Twombly	2	50	Josiah Wentworth Jr	2	00
William Tebbets	3	50	Ephraim Wentworth	.	.
William Tuckey	12	00			
Esqr John Tuckey	14	75	Moses Young	13	00
John Tuckey Jr	4	75			
Joseph Tucker	3	75			
Benjamin Tuttle	2	00			
Josiah Tucker	2	00			
Joshua Tolford	3	25			
Tristram Tucker	2	00			

State of Newhampshire } To John Hanson Jr appointed Collector
Strafford ss } of Taxes for building schoolhouses 1802

Pursuant to a vote of the town of Rochester past May 31st 1802 for raising money for building & compleating School houses in said Town you are hereby Directed & impowered in the name of the State of Newhampshire to levy & collect of all persons named in the foregoing list the several sums set to their names in Dollars and cents and pay the same in to the selectmen in ninetyfive Days from this date and if any person or persons shall neglect or refuse to pay the money after legal warning or notice you are to take the same by distraint and sale as the law directs and for your lawful proceedings this shall be your sufficient warrant given under our hands and seal in Rochester the 2d day of August 1802

Richd Dame } Select
John Odiorne } men

1802

We the Subscribers appointed a Committee to settle Accounts & demands of every description between Rochester & Milton having viewed the Town Accounts and considered the premises & after mature deliberation have agreed that the said Town of Rochester & Milton enjoy all privileges & properties within their own lines Respectively That the Town of Rochester discharge all debts & demands that have arisen against them and Receive all monies now due and that a full discharge of debts prior to the date of the Act of incorporation of the said Milton against each other be... Reserving to the Town of Milton their proportion of all monies the County of Strafford may Refund towards building the Courthouse if any agreeable to their proportion they paid

Rochester Novr 8th 1802

Beard Plumer } Committee
Daniel Hayes } for
Gilman Jewett } Milton

John McDuffee by his son } Committee
Jabez Dame } for
Richd Dame } Rochester
John Odiorne }
Joshua Allen }

order given on Scales for	\$130.00 paid
one Note to be paid in 12 months no int	288.00 paid
one Note to be pd in 24 months on int	288.00 paid
	706.00

The balance to be paid Milton on the above settlement for what lands Rochester Recd more than their proportion.

all this acc settled prior to the Town's Account for 1805

					1.70	3.97
·	·	11	110			491.03
2	1/2	98	48	4.80	· ·	4.50
1	·	90	20	20	89	1.87
	·	70	40	4.00	1.84	3.87
	·	60	24	2.40	1.08	2.25
	10	[illegible]	64	6.40	2.87	6.00
	·	68	38	380	170	356
	·	64	50	500	224	469
1	·		40½	405	190	379
	·	50	22	220	99	206
	·	·	13	130	58	122
4	·		18½	185	[illegible] ·	168
3	·		18	180	80	169
	·	60	7	70	· ·	· ·
	·	26	20	200	· ·	187
	·	·	14	140	· ·	131

Zebulon Dame	·	2	3	·	1	1	1	½	1	3	12	1	·	112	31	310	1			
Wm Downing	1	·	2	2	3	1	[illegible]	·	2	3	8	1	6	·	38	380	·			
Joseph Dame	1	·	·	·	·	·	·	·	·	·	·	·	·	·	8	80	3			
Aaron Downs	1	4	4	·	2	3	[illegible]	·	2	6	8	1	·	38	49	495	2			
Moses Downs	1	2	4	·	·	1	1	·	1½	5	10	·	·	37	38	380	1			
Gersham Downs	1	·	·	·	·	·	·	·	·	·	·	·	·	·	8	80	3			
Gersham Downs Jr	1	2	3	·	·	2	1	·	1	6	4	·	·	200	40	400	18			
Gersham Downs 3^d	1	·	2	6	·	3	[illegible]	½	1	5	12	1	·	32	39	390	17			
Richd Dame	1	4	8	3	2	4	[illegible]	1½	4	10	24	6	1½	320	97	970	· ·			
Richd Dame Jr	1	2	1	3	1	3	1	·	6	10	2	·		68	42	420	18			
Silas Dame	1	4	5	·	1	·	1	·	3½	10	16	2	·	67	61½	615	27			
Silas Dame Jr	1	·	3	·	2	2	·	·	2½	8	16	2	·	113	40	400	18			
Solomon Downs	1	·	3	2	·	2	1	0	1	2	4	1	·	50	29	290	· ·			
Wm Henry Downs	1	·	·	·	·	·	·	·	·	·	·	·	·	·	8	80	3			
Caleb Dame	1	·	1	·	·	·	1	·	1	·	·	·	1	4	20	200	8			
David Dame	1	·	·	·	·	·	·	·	·	·	·	·	·	·	8	80	3			
Paul Downs	1	2	·	·	1	·	·	·	·	·	·	·	·	·	18½	185	8			

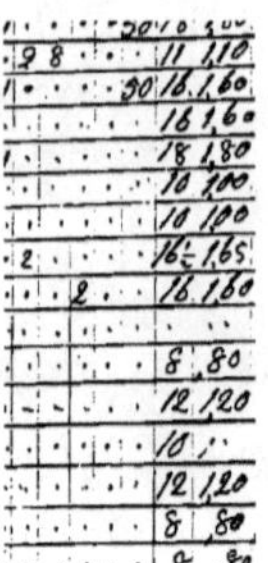

[illegible]	[illegible]	[illegible]	[illegible]
2 8		11	1,10
	30	16	1,60
		16	1,60
		18	1,80
		10	1,00
		10	1,00
2		16½	1,65
2		16	1,60
		8	,80
		12	1,20
		10	[illegible]
		12	1,20
		8	,80
		8	,80

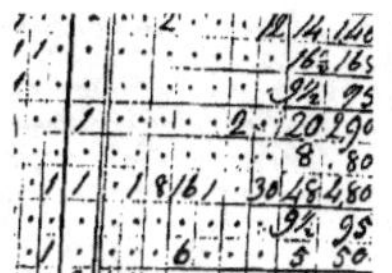

To a Receipt from the Treasurer of said County To Raise Money for said County
You are hereby required in the name of said State to levy & Collect of all Persons named in the foregoing list herewith Committed you to Collect the Same sett to their Names in Dollars and Cents and pay or Cause to be paid to the Treasury of said County one hundred Dollars by the first Day of Decr next and pay the Select Men or their order Three hundred Dollars by the first Day of December — And the whole of the remainer of said list of Town taxes to the Selectmen for the Time being or their order by the first Day of March Next and if any Person or Persons Shall Neglect or Refuse to pay their taxes after legal Warning or Notice you are to take the same by Destraint and Sale as the Law Directs and for your Lawful Proceedings this shall your Sufficient Warrant given under our hands and Seals in Rochester The 28 Day of May 1802

Richd Dame
John Odiorne
Joshua Allen
} Selectmen for 1802

State of New Hampshire
Strafford ss —
} To Benjamin Hayes Appointed Collector of Parish

(28) Taxes for the first Parish in the Town of Rochester for the year 1802 Greeting
Pursuant to Sundry Votes of the Town of Rochester Impowering the Select Men to hire preaching and for Collecting Same You are here by Directed to Collect of all Persons named in the foregoing list of Parish Taxes the Sums sett to their names In Dollars & Cents & pay Joseph Haven Two Hundred & Sixty Six Dollars & Sixty Six Cents by the first Day of March next and the Remainder of said list to the Selectmen for the time being by said first Day of March next or pay the whole of said list to Said Selectmen or their order by Said first Day of March next and if any Person Shall neglect or Refuse to pay Sd Tax after Legal Warning or Notice You are to take the same by Destraint and Sale as the law Directs and for your Lawfull proceedings this Shall be your Sufficient Warrant — Given under our hands and Seals in Rochester this 28th day of May 1802 —

John Odiorne
Joshua Allen
} Selectmen for 1802

abated — 1802 list

		Parish
Abated Caleb Jackson a cow [illegible]	20	
Levi Dearborn Decd	80	36
John Brewster [illegible]	80	—
[illegible] Place a cow lost	20	9
Nathaniel Heard Decd	80	36
Thos Varney 3d horse lost	40	—
Alex Whitehouse a horse	40	18
Edw Cole a dead horse [illegible]	3.00	1.42
Stephen Wentworth sick	80	36
Enos Varney out of town	80	—
Paul Giles not of age	80	—
[illegible] Saml Richards out of town	80	36
Thomas Hanscomb a Cow	20	9
	16.00	3.22

See page 243

State of New Hampshire } To Benjamin Tuttes appointed Collector of
Strafford Ss. } Taxes for the Second Parish
In the Town of Rochester for the year 1802
(LS) Greeting by Virtue of Sundry laws of this State
directing Selectmen to raise Money for the
Support of Schools and Other necessary Expences
and in pursuance of a Precept from the Treasurer
of said County to raise a Sum money for the
for the use of said County — You are hereby
directed in the name of Said State to Levy & Collect
of all Persons named in the foregoing list of [illegible]
Taxes the Several Sums Set to their names in
Dollars & Cents and pay the County Treasury
of said County for the time being Fifty Dollars
& fifty five Cents by the first Day of December
next and one hundred and fifty Dollars more
You are to pay to the Select Man by the by the
first Day of January next and the whole of the
Remainder you are hereby directed to pay the
Selectmen by the first Day of March next and
if any Person or Persons Shall neglect to pay
said Tax or any part thereof after Legal Warning
or Notice You are to take same by Destraint
and Sale as the law Directs and for your lawful
Proceedings This shall be your Sufficient
Warrant Given under our hands and Seals
in Rochester 28th Day of May Anno Dom 1802

Rich.d Dame } Select
John Osborne } men
Joshua Allen } for 1802

State New Hampshire } To Benjamin
Strafford Ss } Tuttes appointed Collector of Taxes
for the Town of Rochester in the Second parish
(LS) for the year 1802 — Greeting
Pursuant to Sundry Votes of the Town of
Rochester for raising money for the Support
of the Gospile and other Parish Expences and
for Raising and Collecting the same You
are hereby required in the name of said State
to Levy and Collect of all Persons named in the
foregoing list the Sums set to their names
under the head parish taxes in Dollars & Cents
and pay the same to the Selectmen or their
order for the time being by the first Day of
March next and if any Person or Persons
Shall neglect or Refuse to pay said Taxes
or any part thereof after legal Warning
or notice you are to take the Same by Destraint
and Sale as the law Directs and for your
lawful proceedings this Shall be your
Sufficient Warrant — Given under our
Hands & Seal in Rochester this 28 Day
of May Anno Domini 1802

John Osborne } Select
Joshua Allen } men 1802

Rec.d March 8th 1806 $
Paul Harford's Town Tax — 1.20
Abel Harris — 1.20
Joseph Tucker — 80
Dudley Hairpole — 65
abated Benja [illegible] 3.85

School account 1802 First [illegible]

No 1 Jacob Hanson 13 dollars	March 10 1804 pd [illegible] Horn by Com orders 1804 [illegible] Horn by Com order	2.31 10.69 [illegible]
No 2 Jabez Dame Esq 24 dollars	paid Daniel [illegible] for keeping the School by Committee order March 10th 1803 See 1803 account	21.00
No 3 Col John McDuffee 36 doll	paid Jacob Main 1802 acct. See 1802 account	36.00
No 4 William Jenness 12 doll.	May 1. 1803 paid Josiah Main [illegible] the Committee order	12.00
No 5 Joseph Hayes 16 dollars	pd Com.ee to pay their Schoolmaster March 7th 1803	16.00
No 6 Joseph Tebbets 19 dollars	paid Josiah Main by [illegible] order March 10th 1804 See 1803 acct.	19.00
No 7 Maj. John Allen 20 dollars	paid Moses Roberts by Committee order March 14th 1803	20.00
No 8 Norway Plains 36 doll	October 14 1803 pd Jacob Main the whole Sum	36.00
No 9 Squamanagonnee 22 dollars	paid Amos Main by Committee order March 10th 1804 pd Richard Henderson for pay Schoolmaster April 20th 1805	16.50 5.50 22.00
No 10 St James Place 15 doll.	1804 pd Schoolmaster by Com. order.	15.00
No 11 Simon Torr Esq 24 dollars	pd Samuel Hurlbut by Committee order March 26. 1803 See 1803 account 1804 Acct.	22.00 2 24.00
No 12 Capt Daniel McDuffee 25 dollars	Paid Thomas [illegible] by [illegible] March 10th 1804 charged [illegible] for [illegible]	25.00
No 13 Abner Hodgdon 12 dollars	1805 Acct pd [illegible] by order of the Committee for pay'g his Schoolmaster	12.00
No 14 Benjamin Meder 20 dollars	pd John Holmes to pay their School March 10th 1806 1804 pd John [illegible] by Com order	10.50 9.50 20.00

School account for Northeast Parish

No 1 Richard Walker 10.50	
No 2 William Palmer Esq 18.70	
Ephraim Twombly $15.80	
John Fish $17.50	
Dudley Burnham $18.50	
Lt Jotham Nute $18.50	
Paul Jewett Esq $24.50	
Samuel Ricker $16.70	

1803 Town accounts for 1802

Returnd in Paul Harfords hands for 1781	85	10
Returnd in Ichabod Corsons hands 1800	361	62
Returnd in Moses Bickfords hands 1801	483	28
Returnd in Benja. Scales hands for 1801	205	45
Returnd in John Odiorn's Nonresid.t list 1800	15	61
Returnd in Stephen Perkins Nonresid.t list 1801	10	24
Due on Moses Canney's Exec. Execution	89	40
Returnd in Notes of hand by Selectmen 1801	56	80
Received of Sales of Town lands	686	77
Rais.d in Benja. Hayes list 1802	960	95
Rais.d in Benja. Scales list 1802	399	15
By a Note Given Daniel Dame Comp.t Courthouse	128	70
	3683	07

The way said Money has been laid out

paid the County Treasurer in full 1802	150	55
pd poor bill in full 1801 and part 1802	132	17
pd Committee Settling with Town of Milton	7	09
pd part of the Sum allowd said Milton	130	00
pd for repairing the pound in full	6	54
pd for Compleating Schoolhouse Jas Hansons	16	81
pd Simon Torr's bill Compleat.g Little falls bridge	9	83
pd Com.ee bill viewing Road by Rich.d Monsons as allowd by Court of Common pleas	3	50
pd Town Clerk in full his Service for 1801	16	00
pd Town Clerk in part his Service for 1802	6	58
pd Selectmen Laying a Road out over Dry hill	3	
pd John Trickey for Work on Chesnut hills road	4	00
pd for Timber and Work Compleat.g Places bridge	36	13
pd Selectmen time & expence Selling Town lands and Settling with purchasers &c	13	78
pd Bills Compleating Norway plain bridge	95	77
pd Selectmen time & expence Settling prosecu-ment on the road by Cap.t Dan.l McDuffee	2	50
paid for taking Inventory for 1802	7	00
pd Making Ratelists & Counterparts 1802	8	00
pd mak.g Surveyors lists & destributing Surveyors	7	00
pd making & giving out School Lists	7	00
pd for recording ratelists & town acc.ts in full	5	00
pd Selectmen appointing Collectors & their bonds	3	50
pd Benja. Scales in full for Collecting tax 1801	20	00
pd abatement of taxes in Benja. Scales list 1801	11	50
pd D.o Thomas Pinkham tax in part 1798 & 1799	4	96
pd D.o Tobias Ricker's Dud Copp taxes in Scales list 1800	2	98
pd John Odiorne in full for a road thro his land	27	00
pd Maj.r Perkins boarding Schoolmaster	20	00
pd Joseph Hayes Dest. 1801 and 1802 in full	34	00
pd Simon Torrs Dest. in full 1801	24	00
pd Cap.t Dan.l McDuffee Dest bal. 1800 & part 1801	23	50
pd Col. Place board.g Schoolmaster in 1802	5	00
pd Abner Hodgdon destrict in full 1801	12	00
pd Jacob Hansons dest in full 1801, bal. 1799 & 1800	23	00
pd Col. McDuffee dest in full 1800 & 1801, 1802	93	50
pd Ens.n John Fish dest. in full 1801	17	50
pd Rich.d Walker dest. in full 1801	10	50
pd Dudley Burnhams dest in full 1801	18	50
pd L.t Jotham Nute's Dest in full 1801	18	50
pd Samuel Ricker dest in full 1801	6	70
	1091	44

1802 town accounts Continued 1802

~~paid Selectmens Services in full thro the year~~		
pd Selectmen opening Road by Eph.m Perkins	2	25
pd Silas Dame J.r for road thro his land in full	25	25
pd Selectmen runing & exchanging Road by Jn.o Chesley	3	00
pd D.o two Deeds for the same & Elisha Wentworth		50
pd D.o runing & opening road at Medenboro 2 days	6	00
pd D.o runing & opening road by Benja. Pages	2	00
pd D.o for two Deeds for the same		50
pd John Cate for runing a road at Medenboro	1	00
pd for recording Deeds rec.d of Odiorne		33
pd Col. Rich.d Furber a Witness in case of presentm.t	2	33
pd Daniel Dame's bills painting Courthouse	233	56
pd Simon Torrs bill for repairing Road	4	10
pd for writing paper through the year	1	50
pd Benja. Medens Destrict the bal. 1801 pt. of 1802	8	33
pd Squamanagonnic Dest the Whole of 1800 & 1801	36	50
paid the Selectmen for 1801 the sum due them last year	65	25
paid the Assessors for 1802 in full	2	00
pd for Compleating Squamanagonnic bridge	5	00
pd D.r Samuel Plumer in full for a Road	1	00
pd Joseph Clark Esq.r for Services in part	5	76
pd Selectmen viewing and appraising School lott	1	00
pd Selectmen fixing place to set Chesnut hills Schoolhouse	2	00
pd Maj. Allens Dest bal 1779 & full 1801	26	71
pd Com.ee Settling road by John Witherells	4	50
pd Joseph Bickford for bridge Covering	1	00
paid the Auditors in full for their Services	6	80
	445	47

Sum cast by Auditors 445.11
Selectmen ... 15.00
... Bickfords abatement 8.80
468.91

Outstanding in Paul Harfords hands 1781	85	10
Remain in Ichabod Corsons hands 1800	362	51
Remain in Moses Bickfords hands for 1801	81	27
~~Remain in Stephen Perkins Nonresid.t list 1801~~		
Remain in Benja. Hayes list for 1802	622	86
Remain in Benja. Scales list for 1802	349	47
Due on Moses Canney Esq. Execution	89	40
Returnd in Notes of hand	661	44
	2252	06
	1091	44
	445	47
	3788	96
	3683	07
Which leaves a balance due the Selectmen	105	89

The foregoing is a true Account of the Debt and Credit of the Town accounts for the year 1802 as Exhibited to the Auditors this 12th of March 1803

Rich.d Dame
Joshua Allen } Select men
John Odiorne

The foregoing account as Rendered to us by the Selectmen apears to be well and accurate, well vouched and just, except Two Dollars Charged for the Selectmens Trouble in fixing the place where to set Chesnut Hills District School House

March 12th 1803

Hatevil Knight
Simeon Gove } Auditors
Jacob Hanson

1802 Parish accounts for first Parish 1802

Returnd in Ichabod Corsons hands for 1800	345	06
Returnd in Moses Bickfords hands 1801	301	07
Rec^d of Selectmen for 1801	29	61
Raisd in Benj^a Hayes list - 1802	318	22
	993	96

The way s^d Money has been laid out		
paid Selectmen making parish list 1802	2	50
p^d for repairs for the parsonage house in part	86	64
p^d Richd Cross taking care of meeting house	6	00
p^d Thomas Brown work on Meeting house & some expences thereon	2	12

Remains in Ichabod Corson list for 1800	285	34
Remains in Moses Bickford list for 1801	301	07
Remain in Benj^a Hayes list for 1802	318	22
	1001	89
	993	96
Which leaves a balance due Selectmen of	7	93

Upper Parish accounts

Returnd in Benj^a Seates list for 1800	68	67
Returnd in D^o for 1801	63	38
Raisd in D^o list for 1802	68	94
	200	99

Paid Selectmen Making Parish list	2	00
Remain in Benj^a Seates list 1800	68	67
Remain in D^o list for 1801	63	38
Remain in D^o list for 1802	68	94
	202	99
Due to the Selectmen	2	00

The foregoing is a true account of the parish affairs as kept by us and presented to the Auditors this 12th day of March 1803

John Dame } Select-
Joshua Allen } men

We have cast the list and examined the foregoing parish accounts as exhibited by the Selectmen and find them accurate and well vouched
March 12 1803 Hatevil Knight
Simon Torr } Auditors
Jacob Hanson

1802 Account Poor bill

p^d Expences Wid^o Waymoth's funeral &c in full	46.25
Samuel Bickford in full	3.00
Josh^a Holmes J^r for Dol Robinsons Child 1801	19.00
Nat Meder & Ephraim for Wid^o Merrows bal^c 1801 in full	21.00
Jon^a Hearl & others Paul Cheslee in full	41.00
Some expences for Matthias Welch in full	00.92
Selectmens bills in full 1802	3.00
	134.17
Deducted for the house Wid^o Waymoth's sold	
Charged in Town acc^t for 1802	132.17

Notes charged in Town acc^t 1802

Stephen Perkins	10.24
Anthony Whitehouse	142.10
D^o	152.10
Richmond Henderson	152.10
D^o	152.10
Benjamin Palmer	8.80
D^o	26.00
D^o and others	2.67
Howard Henderson	8.19
Benjamin Dame	2.93
Lieut. Jotham Nute	2.73
Elijah Varney	1.48
Sum charged in town acc^t 1802	661.44

County precept for 1803 is 132.90

Rochester 11th of April 1803
agreed with the Selectmen to take the Widow Merrow for one year at fifty cents per week exclusive of clothing and extra for sickness
Timothy Roberts

Agreed with Joshua Holmes J^r to take Nancy Robinson for one year from 19th of April 1803 for $13.75 including clothing & all expense

Rochester May 30th 1803
Then agreed with and appointed Hatevil Knight to collect the Town and Parish Taxes for the Town of Rochester for the year 1803 who gave bond to collect the same for 2 & 3/4 Pr Cent of the whole sum or what shall be paid by the first day of March next & to pay Interest for what shall remain unpaid at that time the Town having neglected to chose a Collector

Richd Dame } Sele-
John Dame } ctmen
Joshua Allen }

1803 Settlement with Collectors

March 21 received of Benjamin Hayes Cash	
[illegible] Acct for Selectmen as pr order	21.10
pd. Jacob Mason 23.36: [illegible] for Road [illegible]	39.92
[illegible] Moses Roberts May. Allen Dest 1802	29.44
pd James [illegible] for Wood for Court 6 Doll School 3 Doll	10.00
pd Josh Holmes poor bill 10 Doll Benj Page for road 20	9.00
[illegible] for [illegible] Benj Roberts for wood 92	30.00
pd Abijah Clark for a Road [illegible]	10.92
	2.00
and gave a Rect for 1802 town list in part, for	162.38
May 3d 1803 recd of Moses Bickford as Cash D W [illegible]	2.00
Joseph Clark order for [illegible]	4.06
Benjn Varney School list 1802	12.00
J [illegible] Mr [illegible] Hanscombs Tax	1.45
and gave a recet for 1801 tax in part Town	10.51
June 27th Recd Ichabod Corson as cash to R[illegible]	.88
plank and String for Garlins Bridge	19.59
pd Levi Pickering for work on N [illegible] bridge	1.50
and gave a receipt for 1800 town tax in pt.	21.97
August 8th 1803 Recd of Ichabod Corson 1861 feet of pine plank board measure at 8 Doll pr 1000 as Survey'd by John Hanson Surveyor which was credited to Corson before Extending him	14.88

extent against Ichabod Corson given out August 8th 1803 for three hundred and eight Dollars seventy nine cents given to Major Solomon Perkins to collect [illegible]

August 29th 1803 Settled with Moses Bickford recd Cash	4.55
Cash pd the 8th Instant 20 Doll Abatements 7.30	27.30
for Collecting 22.80 and part of a note 8.66	31.11
and gave a Rect balance in full 1801 town list for	62.96

[illegible]

Also received Joseph Havens rect in full 1801	266.66
Abatements allowd in parish list 1801	5.93
for Collecting parish list for 1801	7.30
took his note for balance for Parish list	
and Rect in full for parish list for 1801	301.07
March 10th 1804 recd of Benj Hayes as cash	5.39
pd Moses [illegible] Acct for work on [illegible] Road	7.00
pd Capt Danl McDuffee Dest for 1802	25.00
pd R Cross for work on N P bridge 3.21 D [illegible] Dest 1801	27.21
Josh Holmes for poor 8: Jn Brown for work on pound 1	9.00
Nat Meder for poor 29.50 Danl Ham for work on [illegible] bridge	30.50
Jabez Dame as Comm 2.50 Jos Tebbets Dest 1802 19.00	21.50
Town Clerk 1802 9.42 Capt Danl McDuffee Dest 1801 4.07	13.49
Capt Hodgdon for wood 7 Jac Hanson Dest 1801 be 12	19.00
Presentment 24.35 Israel Whitehouse for road 2.50	26.85
Jos Holmes Dest 1802 10.50 R Cross for timber 2	12.50
Jac Hanson for postguide 1 Square Dest 1802 13	14.00
Jacob Main for School 53.37 Ed Cole for postguides 8.63	62.00
J. [illegible] for Taxes 7.09 Dav Tebbets Tax to Allen 3.10	10.19
and gave a receipt in part of 1802 Town list for	283.63
Do recd of Richmond Henderson Cash	1.10
Squamanagonnuc School list for 1803	23.00
for Plank for Walker bridge	3.62
	27.72
and Indorsed on his note Dated	
Do received of Ichabod Corson Cash pd at [illegible] times	14.50
for 1576 ft plank for Garlins bridge 9.45 hemlock	9.45
for 1618 feet Do hemlock for [illegible] at [illegible]	6.09
for 2 Stringers for Garlins bridge 2.50 Bark for [illegible] 50	4.80
pd Edward Cole for postguides	3.72
abatements not heretofore allowed for 1800	8.12
and gave a Receipt in part of an Extent 1800	45.90

[illegible]

1803 Settlement with Collectors 1803

June 12 1804 recd [illegible] Cash	7.00
Norway plain District [illegible] orders for 1803	7.50
Thos McDuffee for plank for Norway plain Bridge	1.50
County Tax [illegible] 50: Taxes for Selectmen 20.02	70.62
Simon Tor [illegible] taken to Dame	13.90
Clem Libbys tax to Allen	1.55
and gave a receipt in part of 1803 town tax	112.40
first Extent against I Corson Aug 8th 1803 for $308.79	

An Alias Extent Issued by the Selectmen against Ichabod Corson for three hundred and Eight Dollars seventy nine cents dated October

which not being paid

An Alias Extent Issued by the Selectmen against Ichabod Corson for said Sum Dated January 5th 1804 given to Major Solomon Perkins

which being returned

A new Alias Extent was given out by the Selectmen for 1804 for the same Sum Dated May 25th 1804 given to Major Perkins three hundred and Eight Dollars and seventy nine cents on which was Indorsed Ninety five Dollars and forty two cents.

308.79
95.42
213.37
5.83 cents paid and a n Alias Extent Issued for the balance dated

An alias extent Issued Jany 11th 1805
for 172.54
11.35 paid by Maj Allen
$ 161.19 the sum that ought to have been returned in Town Acct for 1804 see page 317

A new Alias extent Issued out May [illegible] 1805 for One hundred and Sixty one Dollars Nineteen cents Including Three Dollars and fifty Cents for this and former Warrant

The above Extent renewd by an Alias Extent dated September 10th 1805 for one hundred & sixty one Dollars sixty nine Cents & Committed to Hatevil Knight

The above renewd by an Alias Extent dated ~~December 12~~ November 20th 1805 for One hundred thirty ~~six~~ Dollars nineteen cents and Committed to Hatevil Knight

1803 Counterpart of [illegible] Road Tax collecting [illegible]

Name	$	c
Maj. Joshua Allen	3	63
Micah Allen	2	44
Samuel Allen	3	31
Sam'l Adams	1	69
Benj'n Adams	1	20
Amos Adams	-	53
Capt John Brewster	3	00
Thomas Brown	1	13
Isaac Bickford	2	50
Joseph Bickford	3	88
John Brown	1	31
John Baker	2	88
Otis Baker	1	63
David Barker	1	69
Isaac Brown	-	63
John Bickford Jr	3	50
Depen's Bickford	2	44
John Bickford	2	07
Tristram Bickford	-	75
Moses Bickford	1	13
John Bickford 3rd	1	00
Stephen Brewster	-	75
Will'm Blake	1	25
Moses Brown	-	50
Molly Bickford	-	-
Jos. Smith Brown	-	50
Abram Cook	1	75
Dr Sam'l Chamberlain	1	84
Tristram Coffin	-	63
Joseph Clark Esq	1	94
Peter Cushing	1	38
John Clontman	1	72
Hezekiah Clontman	1	50
Ichabod Cousen	5	62
Sr Tim'o Cousen	2	10
James Chessle	3	13
Abijah Clark	2	56
John Clark	-	56
Rich'd Cross	-	88
Edw'd Cole	-	63
Sam'l Chamberlain Jr	1	63
Thomas Chessle	-	69
Samuel Coleman	-	69
Jabez Dame Esqr	4	31
Wid Anna Dearborn	-	72
Benj'n Dame	1	88
[illegible] Dame Estate	1	38

Name	$	c
Sr Sam'l Downing	2	56
Joseph Dame	-	50
Aaron Downs	2	38
Moses Downs	2	50
Gershom Downs	-	50
Gershom Downs Jr	1	51
Gershom Downs 3rd	2	38
~~Paul Down~~		
Rich'd Dame	5	73
Rich'd Dame Jr	3	50
Silas Dame	3	37
Silas Dame Jr	2	56
Solomon Downs	-	50
Ens. Henry Downs	2	19
Caleb Dame	1	06
Daniel Dame	-	50
Paul Downs	1	13
Paul Dame	-	63
Jonathan Downing	-	75
Sam'l Downing Jr	-	50
John H Dearborn	-	56
Jabez Dame Jr	-	50
Aaron Downs Jr	-	50
Thomas Downs	1	31
Thomas Downs Jr	-	50
Benj'n Evans	2	00
Benj'n Hanson Evans	1	16
David Evans	-	59
Benj'n Evans Jr	1	10
Jacob Ellis	2	25
Joshua Ellis	1	06
Jonathan Flagg	-	50
Ens. Rich'd Furber	1	06
Sam'l Downs Foss	2	38
Sam'l Foss Jr	-	50
Eph'm Foss Barron		94
Co. John Gordon	2	25
Daniel Garland	2	44
Dudley Garland	1	75
James Garlin	1	56
Joseph Giles	2	38
Ebenezer Garlin	-	84
Rich'd Hayes	2	38
Humphrey Hanson	-	50
George Heard	-	50
Dr James Ham	1	88
Joseph Heard	1	80
Jacob Hanson	3	56

Name	$	c
Stephen Harford	2	94
Capt Alex'r Hodgdon	1	94
Ens. Nath'l Hayes	2	50
John Hammett	-	63
Joseph Hanson	4	19
Benj'n Hayes	2	50
Sr Joshua Holmes	2	00
Aaron Ham	3	37
Wid Mehitable Ham	4	-6
Stephen Ham	2	69
Paul Harford	-	88
Enoch Hoyt	1	44
Nath'l Heard's Estate	1	81
Tristram Heard	1	69
Benj'n Heard	-	50
Joshua Holmes Jr	-	91
Abram Heard	4	-
Joseph Heard Jr	1	88
Joseph Heard 3rd	-	63
Amos Hodgdon	2	63
Daniel Hancey	3	56
Jacob Hanson Mes	2	38
Nath'l Ham	1	88
Howard Henderson	3	50
Moses Hayes Jr	3	25
Eph'm Ham	2	94
Joseph Hayes	5	38
Will'm Henderson	3	06
Moses Hammett	1	69
Eleazer Ham	1	00
Jonathan Heard	2	44
Jon'a Heard Jr	2	50
Richmond Henderson	2	44
George Hayes	2	07
Reuben Hannaford	-	69
Ebenezer Horn		50
Samuel Ham	1	25
John Hanson		56
Enoch Hoyt Jr	1	06
Temple Hoyt	1	00
Thomas Hanscomb	-	88
Stephen Heard	1	38
Thomas Hoit	1	88

Name	$	c
Mark Hodges	2	28
Benj'n Hoyt	1	94
Joseph Hodgdon	2	16
Dennis Hoit	-	50
Jon'a Henderson	-	50
Eph'm Hammett	-	56
James Horn	2	13
Daniel Ham	1	20
Jon'a Hodgdon Jr	2	63
Eben'r Horn Jr	-	50
Stephen Ham Jr		75
John P Hale Esq	-	88
Paul Ham	-	63
Joshua Hayes	-	50
Benjamin Harford	-	63
John Haven	-	69
John Heard	1	63
Reuben Heard Jr	-	50
John Hoit		50
Eph'm Ham Jr		50
Meshach Heard	1	13
Rich'd Howard		75
Isaac Horn	1	69
Moses Horn Estate	2	69
Paul Jenness	2	44
Will'm Jenness	1	75
Daniel Jenness	1	56
Moses Jenness	2	19
Aaron Jenness	2	44
David Jenness	2	75
Josiah Jenkins	2	81
Caleb Jackson	2	31
Jon'a Jenness	1	6.
Sam'l Jenness	1	8
Dan'l Jenness Jr	1	6
Caleb Jackson Jr	-	5
Will'm Jenness Jr	2	2
Jeremiah Jenness	-	6
Samuel Jackson	-	8
Benjamin Jones	1	[illegible]
Jon'a Jenness Jr		
George Jenness		
Joseph Knight	1	
Joshua Knight	1	
Hatevil Knight	2	
John Kent	1	
Ephraim Kimball		

[illegible] Kimball	1	91
[illegible] Libbey	2	81
David Langley	2	78
Clement Libbey		81
Capt Saml Hamilton	2	25
James Langley		75
[illegible] John McDuffee	6	43
Capt Willm McDuffee	3	31
Capt Danl McDuffee	4	50
John McDuffee	1	94
Jacob McDuffee	3	03
James McDuffee	2	75
David McDuffee	2	72
John McDuffee 3d	2	72
Benjamin Meder	3	03
Nathl Meser	3	25
Jona Meder	2	75
Joseph Meder	-	75
Francis Meder	1	69
Josiah Main	1	50
Amos Main	-	66
Josiah Main Jr		63
Willm McNeal	2	38
Jonathan Morrison	1	28
Lemuel Meder	2	17
Edwd S Moulton	-	81
Micah Meder	1	00
Jonas C March Jr	2	56
Moses L Neal Esqr	1	20
John Nutter	1	44
Jotham Nutter	1	25
Rich Nutter Jr	-	63
John Odiorne	1	44
Elijah Otis	-	-
John Plummer Jr	6	37
Dr Saml Plummer	3	81
Col David Place	3	81
Lt James Place	4	53
Lt Keith Place	2	07
John M Place	2	63
Pearl Place	1	69
James Pickering	1	06
Levi Pickering	1	47
Joseph Page	3	69
Benja Page	4	91
Daniel Page	3	13
Major Solomon Perkins	1	20
Stephen Place	1	23

Dr Saml Pray	-	75
Ebenezer Pearl	2	69
Ephm Perkins	1	56
Diamond Pearl	1	29
Willm Perkins	-	-
Wid Martha Pike	-	50
Joseph Perkins	1	66
Abram Pearl	1	06
Isaac Pearl	1	20
Stephen Pinkham	-	63
John Plummer 3d	-	63
Ebenezer Plummer	1	06
Stephen Perkins	1	00
Andrew Peirce	1	20
Willm Pickering	-	81
Thomas Plummer	-	50
Adam Perkins	-	50
Danl Plummer	-	50
James Pickering Jr	3	03
James Peavy	-	88
Lt Edwd Rollins	2	56
Lt Timo Roberts	2	34
Samuel Robinson	-	50
John Rendall	2	38
John Rendall Jr	2	16
Heard Roberts	3	59
Benja Rollins	1	20
Moses Roberts	3	13
John Richardson	2	83
Timo Richardson	1	38
Jona Richards		50
Daniel Rogers	1	56
Benja Roberts	2	16
John Roberts Jr	2	28
James Robinson	1	94
John Richards	-	50
Joseph Richards	2	44
Ezra Roberts	2	07
Eleazer Rann	-	81
Willm Ripley	-	50
Saml Seavy	2	72
John Smith	1	31
Joseph Sherburne	1	63
James Rabin	-	50
Andrew Simpson		56
Simon Torr Esqr	5	75
Joseph Tebbets	4	31
Benja Tebbets	3	13

David Tebbets	1	92
Robert Tebbets	2	28
Wid Ruth Tebbets	1	69
Silas Tebbets	1	50
John Tebbets	1	81
Ebenr Tebbets	2	94
James Tebbets	1	69
Enoch Tebbets	2	13
David Tebbets Jr	1	20
Joseph Tebbets Jr	-	59
Ezekiel Tebbets	-	50
James Tebbets Jr	-	50
Jedediah Tebbets	2	50
Nicholas Tebbets	-	72
Tobias Twambly	-	31
Isaac Twambly	2	56
Tobias Twambly Jr	3	25
Willm Trickey	2	97
Willm Tebbets	1	63
Joshua Trickey	3	50
John Trickey	1	47
Joseph Tucker	-	59
Benja Tuttle	-	63
Josiah Tucker	-	50
Joshua Tolford	-	88
Henry Tebbets	-	-
Samuel Tebbets	1	23
Nathl Upham	3	23
Moses Varney	1	41
Elijah Varney	1	50
Benja Varney	2	75
Thomas Varney	1	50
Jeremiah Varney	-	50
Tobias Varney	3	20
Thomas Varney Jr	2	53
Thomas Varney 3d	-	94
Moses Varney Jr	-	56
Nicholas Varney	1	00
Silas Varney	-	75
Elijah Varney Jr	-	94

Stephen Wentworth	-	-
Isaac Wentworth	2	19
Josiah Wentworth	2	13
Elihu Wentworth	1	94
Saml Wingate	1	44
David Wingate	4	19
Benja Wingate	1	8[cut off]
George Willand	1	6[cut off]
Enoch Willand		8[cut off]
Jacob Wallingford	2	3[cut off]
Turner Whitehouse	-	9[cut off]
Anthony Whitehouse	1	4[cut off]
Benja Whitehouse	-	8[cut off]
Alexr Whitehouse	-	7[cut off]
Israel Whitehouse		6[cut off]
Daniel Watson	-	5[cut off]
James Waldron	3	2[cut off]
Stephen Wentworth Jr	3	1[cut off]
Elijah Whitehouse	1	[cut off]
Moses Waldron	3	[cut off]
John Wetherill	2	[cut off]
Benja Wentworth	1	-
Thos Wentworth	-	
James Woodhouse	-	
Josiah Wentworth Jr	-	
Ephm Wentworth	-	
Thomas Wentworth Jr	-	
David Wiggin	-	
Moses Young	-	3
Wm Palmer Esqr	-	

Warrants in usual fo[rm] were given to the [Co]… Surveyors to collect above dated Augt 30th directed to be worked on [&] list returned in thirty [days] from date —

pd John Horn by Directors order March 10th 1804 Dec 1803 acct	18.30
1804 pd John Heard by Directors order	$20.00
pd in 1805 acct	1.65
pd Samuel Austin by Comm^ee order June 1805	$20.00
Do balance pd Saml Austin	5.78
	25.78
pd Joseph Richards by Comm^ee order	7.50
pd John Odiorne by order March 12 1804 Dec 1803 acct	4.00
1804 pd John Heard by order	$23.16
paid Joseph Hain for keeping said school by Comm^ee order Dec 1803 acct	23.00
1804 pd schoolmaster by Com order	1.00
1805 July pd Joseph Giles by Directors order to pay Wm Hulse	13.60
	14.60
Nov 3 1804 paid the Committee for paying their schoolmaster	21.00
March 1804 pd S. Tarr for paying his debt to A Tuttle	6.00
	$27.00
1804 paid the whole in 1804 acct to Thos Plummer by Comm^ee order	29.22
1804 acct pd balance of Abner Hodgdon order to D. Clark for 20 Dollars 1st pd in 1800 acct	13.40

1804 James Twombly
January 3^d 1804

Richard Dame
John Odiorne
Joshua Allen
} Selectmen of Rochester

Farmington July 3^d 1814

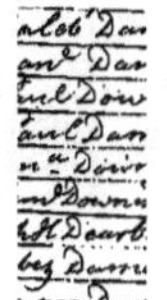

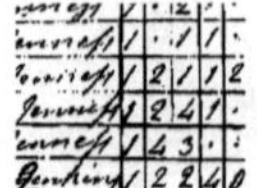

[illegible]	1	·	2	·	·
[illegible]	1	·	1	1	·
[illegible]	1	2	1	1	2
[illegible]	1	2	4	1	·
[illegible]	1	4	3	·	·
Jenkins	1	2	2	4	0

Warrants to the ~~a~~ foregoing Town & Parish lists — 1803 —

State of New Hampshire } To Hatevil Knight
Strafford Ss — — — — } Appointed Collector
of Taxes for the Town of Rochester for the year
1803 Greeting —

(Seal) By Virtue of Sundry laws of said State
directing Select Men to raise money for
the Support of Schools and other necessary
Purposes and agreeable to a Vote of said
Town to Raise money for the use of said
Town and in pursuance of a Precept from
the Treasury of said County — to rase money
for said County You are hereby required in
the name of said State to levy and Collect of
all Persons named in the foregoing list the
Sums set to their names in Dollars & Cents
And pay or Cause to be paid into the Treasury
of said County the sum of one hundred thirty
Two Dollars & ninety Cents by the first day
of December next & pay the Select Men or
their order Three hundred more by the first
Day of January next and the whole of the
Remainder of said Town list by the first day
of March Next Insueing the date hereof and
if any Person or Persons shall Neglect or refuse
to pay his or their said Taxes after legal
Warning or Notice you are to take the same
by Destraint & Sale as the law Directs and
for your lawfull proceedings this shall be
your sufficient Warrant Given under our
hands and Seals this Thirtieth Day of May
1803

Richd Dame } Select Men
John Odiorne } of Rochester
Joshua Allan

1803

Names under the head Parish Taxes in Dollars and Cents and pay the same to the Select Men or their order for the time being by the first Day of March Next and if any Person or Persons shall Refuse or neglect to pay said Taxes or any part thereof after having Legal Warning or Notice you are to take the same by Destraint and Sale as the law Directs and for your lawful proceedings this shall be your Sufficient Warrant given under our Hand and Seals this Thirtieth Day of May – 1803

John Odiorne } Selectmen
Joshua Allen } of Rochester

Abatements	town	parish
John Odiorne a horse lost	0.46	0.15
Benj Whitehouse a Cow too much	20	0.8
Paul Libbey a Cow lost	20	0.9
Jos Smith Brown	80	36
Saml Jeff Jr	80	34
Ebenezer Garlin	1.35	0.60
Ebenezer Ham Jr	80	36
Caleb Jackson Jr	80	00
Ephraim Langley	80	
John Plumer 3d	1.00	..
Adam Perkins	80	..
Daniel Rogers	2.50	1.12
John Raynall	80	36
James Rann	80	36
Dudley Stackpole	70	..
Joseph Tucker	95	42
Josiah Tucker	80	36
Jacob Hanson	—	2.56
Moses Jenness		1.17
Eleazar Rann	1.30	58
Stephen Wentworth	90	40
John Wilson	80	00
John Roberts	80	36
Ezekiel Tebbets	80	00
Paul Harford	1.40	63
	20.50	10.35

Recd Novr 2d 1805 of the Selectmen twenty Dollars fifty cents for the above abatements in my town list for 1803 recd of the Select men.

H Knight

Moses Canney poor — 1.20
James Tebbets gone away — 80

March 8th 1806 recd two Dollars for the above and Twenty Dollars for collecting town tax for 1803

Hatevil Knight

March 7th 1812 Recd the above Parish abatements and six dollars and fifty eight in full for collecting parish Taxes for the year 1803 by me

Hatevil Knight

Town accounts for Rochester 1803

		$	cts
Returnd in Paul Harfords list	1781	85	10
Returnd in Ichabod Corsons hands	1800	362	51
Returnd in Moses Bickfords hands	1801	81	27
Returnd in Benjamin Hayes list	1802	622	88
Returnd in Benjamin Scales list	1802	349	47
D°. Sum due on Moses Canney Esqr Execution		89	40
Rec^d in Notes of hand of Selectmen of	1802	661	44
Raisd in Hateivl Knights Town list	1803	989	20
Rec^d for Town lands sold in	1802	77	09
Rec^d of Elijah Whitham for a piece of a Road [illegible]		5	00
		3323	34

The way said money has been laid out

		$	cts
Paid County Treasurer in part	1803	50	00
Pd Poor's bill balance of 1802 and in part	1803	53	28
pd Selectmens services for 1802 omitted last year		15	00
pd Extra for Jacob Mains service keeping school over what the several Districts [illegible]	1802	108	61
pd Moses Canney Esqr for Quitting his Claim to land sold him near the Courthouse by the Town		195	00
pd Selectmen for laying a road over Jos. Hayes & Eph^m Hams land		3	00
pd Joseph Hayes in full for a road thro his land		5	00
pd Eph^{rm} Ham in full for a Road thro his land		4	00
pd Selectmen Laying a road thro Joseph Waldrons land		3	00
pd Joseph Waldron in full for Road & two deeds		12	60
pd Abatement in Benj Scales list 1799 as agreed by former Selectmen		4	84
pd Selectmen viewing Road over chesnut hill and settling the same after Presentment		3	00
pd D° attending court on account of Presentments		2	00
pd D° Viewing the road from Norway plain to Eph^m Hams		3	00
pd James McDuffee in full for land turnd out for the Road		6	08
pd Benjamin Page in full for a Road thro his land		20	00
pd for Strings and covering for Garlins Bridge		37	53
pd Moses Jones Acc^t for cutting a road from Danl pages to meaderboro Road in part		7	00
pd Wm Henderson for a Door stone & other repairs underpinning Courthouse		10	00
pd Joseph Clark Esqr for services he says he has done the town		4	06
pd Selectmen making Ratelist & Counterpart	1803	6	00
pd D° taking Inventory and making return to Gen Court		8	00
pd D° Making & Giving out Surveyors list	1803	4	00
pd D° Making School list Districting Schools and settling with schoolmasters &c		4	00
pd D° time & expence app^g Collectors writing bonds &c		3	50
pd for recording Ratelists & Town acc^ts in full		3	00
pd for firewood for Norway plain Town school	1802	3	92
pd Abijah Clark in full for land improv^d for a Road from Norway plain to Salmon falls & laying out		2	50
pd Moses Bickford for collecting Town tax	1801	22	50
pd abatements in Moses Bickfords Town list	1801	15	60
pd abatements in Ichabod Corsons Town list	1800	25	09
pd the balance due the Selectmen for	1802	105	89
pd for postage of Journals of the Gen Court	1802	--	23
pd for timber & work on Norway plain bridge	1803	19	13
pd the Selectmen settling with Collectors arranging town accounts and other like services	1803	12	00
pd for writing paper thro the year		1	00
		783	27

	$	cts
P^d Simon Torr Esqr District in part 1802	22	-
Pd Norway plain Dist. balance 1801 in full 1802	47	40
Pd Squamanagonnic Dist balance 1801 & part 1802 & in full 1803	47	00
Pd Maj. Allens Dist 1802	20	00
Pd Jacob McDuffees Dist 1802	12	-
Pd C^pt John McDuffee Dist in p^t 1803 in part	24	00
Pd Capt Danl McDuffee Dist for 1803 & balance of 1801	29	07
Pd Joseph Tebbet District for 1801	19	00
Pd Jabez Dame Esq Dist for 1802	22	00
P^d Jacob Hanson's Dist bal^ce for 1800 & part 1802	12	00
P^d Benjamin Meder District in part 1802	10	50
Paid Joseph Hayes District for 1803	18	30
paid John Wetherell in part for a Road thro his land	21	80
paid Norway plain School in part 1803	10	50
Paid Selectmen making second highway tax & giving out	4	00
P^d Interest money on notes more than we received	7	..
Pd for timber & extra work on Norway plain brook bridge	3	21
Pd for work repairing the Pound	1	-
Pd Balance for Compleating Walkers bridge	4	62
Pd for wood for Grammar School in 1802	7	00
Pd for Execution on presentment for bad Roads	24	35
Pd Israel Whitehouse in full for land turnd out for Road	2	50
Pd Edward Cole and others for Erecting post Guides	18	75
Pd Josiah Main for service as town Clerk 1802 the balance	9	48
pd for Plank for bridge by Hezekiah Chamberlain	6	09
pd Selectmen & others for time & expence carrying poor person out of the town	4	70
paid the Auditors in full for their services 1803	4	00
Pd for making out & for Acknowledge 3 Deeds	1	00
	417	17

		$	cts
Outstanding in Paul Harfords hands for	1781	85	10
On Execut against Ichabod Corson for	1800	264	39
In Benjamin Hayes hands for	1802	176	85
In Hateivl Knights hands for	1803	876	80
In Benjamin Scales hands for	1802	349	47
Returned in Notes of hand		500	28
		2252	89
		417	17
		783	27
		3453	33
		3323	34
which leaves a balance due Selectmen		129	99

The foregoing is a true account of Debt and Credit for the present year 1803 as Exhibited by us to the Auditors this 12th day of March 1804

Richd Dame
John Odiorne
Joshua Allen } Selectmen

the foregoing Acc^t as Rendered to us by the Select Men appears to be well Cast & well Vouched this 12 Day of March 1804

Joseph Hanson } Auditors
Moses Roberts Jr

1803 270

Parish Account for Rochester 1803

		Dollars	cents
Returned in Ichabod Corsons list for	1800	285	34
Returned in Moses Bickfords list for	1801	301	07
Returned in Benjamin Hayes list	1802	318	22
Raised in Hatevil Knights list	1803	325	51
		1230	14

The way said money has been laid out

Paid Selectmen making parish list	1803	2	50
pd the balance due Selectmen	1802	7	93
pd Abatement in Moses Bickfords list	1801	5	93
pd Moses Bickford for Collecting parish list	1801	7	50
pd Joseph Havens salary in full 1801		266	66
pd Repairs on the Meeting House		3	83
Returned in Ichabod Corsons list	1800	285	34
Returned in Benj Hayes list	1802	318	22
Raised in Hatevil Knights list	1803	325	51
		1223	44
which leaves a balance due from Selectmen		6	70
	7 86.70	1230	14

The foregoing is a true account of parish matters as kept by us and presented this 12th day of March 1814

John Odiorne } Select
Joshua Allen } men

The foregoing parish account appears to be accurate and Just and well vouched

Joseph W Hanson } auditor

1803 271

Sums paid towards Support of The poor 1803

	$
Nathaniel Meder the balance in full for Wido Merrow for 1802 & to 1st of April 1803	29.50
Joshua Holmes in full for 1802 & to 19th April 1803	18.00
for Wood Supplied Raynall family in the house	1.00
Selectmen time & expence about poor	3.33
Some Supplies from J. C. Ward for Raynals fam	1.45
Charged in Town account 1803	53.28

Notes Charged in Town accounts 1803

Anthony Whitehouse	90.10
Ditto	152.10
Richmond Henderson	35.98
Ditto	152.10
Benjamin Dame	2.93
× Howard Henderson ×	8.19
Benjamin Palmer	26.00
Ditto	8.80
Elijah Varney	1.48
Stephen Perkins	10.24
Benjamin Hayes	2.67
× John Kent paid ×	9.69
Charged in Town Acct. 1803	500.28

Rochester May 28th 1804

Then agreed with and appointed Joshua Holmes Junr Collector of Taxes for 1804 who is to Collect and pay in the same for Two & one Quarter percent of what is paid in before the first day of March next and to give Six percent on all that shall then remain unpaid till the whole is paid. The Town having neglected to Choose any Collector for the present year.

John Odiorne } Select
Richd Dame } men of
Joshua Allen } Rochester

Nov 3d 1804 Settled with Simon Torrly and renewed his Note given Decr 17 1798 for one hundred Dollars and gave a note for Thirty five Dollars and Twenty five cents the Interest due up to this date ——

Do Renewed Daniel Dames note dated December 18th 1802 for One hundred and Twenty eight Dollars and seventy cents principal and Fifteen Dollars and forty four cents in all one hundred forty four Dollars fourteen cents ——

1804; Settlement with Collectors 1804.

	$ cts
March 13. after 1803 rect [illegible] Clerk received of	
Ichabod Corson Abij Allen's school list 1797	18.19
pd Micah Allen for Esq Corsons list balance of 1797	17.36
Do in part do 1798 only 325 had before been paid	14.64
pd David Wingate for [illegible] for [illegible] bridge	6.
pd Do for helping carry B. Wentworth out of town	9.77
~~and gave a receipt in part of 1800 list~~	53.77
paid by [illegible] as above	
and gave a receipt in part of 1800 list for	49.52
Aug 27. 1804 Recd of Benj Hayes Milton Order	23.68
Micah Allen. Jos Tebbets Dect 6.96.	6.96
B. Wentworths Tax in Hayes list to Allen 3 [illegible] for [illegible]	8.60
R Nutter. Jas Ellis Abij Clark Tax to Hayes	3.85
Jo Wentworth to Milton 6.53. Watson for Dame 5.94	12.47
Jacob Hansons District to Jno Wetherels Road 5.07	16.07
and gave a Recct in part Town list 1802	74.63
Novr 5th 1804 Settled with H Knight Recd Cash	28.18
*Co Treasurer Rect 132.90 Co Exs 55.47. S. Tords 21	209.37
Saml Ham 50c. N Meder for Welch 100. J. Wetherel 48.30	49.23
Jas Hanson District 15.60 Davd Dame Dect 28.50	41.10
Norway plain Dect 1803. 23.56 W Henderson 7.00	30.56
Mark Hurd [illegible] for Odiorne 4.00. T. Roberts poor 30.	34.00
Meder for Odiorne 3.40. Lower Plain Dect 16.00	19.40
Cap Davd McDuffee Dect 1803. 29.22. Do 1801. 2.78	32.00
Caleb Jackson for poor boy 3.00 Ezra Roberts 1.00	4.00
Abner Hodgdon for School 20.00. J Holmes 2.33	22.33
John P Hale Acct	3.00
and gave a Rect in part Town list 1803	473.17
1805. March 9. Recd Hatevil Knight Cash	16.00
Jacob McDuffee Dect 1804. 15. Cash to Odiorn 10.	25.00
Davd Dame [illegible] money 7.00 Jos Tebbets Dect 1803. 20.	27.00
Work on Pages Road 2.00. Taxes for Odiorne 8.98.	10.98
Meder [illegible] Dect pd Coborn 22. remains of Meder 20c	22.20
Benj Tuttle. Tax toward keeping poor 1 Doll	1.00
and Gave a Rect in pt Town list 1803	102.18
Do Recd of Joshua Holmes Jr Cash & Taxs for Dame	28.52
N plain Dect 14.00: his Dect 1804. 15.00: Square 1804. 5.50	34.50
J Plumer Dect 12.50. for Tuttle 2.50. Road 5.00 J [illegible]	20.00
R Mellen for Dr Howe 10: March for supplies 6.50	16.50
J Hanson order 12.71: D Page bridge 15. J. O. 4.00	31.71
Co Treas: 81.55: Town Clerk 1803: 15.00: D Dame Dect 25	121.55
Jos Richards for hal [illegible] 75c. Int for Torr. 4.66	5.41
R Cross for Meethouse 6.00: B Tuttle for poor 6.	12.00
Wm Henderson Dect 1803: 8.31. Do 1804. 9.48	17.79
Abatement in Cap Brewsters tax: S Tords Dect 8	.29
Col Place for bridge 6.69: J. O. taxes 5.27	11.96
And gave a Rect in pt Town list 1804	308.15
March 11th Recd of Hatevil Knight Cash 25 Dolls	25.00
& David Tebbets & Silas Tebbets Taxes 5.45	5.45
and gave a rect in pt Town list for	30.45

See page 320 [illegible]

Settlement with Collectors 1804.

Recd of Benjamin Hayes Cash	10.55
pd Ichamel [illegible] 2.00: pd B Tuttle towards poor 1.00	3.00
pd Do Thos Town tax for Dame. 3.35. and a tax in Milton .35	3.70
Abatements 33.60. Colls [illegible] 20.00. Note. 31.37.	84.97
and gave a Receipt in full for 1803 town tax	102.22
Also recd March 1805 of Benjamin Hayes	
Joseph Havens Rect for Salary in full 1802	26.66

Dol. Ct.

1804 acct pd Susan Tebbets balance due her by Com. order 3.71
To pd Josiah Main for keeping said School 1805 acct - 9.79

March 9. 1805.
pd Daniel Dame in full by Directors order $25.00

1804 pd in part Moses Dame $24.00
1805: Acct. paid 12 Dollars 12..
36..00

pd Josiah Main per Comee order June 9th 1805 - 11.50

1804
pd by Comee order to Anthony Whitehouse - 18.50

in 1805 acct paid Moses Roberts Jr. by the Directors order 16.50
ind 1805 acct pd Micah Allen - 5.00
21.50

1805 Acct pd Saml Austin 4.22
Do. pd Benj Wingate 4.00
pd Mary Horne 8.00
pd Committee 7.78
24.00

1804 acct
Settled the whole per orders 45.00

pd per Comee order to Eleazer Horne 1804 5.50
pd Josiah Main per order 1805 18.36
23.86

1805 July pd Joseph Giles to pay Wm. Clark by Director order balance $2.40
pd Josiah Main per committee order 9.10
Charged in 1806 acct
pd to [illegible] 1806 - 3.50

pd John Tanner by Directors order. Chargd in 1805 acct $20.00
pd committee 5 dollars in full chargd in 1806 Accounts -

pd Capt Danl McDuffee in pt see 1805 acct 12.25
pd Wm Henderson in 1805 acct 9.48

1804 Acct pd John Wingate by order of Committee - 12.50

pd Stevenwingate in 1805 accts by Committee order - 1.40

An account of land sold at Public Auction January 4th 1803..

The Parsonage first Division Sold to Richmond Henderson and Anthony whitehouse for - 676..00
The Grammar School lot first Division Sold Paul Roberts 2/3 & Silas Tebbets 1/3 - - 189..00
The Parsonage forth Division Sold John Clark - 111..00
One Acre back of the Courthouse Sold John Kent 15.25
One Acre Do. Sold H Knight & D Barker - 35.05
One Acre Do. Sold John Smith - - - 35..05
The remainder of Do. Sold John Smith - - 37.62
$1108.97

Henderson & whitehouse settled and paid Cash and in Notes the whole - $676..00
Abijah Clark for John pd pt of 10 per ct. - - 6.50
Hateril Knight pd Do. - - - - - 2.75
John Kent pd Do. - - - - - 1.52
Credited in Town Acct. 1802 - - - 686..77 - 686..77

Abijah Clark pd for John Clark $29..25
John Smith paid - - - 33.14
John Kent paid in full 14..69
Credited in Town Acct. 1803 - - - 77.08 77.08

Paul Roberts paid by Gilman Jewett - 57..20
John Smith 10..00
Credited in Town Acct. 1804 - 67..20 67.20

Recd of John Clark in Cash & Notes exclusive of Interest - - 75.25
Do David Barker notes for the whole 36.73
Of John Smith the balance in full 29.57
Of Paul Roberts bal. in full 36.20
Of Paul Roberts omitted being his 10 per cent - - 12..60
Of Silas Tebbets his 10 per ct. 6.30 and 2..60 towards principle - - 8.90
and $1.10 Interest on 10 per ct. - - 4.57
Credited in Town Acct. 1805 223..82 223.82

Due from Silas Tebbets principal not settled 54..10
$1108..97

Interest due on the above on Settlement and Credited in 1805 from David Barker 5..14
not included in the above - John Smith - - 6..94
of Paul Roberts - 12.80
of John Clark - 10..19
of Silas Tebbets interest 1.10
36..17

0	4.60	3.54
·	1.40	1.07
·	4.30	3.39

1	1	4
1	5	12
4	12	24
2	8	10
$2\frac{1}{2}$	10	18
$2\frac{1}{2}$	8	16

2.	4
3	1:
2.	6
$\div$ 1	1

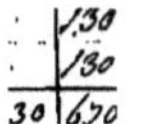

..	..	25
6 ...	--	17
.	..	130

1	3	8
1	4	12
1	1	·
1	·	·
2	12	16
$2\frac{1}{2}$	15	20
$1\frac{1}{2}$	8	12

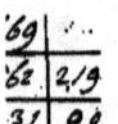

.	.	.	.	.	130
.	.	.	.	150	75
.	.	.	.	.	250
.	.	.	B	.	150
8	250	.	1000	.	1155
4	40	.	.	.	2,9
2	100	.	.	.	320

State of New Hampshire } To Joshua Holmes Jun.
Strafford ss — } appointed Colector
for the Town of Rochester for the Year 1804,
Greeting
By Virtue of Sundry Laws of said State directing
Selectmen to raise money for the Support of
Schools and other purposes, and Agreeably to a Vote
of said Town to Raise money for the Towns use
and in pursuance of a precept from the Treasurer
of said County to raise money for said State &
County use — You are hereby required in
the name of said State to levy and collect of all
Persons named in the foregoing List the several
sums set to their names in Dollars & Cents & pay
or cause to be paid into the Treasurer of said
State the sum of Two hundred & eighty eight
Dollars and thirty Cents by the first day of December
next also pay or cause to be paid to the treasurer of said
County Eighty one Dollars & fifty five Cents, by the
first day of December next also you are to pay
or cause to be paid to the Selectmen in Office three
hundred Dollars more by the first day of January
next, and the whole of the remainder of said List
to the Selectmen in Office by the first day of
March next and if any Person shall neglect or
refuse to pay his or their Tax after Legal Warning
or notice You are to take the same by destraint &
Sale as the Law Directs, and for your lawful
proceedings this shall be your sufficient Warrant
Given under our hands and Seals this Twenty fifth
Day of May 1804 —

John Osborne } Select
Richd Dame } Men
Joshua Allen

Strafford ss State of } To Joshua Holmes Jr appointed

Town's account for 1804

		Doll.	cent
Returnd in Paul Harfords hands	1781	85	10
Due on an Extent against Ichd Corson	1800	264	39
Returnd in Benja Hayes hands	1802	176	85
Returnd in Hatevil Knights list	1803	876	80
Returnd in Benjamin Seates list	1802	349	47
Returnd in Notes of hand by Selectmen	1803	500	28
Recd in Joshua Holmes Townlist	1804	1263	46
Recd for Sale of Town lands Sold in	1802	67	20
		3583	55

The way Said Money has been laid out

	Doll.	cent
To paid the County Treasurer in full 1804	81	55
To pd in part of the Debt due to Town of Milton	288	90
To pd the balance of Poor 1803 and part 1804	52	95
pd an Extent County against the Town for neglect of repairs of Road Chemist hill	55	47
To pd the demand of Wm K. Atkinson against the Town promised by Selectmen 1794	17	67
To pd repairs on Norway plains bridge	10	82
To pd John P. Hale Esqr for Services in full	3	00
To pd Howard Henderson for Interest on a Sum voted for a Road thro his land in 1795	7	00
To pd County Treasurer in full for 1803	82	90
To pd for Timber for Garlins bridge	6	00
To pd John Witherell in full for road round and thro his land	58	20
To pd for work done on Dan Pages Road in 1803	2	00
To pd Joseph Sherburne his Service as Town Clerk for 1803	15	00
To pd for building a bridge by Dan Pages as pr acct	15	00
To pd Col David Place bill for Timber for bridge	6	69
To pd Prentiss Mellens bill for fees in Dr Howard case with Lt Rollins and costs	11	82
To pd John Plumer in full for a Road	5	00
To pd the Selectmen Opening Road to Gerlins mill	3	00
To pd Selectmen for taking Inventory	5	00
To pd Do for making Ratelist & Counterparts	6	00
To making & Giving out Surveyors lists	4	00
To making School lists Giving out and Settling with School master	6	00
To pd Selectmen appointing Collectors and ~~[illegible]~~ bonds	4	00
To time & expence letting out the pound	3	67
To pd Selectmen Settling with Collectors arranging town accounts &c	12	00
To pd Selectmen Runing roads by Timothy Roberts and Lemuel Medens ~~two days~~	6	00
To Runing & opening Road by Jos: Burkford	3	00
To pd for Writing paper thro the year	1	00
To pd Sum due Selectmen of 1803	129	99
To pd for Recording Ratelists &c	3	00
To pd Samuel Ham for erecting post guide		50

	Doll.	cent
pd the balance Col McDuffees Dedt 1803 & pt 1804	36	50
pd Benja Medens Debt in full 1802 pt 1803 & 1804	46	33
pd Dr James Places Debt in full 1802 & pt 1803	16	00
pd Maj. Joth Allens Debt in full 1797	18	19
pd Norway plain Debt in pt 1803 in full 1804	68	56
pd Dr James Howes Debt in full 1803 & 1804	50	50
pd David McDuffees Debt in full 1804	18	50
pd Joseph Tebbets Debt balance of 1797 1798 & pt 1803	48	96
pd Abner Hodgdons Debt in part 1800 & 1803	20	
pd Simon Torrs Debt in ~~full~~ 1803 ~~part~~ 1802	29	
pd Jacob Hansons Debt balance 1802 1803	30	
pd Jacob McDuffees Debt in full 1803	15	
pd bal of Capt Dan McDuffees Debt 1801 ~~in full~~ 1803 pt 1804	49	89
pd Squamanagamic Debt in part 1804	5	50
pd Some expence for Gram mar School to J. Richards		75
To pd Capt John Odiorne a Journey to Exeter for paying in Dr Howes case	4	00
To making out a plan of the Town of Rochester agreable to an act of the General Court past Decr 1803	31	50
paid the Assessors in full for 1804	4	00
pd Jacob Hanson for marking a Rock in the river between Rochester and Somersworth		50
		33
to procuring key & hinges for Jury box		42
to a Pad lock for the pound		
to pd Some expence on Walkers bridge deliverd Col David Place	2	75
To paid Interest to Milton Selectmen & others more than we have received	44	97
	33	80
To paid Abatements in Benja Hayes Town list	20	00
To pd B. Hayes in full for collectg Town Tax 1803	4	00
To paid the Auditors in full		
Remains in Paul Harfords hands 1781	85	10
Due on a Execution Ichabod Corson 1800	172	66
Remains in Hatevil Knights hands 1803	371	00
Remains in Joshua Holmes list 1804	955	31
Returnd in Notes of hand	373	29
	2506	71
	915	73
	3422	44
Returnd in Benja Seates hands 1802	349	47
	3771	91
	3583	55
	188	36
	balance due Selectmen	

The foregoing is a true Statement of the Towns account both Debt and Credit for the year 1804 and as such exhibited to the Auditors this 11th of March 1805

John Odiorne, Rich. Dame, Joshua Allen — Selectmen

the above Accts as handed by the Selectmen appears Right to us — 11 March 1805

Joseph Hanson, Moses Roberts — Auditors

1804. Parish Accounts for 1804

Returned in Ichabod Corsons list for 1800	285	34
Returned in Benj^a Hayes list for 1802	318	22
Returned in Hatevil Knights list 1803	325	51
Rais'd in Joshua Holmes list for 1804	365	86
Rec^d of Selectmen for 1803 ---	6	70
	1301	63

The way said Money has been laid out

Paid Selectmen Making parish list	2	50
Paid Joseph Haven acct. for board of workmen	14	33
pd Richard Cross for taking care of Meetinghouse 1803	6	00
pd for Repairs of the Meeting house	3	96
pd Joseph Havens Salary in full 1802	266	67
	293	46

Remains in Ichabod Corsons hands 1800	285	34
Remains in Benj^a Hayes hands 1802	47	60
Remains in Hatevil Knights hands 1803	325	51
Remains in Joshua Holmes Jr hands 1804	365	86
	1024	31
	293	46
	1317	77
which leaves a Balance due Selectmen of	16	14
	1301	63

~~the above Acct appears [illegible]~~

~~11 March 1805~~ [illegible]

the Above is a true Statement of the parish accounts March 11th 1805

John Osborne } Select
Joshua Allen } men

the above Acct Exhibited appears Just & Right
11 March 1805 Joseph Hanson } Auditor

Decr 7th 1805 Hatevil Knights list $989.20
his Rec^ts $112.40
473.17
102.18
30.45
96.55
53.38
868.13

868.13
121.07
Extended for this Day

D^o Joshua Holmes list 1804 - $1263.46
his Rec^ts $308.55
516.86
152.20
80.00
1057.21

1057.21
206.25
Extended for this Day

Notes of hand returned to Selectmen of 1805

Anthony Whitehouse	152.10
Ditto	28.70
Richmond Henderson	134.05
Benjamin Palmer	10.30
Ditto	26.00
Stephen Perkins	10.24
Benjamin Dame	2.93
Benjamin Hoyt	2.67
Silas Tebbets & Co	6.30
Sum Charged in Town Acct 1804 }	373.29

paid for Support of Poor 1804

pd Benj^a Tuttle for Nancy Robinson in f. 1804	12.50
pd Tim^o Roberts for Wid^o E Henow in full 1803	31.17
pd Elijah Varney for Shoes for Ed^o Waymoth	1.43
Supplied J. Raynells Wife 1804	0.28
Do. Matthias Welch 1804	2.00
Caleb Jackson for Sargeant boy 1804	3.00
Selectmens bill 1804	2.00
Charged in Town Acct for 1804 =	52.38

Rochester June 1805

These are to certify that on the above day we agreed with Moses Bickford to Collect the Taxes in Rochester for said year for which we were to give him forty Dollars Provided he collected and paid in the whole amount of his Lists by the tenth day of March 1806. Otherwise he was to receive nothing for which he gave bonds according by

John Osborne } Selectmen
Richd Dame } of Rochester for 1805

Settlement with Collectors

	Dolls
June 9th 1805 Recd of Joshua Holmes Jr Cash	13.00
pd Saml McDuffee Dest 1804. 16.50 — Squam[illegible] 1804. 13.30	29.80
David McDuffe for Road 3.62 — Norway pt Dest 1804: 17.66.	21.28
Capt Danl McDuffe Dest 1804. 12.25: Jos Tebbets Dest 16.50	28.75
* pd March 12th last 83.76. pd J.O. balance due him. 5.25	89.01
pd State Treasr 1804. 288.30: Cash pd March 16. 33.00 Cash	321.30
pd Moses L. Neal towards School. Sundry orders	13.72
and gave a Rect in pt of 1804 town list for	516.86
Do Recd of Hatevil Knight Cash 17.00	17.00
pd Saml Austin for Maj Allen Dest 1803 20.00	20.00
Jos Pages Dest 1802. 12.00. Mos L Neal Esq. towd School 4.38	16.38
gave a rect in pt of town list for 1803	53.38
Do Recd Joseph Haven. Rect Parish tax 1803 in full	266.66
pd Richd Cross for taking care of Meetg house	6.00
and gave a rect in part of Parish list 1803	272.66

*The above $83.76 pd by Joshua Holmes was for
pd Maj Allen balance Selectman 1804: 17.18
pd John Tanner S Torr's Dest 1804 20.00
pd David Ham for wood for N P school 3.12
pd Saml Chamberlin Jr for Road in pt 4.66
pd Micah Allen pt Jos Tebbets dest. 7.41
pd David Wingate pt his Dest. 1804 10.00
pd Cash 20 Doll. Reuben Hams Tax for Damm 21.39
Rect for Town list 1804 which was Given up on the above settlement 83.76

Novr 2, 1805 Settled with Hatevil Knight recd in Cash pd Aug: 30: 10.00 & Taxes offst 6.92	16.92
Pd Moses L Neal Esq towards Town School 35.00. abatemt 20.50	55.50
Pd Do towards N.P. School 1805. 50.00. H Coleman Dest 5.00	55.00
Pd Micah Allen towards Salmonfalls lower dest.	18.13
Silas Varney for Post for postguide	1.00
	146.55
from which we deducted $50: for a mistake for that sum receipted to him too much in settlemt made March 12th 1804 ~~four~~ fifty Dollars pd Co Treasr and in settlement Novr 5th 1804 for $132.90 pd Do See page 272 the whole sum he had to pay being only $132.90 which mistake he agreed to rectify	50.00
and gave a receipt towards Town tax 1803 for	96.55
Do Recd of Joshua Holmes Cash 34.00 Taxes 1.15	35.15
pd himself for keeping Nanc Robinson in full 1805	14.83
pd Jacob McDuffee Assessor 1803. 1.00: Cash Sep 19. 15.00	16.00
pd Jos Pages Dest bal. 1799: 4.17 whole 1803: 17.80	21.97
pd Dennis Hoyt for work on the Courthouse	2.50
pd Moses Downs for keeping poor child Cooke	8.00
pd Medenboro School balance of 1804	8.00
pd Jacob McDuffee toward pound [illegible] Cash Aug: 10	31.00
pd Enoch Tebbets School 1804: 13.[illegible]	13.50
pd Moses L Neal towards Town School	1.25
and gave a receipt in pt Town list 1804 for	152.20
Dec 7th 1805 Recd of Silas Tebbets in part for [illegible]	10.00
Dec 27th 1806 Recd of Silas Tebbets by Paul Roberts	30.00
Recd an order for six dollars	06.00

Dec 7th 1805 recd of Joshua Holmes Jr Cash & Taxes	25.80
pd Jos Hodgdon Jr for wood for Grammar School	3.12
pd Thos Cheslee for wood for N P school 1805	75
pd Maj Allen by David Tebbets Tax	3.65
pd Abatements in Town list 1804	16.68
pd Samuel Meder towards a Road	30.00
and gave a Rect in pt of Town list 1804	80.00
March 7th Recd of Hatevil Knight in cash	26.00
Benj Wingates Rect for 4 Doll pd Benj Dest School 10 Dolls 14 and for paying for work on the Road by Amos [illegible]	40.00
and Gave a Rect in part of his Town tax 1803	
pd for collecting town tax for 1803	23.00
Sundry taxes discounted 5.04: abatements 2.00	7.04
a note Given for the balance	54.00
took up the above and gave a new receipt in full for his Town list 1803	121.4
March 8 Recd of Ichabod Corson Cash at Different times	76.00
abatements 6.13: pd Milton order 50.00	56.13
pd Aug 9th 1804: 5.83. Oct 26th 12.00 Novr 1804. 26.2	43.85
pd Maj Allen Schoolhouse tax 11.35: for plank 14.88	26.23
pd by John Harrison his School house list the balance	37.07
and gave his notes for the balance	5.86
The balance Receipted for of his Town list 1800	245.14
he also settled for Sunday extents $4.00 included in his note for 11.92 given this day	
Settled his Parish list pd Jos Haven for 1800	266.67
abatements 8.87. Collecting 7.74 — Note 2.06	18.67
and gave a Rect in full for balance of Parish list	285.34
Recd of Benj Hayes Cash	2.26
Abatements 14.53. Collecting 7.96: pd Cole 7.00	29.49
pd Schoolmistress in Col McDuffees District 1804	12.00
pd Abatements. Paul Hayford — Abel Harris: Josiah Tucker [illegible] Douglas Hasp poles Town Taxes for 1802	3.85
and gave a rect in full of his Parish list 1802	47.60
Recd of Moses Bickford pd Moses L Neal for School	7.00
pd David McDuffee towards Road	10.62
pd Joseph Sherburne Town Clerk 1804	15.00
pd Hezekiah Hayes for wood N Plains school	1.25
pd Joseph Hayes Dest 1805 $34.50 — Esq Damm. 30	64.50
Squamanagonic Dest 1805 pd Nich Varney	6.12
pd H Clouter for School 2.20: Assessor 1.00	3.20
pd Selectmen in Cash & Taxes [illegible]	94.12
pd County tax 1805 81.55	81.55
and gave a receipt in part of 1805 tax for	273.36
Recd after the accounts were Closed March 10th 1806 Cash 111 Dollars Danl McDuffees Dest 1805 40.33	151.33
pd Eben Plummer towards poor	13.00
and Gave a Rect for 1805 list in pt	164.33

Delivered the Selectmen the above $40.33 and 13.00

1805: School account for 1805

No. 1. Jacob Hanson $.17..00	To paid Benj. Tebbets for keep. said School in full Charg^d in 1806 Acct.
No. 2. Jabez Dame Esq. $.30..00	paid Daniel Dame by Com order in 1805 Acct
No. 3. Col. John McDuffee $.50..00	To paid for said school by committees order pd Polly [illegible] charged in 1806 account
No. 4 Jacob McDuffee $ 16..50	pd committees order Charg^d. in 1806 Acct
No. 5 Joseph Hayes $.24..00	paid Committee in 1805 Acct
No. 6 Joseph Tebbets $.27..00	paid in 1806 to Saml Allen to pay Josiah Main paid Moses [illegible] per com. order paid 2 dollars to Joseph [illegible] per committees order Charged in [illegible]

'00	555	3.84	..	4
.	5.35	3.70	1.62	4.6
75	790	5.47	..	6.8
0	5.22	3.61	1.56	4.5
.	6.22	4.31	..	5.3
00	6.13	4.25	1.84	5.3

Moses Hale
George Heard
Hezekiah Hayes
John Hoyt
Ephm. Hain Jr.

Clement Libbey	1	·	·	2	·	·	·	·	
Capt. Saml Langton	·	2	·	2	·	·	·	·	
John Libbey	1	·	·	·	·	·	·	·	
John Leck Barington 2d division				·	·	·	·	·	
Jeremiah Libbey Lebanon				·	·	·	·	·	
Col. John McDuffee	1	4	·	3	6	8	2	·	
Capt. Davd McDuffee	1	2	··	2	5	5	1	23°	1
2d John McDuffee Esq	1	2	·	1	·	·	·	13°	·
Jacob McDuffee	1	·	2	2	5	4	1	·	
James McDuffee	1	2	·	1	5	3	1	·	
David McDuffee	1	2	·	2½	2	2	·	33°	1
John McDuffee 3d	1	2	·	2½	2	2	·	23°	1
Benjn Meader	2	2	·	2	2	·	1	·	¼
Nathl Meader	2	2	2	4	2	3	2	·	1
Jonathan Meader	2	·	2	4	7	1	2	·	½
Joseph Meader	1	·	·	·	·	·	·	·	¼
Josias C. Marchkey	1	·	·	1	·	·	·	·	

											1	2	4	40			[illegible]	[illegible]	[illegible]	· ·	[illegible]
Isaac McDuffee	·	·	·	·	·	·	·	·			·	1	4	·		0	200	140	98	· ·	12
John McCrillis Lebanon			·	·	·	·	·	·			·		·	·	66/30	·	100	80	55	· ·	· ·
Majr Jotham Morrow	1	·	·	·	·	·	·	·			·		·	·	·	·	·	130	90	· ·	[illegible]
Saml McDuffee	1	2	·	4	4	4	1	·	1		1	9	20	100	·	·	30	825	561	247	71[illegible]
Jona Morrison	1	·	2	1	2	2	1	·			½	3	8	·	·	·	·	420	291	· ·	36
James McDuffee Jr	1	·	·	·	·	·	·	·			·	·	·	·		·	·	130	90	39	112
Henry ~~Mellen~~ Esqr Dover for [illegible] Gorlines Hill											· ·	·	·	·	66/30	·	· ·	50	50	· ·	· ·
Moses L Neal Esqr	1	·	·	1	·	·	·	·			1	·	·	300	·	·	·	320	222	96	27[illegible]
John Nutter	1	·	·	2	2	2	1	·	½		½	2	8	50	·	·	3	400	277	120	34[illegible]
Jotham Nutter	1	·	4	2	1	·	·	·			1	2	4	·	·	·	·	480	333	144	414
Richd Nutter Jr	1	·	·	·	·	·	·	·			·	·	·	·	·	·	·	130	90	39	112
Winthrop Nutter Farmington				·	·	·	·	·			·	·	·	·	·	·	190	75	52	· ·	· ·
John Nutter Jr	1	·	·	·	·	·	·	·			·	·	·	·	·	·	·	130	90	39	112
Capt John Odiorne	1	·	·	1	·	·	1	·			1	·	·	400	·	66	150	548	370	164	473
Elijah Otis	1	·	·	1	·	2	·	·			1	·	·	·	·	· ·	·	180	125	· ·	· ·

John Rann
Ichabod Rich.
Samuel Richa
Joseph Richar
Lt. Timothy Robe
Lt. Ewd. Rollin

2	10	20	100	.	.	70	8.40	5.
2½	12	20	100	.	.	100	8.25	5.
.	.	.	.	.	.	.	3.15	2.
1½	8	16	75	.	.	.	9.99	6.

Inventory and Counter part 1805	Polls	Oxen 4	Oxen 3	Cows	2 yr old	1 yr old	Horses	[illegible]	[illegible]	Tillage	Mowing	Pasturing	Buildings	Mills	Stock	Land &c	Total Assessed	Town Tax	[illegible]	Road Tax
Jered Varney	1	2		2					4	14	3	8				18	395	273		3.30
Thos Varney	1	2	2	3	5		1			14	5	8	75			140	728	5.04		6.30
Thos Varney Jr	1			1							1						170	118		146
Moses Varney Jr	1				1												140	98		121
Nicholas Varney	1			2				345	½	1½	6	8	50		40		480	3.33		4.14
Silas Varney	1																130	90		112
Elijah Varney Jr	1	2		3						1	2	4	30				375	259		3.23
Charles Varney	1							345									180	1.25		155
Edmund Varney	1														80		170	118	.51	146
Richd Varney	1																130	90		1.12
Dudley Varney	1	2															210	146		182
Paul Varney	1																130	90		112
Solomon Varney Dover																80	45	29		
Amos Varney Dover										1	2					80	100	69		86
Aaron Varney Dover																200	100	69		86
Caleb Varney Barrington																30	20	14		14
Isaac Wentworth	1		2	3	3	1	1		2/3	1	8	10	60				6.35	4.40	1.90	5.49
Josiah Wentworth	1			1	4	1	1			1	3		100			50	440	3.06	1.32	3.80
Elihu Wentworth	2	4		3	1	2	1			1	5	6	50				730	5.06	2.19	6.31
Saml Wingate				1		1			¼	2	6	12	40				275	1.91	.82	2.37

Abatements in Moses Bickford's list fo[r]
the year 1805

Name	Town $	cents				Parish $	cts
Edward Cole	1	23	—	—	—	0	5.
James Clark	1	04	—	—	—	0	4.
Aron Downs Jr.	0	90	—	—	—	0.	3
Jershim Dennis	0	90	—	—	—	0	3
Saml. Harford	1	53	—	—	—	0	6
Ebenezer Horne	0	90	—	—	—	—	—
Mr. Joseph Morrow	0	90	—	—	—	—	
James McDuffee	0	90	—	—	—	0	3
Daniel Cd. Tubner	0	90	—	—	—	—	—
Jonathan Richard	0	90	—	—	—	—	—
Thos. Varney Jun.	1	18	Thomas How			2	0
Benj. Roberts lost at Horse	0	49	—	—	—	—	
Col. John Goodwin, pole	0	90	—	—	—	—	
Benja. Young Jun.	1	55	—	—	—	0	6
Elijah Tebbett Jun.	1	04	Stephen Wentworth				6
		[illegible]					

Rec.d the above abatements in
Town Taxes in my list for 1805
of the Selectmen this 7th
day of March 1807
Moses Bickford

March 5th [illegible] $ 6.
March 5th 1808 8 [illegible]
Rec.d the above parish abatement of the Selectmen
Moses Bickford

… Holmes' list
		$	cts
…	39	0	78
…	48	0	87
…	39		78
…	39	1	17
		4	45
…		1	05

… 1804
… Holmes Jr.
… 59
… in the list of Town
March 5th 1808
… of the Selectmen
Moses Bickford
Holmes list with
parish account
… in the acct.
… deducted from the

Damages 1805 — Dollars 344

Joseph Hanson Stock in trade	$	12.00
Jonas C. March Esqr.	D°	1,000
Nathl. Upham	D°	15.00
Joseph Sherburne	D°	1.50
Andrew Pierce	D°	3.00
David Barker	D°	5.00
Wm. & George Dame	D°	4.00
Joseph Haven Junr.	D°	3.00
Edmund Varney	D°	80.00
Jabez Dame Esqr. Tanner		3.00
Anthony Whitehouse	D°	
Simon Torr Esqr.	D°	150.00
Caleb Jackson	D°	
Moses Hale	D°	1.50
James Tibbets blacksmith	D°	5.00
John Smith	D°	1.00
Nicholas Varney	D°	.40
John Odiorne	D°	66
Norway Plain upper Saw Mill		24.00
Garlands Saw Mill		18.00
McDuffee & Dames fulling Mill		2.00
Edwd. S. Moultons Stock		3.00
Jabez Dame Junr.		4.00
Hains & Elo		1.00

1836

Abatements in Moses Bickfords List
For the year 1805
As follows

Edward Cole $1.23
James Clark 1.04

State of New Hampshire } To Moses Bickford
Strafford SS. } appointed Collector
of taxes for the Town of Rochester for the Year 1805
Greeting

(LS) By Virtue of Sundry laws of said State directing Select Men to raise money for the support of schools and other necessary purposes and in pursuance of a Vote of said Town directing the Selectmen to raise such sums of money as they should judge necessary and in pursuance of a precept from the Treasurer of said County

You are hereby required in the name of said State to levy and Collect of all Persons named in the foregoing list the sums set to their names in Dollars and Cents and pay into the receiver of said County by the first day of December next the sum of Eighty one Dollars and fifty Cents and pay the Selectmen for the time being Three hundred Dollars more by the first day of January next and the whole of the Remainder of said list by the first Day of March next ensuing the Date hereof and if any Person or Persons shall neglect or Refuse to pay his or their said taxes after legal Warning or notice you are to take the same by Distress and sale as the law directs and for your lawful proceedings this shall be your Sufficient Warrant given under our hands & Seals this 2d Day of May 1805

John Bodiome }
Richd Dame } Select
Joshua Allen } men

Strafford SS State of } To Moses Bickford
New Hampshire } appointed Collector for
the Town & Parish of Rochester for the Year 1805
Greeting

(LS) Pursuant to Sundry Votes of the Town of Rochester for Raising of Money for the Support of of the Gospel and other necessary parish Expences and for Collecting the same you are hereby required and directed in the name of said State to levy and Collect of all Persons Named in the foregoing List the sum set to their names under the head Parish Taxes in Dollars & Cents and pay the same to the Selectmen or their Order for the time being by the first day of March next and if any Person or Persons Taxed in the said parish List shall Refuse or neglect to pay their said Taxes as aforesaid or any part thereof after after having legal notice you are to take the same by Distraint and sale as the law Directs — And and for your lawful proceedings this shall be your sufficient Warrant — Given under our hand and Seals at Rochester May 2d 1805

John Bodiome } Select
Joshua Allen } men

Town Accounts for 1805

To an Execution against Jch. Cowon for 1800	172	66
In Hatevil Knights hands for .. 1803	321	00
In Joshua Holmes Junr. hands for 1804	955	31
Raised in Moses Bickfords list for 1805	1095	16
Rec. notes of Selectmen for . 1805	573	24
Recd for lands sold in 1803	223	82
Remains in Benj Teates list - 1802	349	47
By Interest money received in 1805	84	34
By Note due at N.H. Strafford Bank ...	175	00
By received for the Old pound ...	2	75
	3752	80

The way said Money is accounted for		
To paid State Treasurer in full for 1804	238	3[illegible]
To pd. County Treasurer in full for 1805	81	9[illegible]
To pd. Moses L. Neal Esqr for keeping Grammar school	90	00
To pd Poors bill the balance for 1804 and in part for 1805	52	0[illegible]
To pd. Selectmen the balance due in 1804	188	3[illegible]
To pd. for erecting Post & Post Guides	1	
To pd Dennis Hoyt for work on Meetinghouse hearth	2	5[illegible]
To pd. Joseph Hayes in full for road on his land	2	0[illegible]
To pd Betty Richards for road through her land in part	10	
To pd. the debt due to the town of Milton in full	346	7[illegible]
To pd. Jacob McDuffee in full for building the Pound	41	4[illegible]
To pd. Saml. Chamberlain Jr. for road through his land		
To pd David McDuffee the sum voted him by the town for a road thro' his land 1795	18	2[illegible]
To pd. the Selectmen for taking Inventory in 1805	6	0[illegible]
To pd. Ditto for making & giving out Invoices list	4	0[illegible]
To pd. Do. for making rates lists & school lists	12	0[illegible]
To pd. Do. for appointing collectors & taking bonds	3	9[illegible]
To pd. Do. for recording Lists $300. Papers $400	4	0[illegible]
To pd. Do. for laying out a road to Garlands Mill	3	0[illegible]
To pd. Do. for running & settling a road thro' Lieut. Meder's land	2	0[illegible]
To pd Do. for running a road by Dimond Peaks	1	0[illegible]
To pd. Do. for running & settling a road by Joseph Meader's land	2	0[illegible]
To pd. Do. for their services through the Year	12	0[illegible]
To pd. Abatements in Hatevil Knights list for 1803	22	5[illegible]
To pd. Samuel Meder in full for road through his land	30	0[illegible]
To pd. Abatements in Joshua Holmes Jr. list for 1804	16	8
To pd. Selectmen for running land sold & five deeds	4	0[illegible]
To pd. Col. David Place's bill for rocks for roads	1	5[illegible]
To pd John Plumer 3d tax in M. Bickfords list in 1802	1	0[illegible]
To pd. Selectmen for attending court & settling an indictment	1	30
To pd. Do. for attending committee from Court on Chesnut hill road	2	
To pd. the Assessor in full for 1805	2	
To pd Selectmen attending the committee from Court on Chesnut hill road		
To pd. Select of Milton Benj. Teates taxes 1802	349	4[illegible]
To pd. Sundries for work on the road by Ham. Jenny	10	00
To pd. Hatevil Knight for collecting town tax 1803	20	00
	1632	[illegible]

Town Accounts for 1805.

	Year	$	cts
By Amount of debt brought over		1632	60
To pd. Norway Plains district in full	1805	59	00
To pd. Jacob Hanson's district in full	1804	13	50
To pd. Squamanagonic district balance of	1802	5	50
To pd. Do. for the balance in full for	1804	18	30
To pd. Hezekiah Cloutman's Dist. 1803 & part 1804		7	30
To pd. Capt. Saml. Allen's District 1800 $9.00. 1802 19.00		28	00
To pd. Benjn. Meder's district in full for	1804	23	00
To pd. Abner Hodgdon's district for	1803	17	90
To pd. Do. balance 1799 $4.17 & in full	1802	16	17
To pd. Majr. J. Allen's District in full for	1803	25	78
To pd. Jacob McDuffee's district for	1804	11	50
To pd. Simon Torr Esqr. District for part for	1804	20	00
To pd. balance Capt. Danl. McDuffee's district for	1804	12	25
To pd. Do. in part for 1805			
To pd. balance Col. John McDuffee's district	1804	12	00
To pd. Do. in part for			
To pd. James Place's District for	1805	38	00
To pd. Joshua Allen's Dist.	1803	16	00
To pd. Samuel Allen's Dist. 1803 $1.65	1804	8	28
To pd. Dr. James How Dist. in full	1804	33	4
To pd. Joseph Hayes Dist. in full	1805	30	00
To pd. Squamanagonnic Dist. in part	1805	24	50
	1805	6	12
To pd. Abatements in Ichabod Corson's hands 1800		6	13
To pd. Some abatements or Salmon fall upper district for their School house		8	51
To paid Edwd. Cole for painting post guides		5	50
Abatements in Benjn. Hayes list 1802		3	85
To paid Town Clerk his Services in full 1804		15	00
To pd. Some expence for Wood for Gram. School		6	26
To district paid more than we have Charged		28	55
To pd. Selectmen reviewing & setting about the pound		3	..
To pd. John Brown for work on Court house		2	..
		2137	33
To paid the Commissioners 4 Dollars		4	00
Remain in Joshua Holmes Jr. hands 1804		206	25
Remain in Moses Bickford's hands 1805		821	80
Due on Notes in Selectmen hands		461	33
Cash remaining in the Selectmen hands		122	09
		3752	80

The above account is a true Statement of the towns account Debt and Credit for the Year 1805 and as such we Exhibit the Same to the Commissioners

March 10. 1806 John Odiorne } Select
R. Dame } Men of
Joshua Allen } Rochester

The above account as handed to us by the Selectmen appears to us to be well vouched

Moses Roberts Jr. } Audit
Jacob McDuffee } ors

Parish accounts 1805

	Year	$
Returned in Ichabod Corsons hands	1800	285
In Benjamin Hayes hands	1802	47
In Hatevil Knights hands	1803	325
In Joshua Holmes Jr. hands	1804	365
Raised in Moses Bickfords list	1805	336
		1360
The way said money has been laid out		
To paid the Selectmen the balance due 1804		16
To paid Do. for making parish list		2
To pd. Joseph Haven Salary in full	1800	266
To pd. Joseph Haven Salary in full	1803	266
To pd. Richd. Cross for taking care of meeting house		6
To pd. Ichabod Corson for Collecting Parish Tax	1800	7
To pd. Abatements in parish list for	1800	8
To pd. Benjamin Hayes for Collecting in	1802	7
To pd. Abatement in Benjn. Hayes list	1802	14
To pd. Edwd. Cole for setting Glass putty &c for the meeting house		3
		600
To paid Joseph Haven his Salary in full 1804		266
		867
Remain in Hatevil Knights hands	1803	53
Remain in Joshua Holmes Jr. hands	1804	99
Remain in Moses Bickfords hands	1805	336
		1356
which leaves due from the Selectmen		4
		1360

The above is a true Statement of the parish account for the Year 1805 and as such we Exhibited them to the Commissioners

March 10-1806 John Odiorne } Se[lectmen]
Joshua Allen

The above account as Exhibited app[ears] to be well vouched — Jacob McDuffee

Abatements allowed in Joshua Holmes list for ... allowed September 27th. 1806 — Towns List	
Ebenezer Cooks Poll Tax	1
Wm. Jennis 3d. do	1
Aaron Jennis Jr. do	1
John Libbey do	1
Jacob Jennis do	1
	5
Abatement Joshua Holmes List 1804 — January 28th. 1807 — Town List	
Stephen Hanson Tax 1.9	1
Edward Cole do 1.36	1
John Grey do 1.84	1
Recd. the above abatements in my list for 1804 ... me — Joshua Holmes Jr.	9
	1
also Thomas Plummer Jun. Tax Town 1.39	10

Settlement with Joshua Holmes Jun September 27th 1806

allowed abatements	5.27
B. Tuttles order	1.15
Isaiah Jenkins School list	28.00
Rec'd Cash one hundred & five dolls and Sixteen cents	105.16
	$ 139.58

and gave him a receipt for the above Sum

Settlement with Moses Bickford Collector

	$
an order for school money S. Tors district	1.69
Joseph Tibbets district for order	22.00
pd order Squamscot district	5.00
pd order Abner Hodgdons district	16.00
pd Jon. Heard in part	10.07
pd Maj Allens district 1805	33.00
pd Abner Hodgdons distr 1805 in full	3.18
pd Joseph Tibbets district in full 1805	11.59
pd Jacob M Duffs district in full 1805	17.17
pd Squamscot district 1805 pd same	16.11
pd do Benj. Jewett	7.50
pd Simon Tors district 1805 [illegible]	15.88
pd S. Chamberlain Jun in full for a road	9.09
pd. ~~[illegible]~~	— 0 — 0
pd J. Places district 1815	20.00
pd B. Tuttles order for the poor	9.35
pd Col. Joshua Allens dist 1804 in p.	8.00
Rec'd Cash one hundred & thirty dollars	130.00
November 3d 1806	329.57

and gave a receipt for the above

Settlement with Moses Bickford February 27th

	$ Cents
by Cash	30.00
by paid Dea. Saml. Chamberlain's Note	4.75
pd Tim. Corsons order	1.00
Cash	4.74
and gave a receipt for the above	40.49

361) abatements in the parish tax of 1805, this 15th of December 1806 in Moses Bickford's list for 1805

	$
Thomas Hows parish Tax	2.
Col. John Goodwin Esq pole Tax	— .
carried to page 343	2.

abatements in Moses Bickford's list of town Tax for 1805

	$
Col John Goodwins pole Tax to page 343	[illegible]

Jan. 1808 Austin

Comittees order in full —
Discharg'd in 1806 Austin

id Comittee in full —
harg'd in 1806 Austin
[illegible] Recei— for soldier

1	2
·	·
·	½
1	1½
·	1½
·	1
1	3

·	1	·	·	·
2	·	·	·	·
·	1	·	·	·
·	1			
1	1	·	·	·
3	1	·	·	·
1	1	·	·	·
3	1	·	·	·
4	2	·	1	·
1	1	·	·	1
·	·	1	·	·
·	·	·	1	·
·	1	·	·	·
2	1	·	·	·
·	·	·	·	·

	2	6	12	75	
[illegible]					
		1	8		
	1	3	8	31	
1	2	5	10	75	
½	1½	6	8	50	
	3				
½	1½	5	8	75	
	1½	5	12		
½	1	4	10	75	
	1½	4	12		

Jonathan Jennes Jr	1	.	.	1	.	.			
Moses Jennes Jr	1	.	2	2	.	.			
John Flint Resident Berwick									
Joseph Knight	1	1	.	1	1	2			
Joshua Knight	1	1	2	2	1	2	1		
Hatevil Knight	1	.	.	2	1	.	2		
Paul Kimball	1	.	.	2	4	.	1		
Ephraim Kimball Farmington									
John & Paul Kimball Dover									
Widw Sally Knowles	.	.	.	2					
Paul Libbey	1	.	2	3	1	3	1		
Clement Libbey	1	.	.	2					
Jethro Lock Barrington									
Capt Timo Langton	1	.	.	2	2	1	1		
John Libbey	1								
Joseph Langton [illegible]									
Edward Lock	1	.	.	2	1	.	1		
Col John McDuffee Esq	.	4	2	7	2	4	2	.	1
Capt Daniel McDuffee	1	.	4	3	4	3	1		
Lt John McDuffee Jr	1								
Jacob McDuffee	1	.	2	5	5	4	1		
James McDuffee	1	2	2	1	2	1	1	.	1
David McDuffee	1	2	2	3	1	2	1		
John McDuffee 3d	1	2	.	3	3	2	.	1	
Benja Meder	1	.	2	4	1	2			
Nathl Meder	2	2	.	5	2	3	1		
Jonathan Meder	2	.	4	4	1	2	1		
Joseph Meder Farmington									
Jonas C. March Esq	1	.	.	2	Chaise $20				
Francis Meder	1	.	.	4					
Josiah Main	.	.	2	1	5	.	.	.	1
Amos Main	1	.	.	1	2				
Josiah Main Jr	1	.	.	1					
Lemuel Meder	1	.	.	1	.	.	1		
Edward S Moulton	1	.	.	1	.	.	1		
Micah Meder	1	.	.	1	.	.	1		
Isaac McDuffee	1								
Samuel McDuffee	1	2	.	4	5	3	1		
Jonathan Harrison	1	2	.	3	.	.	1		
James McDuffee Jr	1								
John Ct Relis Lebanon									
John Nutter	1	.	.	1	2	2	0	1	

		2.30	1.77	.	2.[illegible]
		1.00	77	.	1.[illegible]
200		4.93	1.75	126	1.[illegible]
½ 1 4 19 75		3.60	2.57	108	4.2
9 4 . 350 140	75	7.93	6.10	237	9[illegible]
½ 1 4 7		4.30	3.31	129	5.[illegible]
19	100	7.10	.84	.	12.[illegible]
	75	38	.51 Farmington		
		40	.	.	5.[illegible]
½ 1½ 5 12 100		6.00	4.62	180	7.[illegible]
1	40	2.10	1.61	63	2.[illegible]
1 2 4	100	1.30	1.00		1.[illegible]
¾ 60	50	3.35	2.51	75	3.[illegible]
		1.50	1.00	39	1.[illegible]
¾	.50	40	.30	.	4[illegible]
¾ 2 8 100		3.93	3.04	.	4[illegible]
4 24 36 400	300	16.40	12.62	4.92	1[illegible]
1 4 14 28 150	200	11.20	8.77	349	1[illegible]
1½ 3½ 8 125 60	100	4.18	3.21	125	4[illegible]
2 8 12 75	200	8.78	6.37	248	2[illegible]
2 7 12 75	100	7.23	5.56	292	[illegible]
1 3 4 10 100	150	7.86	6.05	299	9[illegible]
1 3 7 10 100	150	7.65	5.89	337	8[illegible]
½ 1½ 5 12 100		5.45	4.19	.	6[illegible]
1 2 7 16 100	50	9.00	6.93	.	1[illegible]
½ 2 8 16 100	50	9.10	7.00		1[illegible]
½ ½ 1 . 50		70	.53		[illegible]
1 . . 550 1300		11.25	8.68	337	[illegible]
½ 1 5 12 100		4.55	3.50	.	[illegible]
½ 1 4 10 50		3.50	2.69	105	[illegible]
		1.70	1.30	57	
		1.50	1.15	[illegible]	
1 4	100	3.10	2.88	.	
150 200		3.95	3.07	92	
1 2 4 40		3.20	2.46	.	
0 1 4	200	2.70	2.07	64	
1 1 9 20 100	50	8.30	6.39	249	
½ 3 8 25		4.62	3.55	.	
		1.30	1.00	39	
	100	50	38	.	
½ ½ 1 8 50		3.40	2.61	102	
1 2 4		3.60	2.77	100	

2	2	5	4	4	2	.	.	1
.	.	3	2	1	.	1	.	.
2	2	4	5	4	1	2	.	.
2	2	6	4	2	1	.	.	1
2	.	2	2	6	2	.	.	1
.	.	2	3	1	1	.	.	.
2	.	3	.	.	.	.	.	1
2	.	2	.	3	1	.	.	.
.	2	1	.	3	1	.	.	.
.	.	.	.	.	.	.	.	.
.	.	1	.	.	1	.	.	.
.	.	3	1	2	.	.	.	.
2	.	3	1	3	1	.	.	.
.	.	.	.	.	.	.	.	.
.	.	1	5	1	.	.	.	.
.	.	4	.	2	.	.	.	.
2	.	1	.	.	2	.	.	.
.	.	.	.	.	.	.	.	.
.	.	.	.	.	.	.	.	.
2	2	4	3	2	1	.	.	.
.	.	1	.	.	.	.	.	.
.	.	1	.	.	.	.	.	.
2	?	2	.	2	.	.	2	.
.	.	.	.	.	.	.	.	.
.	.	.	.	2	1	.	1	.
.	.	2	.	2	1	.	.	.
2	.	2	.	.	.	.	.	.
.	.	2	.	.	.	.	.	.
Wakefield				.	.	.	.	.
.	.	.	.	.	.	.	.	.

2	4	15	24	100	.	—	[illegible]	[illegible]	[illegible]		[illegible]
.	1	4	12	150	.	.	.	4.75	3.65	1.42	5.5
2	2½	15	20	200	Cham[illegible]	40	100	12.70	9.77	3.71	14.0
½	2	12	16	75	.	.	100	10.23	7.87	3.06	11.9
½	1½	8	12	75	.	.	100	8.18	6.29	2.45	9.5
½	1	3	8	.	.	.	.	4.10	3.15	1.23	4.7
.	1	2	12	.	.	.	50	4.65	3.58	1.39	5.4
1	2½	10	12	75	.	.	50	7.38	5.68	2.21	8.6
.	1	.	.	.	.	.	.	3.15	2.42	.	3.6
.	1	.	.	200	.	.	.	1.20	.92	.36	1.4
.	½	.	.	50	.	.	.	2.55	1.96	.76	2.9
.	.	.	.	.	.	.	.	.80	.61	.	.9
½	2	5	12	50	.	.	100	6.55	5.04	1.96	7.0
.	.	.	.	.	.	.	.	1.30	1.00	.	1.3
.	1	1	.	.	.	.	70	1.80	1.38	.	2.
.	2	2	8	75	.	.	.	3.78	2.91	.	4.
.	1	1	.	.	.	.	50	4.35	3.39	.	5.
.	.	.	.	50	.	.	.	1.55	1.19	.46	1.
.	.	.	.	.	.	.	.	1.30	1.00	.39	1.
1	3	17	24	150	.	.	150	11.55	8.89	2.66	13
.	.	.	.	.	.	.	.	1.50	1.15	.	1
.	.	.	.	120	.	300	.	3.60	2.77	1.00	4
.	1	.	4	.	.	.	80	3.70	2.84	1.11	4
.	.	.	.	.	.	.	.	1.30	.	.	1
.	.	.	.	.	.	.	.	2.40	1.84	.72	2
.	.	.	.	.	.	.	.	2.50	1.92	.75	2
.	.	.	.	.	.	.	100	4.35	3.34	1.30	[illegible]
.	½	3	8	50	.	.	.	1.70	1.30	.	[illegible]
.	.	.	.	.	.	.	200	1.00	.77	.	[illegible]
.	.	.	.	.	.	.	.	1.30	1.00	.39	[illegible]
.	.	.	.	.	.	.	.	1.50	1.15	.	[illegible]

Name	1	2	3	4	5	6	7	8	9	10	11	12	13	14	15	16	17	18	19	20	21
John Randal	1		2	2		3	1				⅓	1½	7	8	75				5.73	4.41	1.71
John Randal Jr	1	2		4			1				1	1	5	8	75				5.88	4.52	1.76
Lt Daniel Ricker	Somersworth																	133	.66	51	
Heard Roberts	3	4		3	3		1		1		1	2	9	16	50			80	11.35	8.73	3.40
Benj.a Roberts	1	2		3		2						1	4	4	50			50	4.50	3.46	
Benj.a Rollins	1						1								150				2.75	2.11	82
Moses Roberts Jun	1	2		3		1	1		1			2	8	20	100			300	8.55	6.58	
John Richardson	1	4		4	3	2	1		1		½	2	6	12	0			100	7.95	6.12	2.38
Tim.o Richardson	1			2	5	2				1		1	1						2.80	2.15	.84
Jotham Richards	1			1															1.50	1.15	
John Roberts	1																		1.30	1.00	.39
John Roberts Jun	1	2	2	5	1	2	1					1	6	4		40			6.40	4.92	
James Robinson	1	4		3	1	1						1	2	4	50				4.70	3.61	
Ezra Roberts	1			2		1	1					½	1						2.75	2.11	.82
Levi Robinson	1				1				1										1.70	1.30	.51
Wid.o Hannah Rogers				2	1		1					1	2	4					2.30	1.77	
Thom.s Richardson												1	3	8	50			40	1.65	1.27	.49
John Richardson Jr	1			1															1.50	1.15	49
Capt Moses Roberts	1			2								½	4	4	100				3.30	2.54	
John Remmick											½	1	3	12	75				1.93	1.48	57
Capt John Rollins	Somersworth																	133	.66	51	
Sam.l Seavey	1			2	4	2	1		1		1	2	6	16	120			100	7.00	5.39	2.10
John Smith	1			1								1			250	100	150		4.70	3.61	1.41
[illegible]	1			2											150		50		[illegible]	[illegible]	[illegible]

Inventory and [illegible] 1806

368 | 369

Name	Polls	Oxen 4 yrs	Steers 3 yrs	Cows	2 yrs	1 yr	Horses	Colts 3 yrs	Colts 2 yrs	Colts 1 yr	Orchard	Tillage	Mowing	Pasture	Buildings	Mills	Stocks	Land	Total Amount	Town Taxes	[illegible] Tax	Taxes
Ebenezer Tebbets	1	2	2	3	1	4	1	.	.		1	2	1	12	75	130	.	90	842	648	2.51	1.80
James Tebbets	1	.	.	2	.	.	1	.	.		.	1	4	.	150	.	400	.	615	473	1.84	7.17
Enoch Tebbets	1	.	.	4	.	.	1				¼	½	3	4	62	.	.	.	424	326	.	494
David Tebbets Jr	1	2	.	2							.	.	.	.	.	.	.	.	2.50	1.92	.	2.91
Joseph Tebbets Jr	1																		1.30	1.00	.	1.50
Jonathan Tebbets	1	2	.	2															2.50	1.92		2.91
Jeddediah Tebbets	1	4	.	4	1	4	1	.	.	1	½	1	5	8	130	.	.	50	7.55	5.81	2.26	8.80
Nicholas Tebbets	1	2	.	2															2.50	1.92		2.91
Tobias Twombly				1															.50	.38		.58
Isaac Twombly	2	2	.	2	.	2	1				½	1	1½	6 4	75				5.80	4.48		6.80
Wm Trickey	1	.	2	3	2	1	1				.	2½	12	20	100			100	8.35	6.36	2.50	9.74
John Trickey	1	2	.	2	1	.	1								50				3.55	2.73	1.36	4.14
Tobias Twombly Jr	1	2	2	4	2	2	1	.	.	1	.	2	10	20	119			70	8.85	6.81	2.65	10.32
Joshua Trickey	2	3	.	4	3	.	1				½	2	8	16	75				8.93	6.87	2.67	10.41
Saml Tebbets	1	.	.	3	2														2.10	1.61		2.45
Ichabod Tebbets Dover																		150	.75	.57		.87
Joseph Tilton Esq	1	.	.	.	.	.	1				.	.	[illegible]		1050				7.45	5.73	2.23	8.69
Seth Upham	1	.	.	1	.	.	1	Chaise 840			½	1	8	12	1100	.	1500	.	18.00	13.86	5.40	21.00
Moses Varney	.	.	.	2															.40	.30		.46
Elijah Varney	1	.	.	3							½	1½	2	4	[illegible]			200	3.35	2.57		3.90
Benjamin Varney	1	.	4	3	3	1					1	1½	5	12	50			100	6.40	4.92		7.46
Tobias Varney	2	2	.	3	1	4	1	1			½	2	8	16	100				8.90	6.85		10.38
Jeremiah Varney	1	2	.	2							½	1½	3	8					3.95	3.04		4.61
Thomas Varney	1	2	.	4	.	.	1				.	1½	5	8	75			140	6.38	4.91		7.44
Thomas Varney Jr	1																		1.30	1.00		1.50
Moses Varney Jr	1																		1.30	1.00		1.50
Nicholas Varney	1	.	.	1	.	.	1				½								2.35	1.80		2.67
Silas Varney	1																		1.30	1.00		1.50
Elijah Varney Jr	1	.	.	1	.	2					.	1	2	4	50				2.65	2.15		3.09
Richd Varney	1																		1.30	1.00		1.50
Dudley Varney	1																		1.30	1.00		1.50
Solomon Varney Dover																		80	.40	.30		.46
Shobal Varney Dover											.	1						50	.45	.34		.47
Aaron Varney Dover																		200	1.00	.77		1.16
Caleb Varney Farmington																		30	.15	.11		.17
Amos Varney Dover											.	1½	2					80	1.10	.84		1.28
Jacob Varney & Jacob Varney Dover																		25	.13	.10		.15
Benjamin Wentworth Berwick											.	2	1					100	.60	.46		
Isaac Wentworth	1	.	.	3	4	2					⅔	1	3	10	60				5.20	4.00	1.56	6.06
Josiah Wentworth	1	.	.	1	.	2	1				.	1	3	.	100			30	3.85	2.74	1.15	4.49
Elihu Wentworth	1	4	.	3	1	2	1				⅓	1	5	6	30				6.25	4.81	1.87	7.2[illegible]
Saml Wingate	.	.	.	1							1	1	6	12	40			100	3.20	2.46	.96	3.7[illegible]
David Wingate	1	4	.	5	.	1	1				1	2	10	20	100			150	9.60	7.39	2.88	12.2[illegible]
George Willand	.	2	.	2							.	1½	3	4	50				2.55	1.96	.76	2.9[illegible]
Enoch Willand	1	0	2	2														70	2.45	1.88	.73	2.9[illegible]
Jacob Wallingford	1	.	2	2	3	1	1				½	1½	3	12	50			80	5.45	4.19	1.63	6.4[illegible]
Turner Whitehouse	1	.	.	3	.	1					.	.	1	.	25			50	2.52	1.94	.	2.9[illegible]
Anthony Whitehouse	1	.	.	2	1	.	1				.	1	2	4	25		50	100	4.17	3.21	1.25	4.8[illegible]
Stephen Whitehouse	1																		1.30	1.00	.39	1.50
Benjn Whitehouse	1	.	.	2							.	1							1.90	1.46	.57	2.2[illegible]
Alexander Whitehouse	1	.	.	1	.	1					.	1							1.80	1.38	.54	2.1[illegible]
Israel Whitehouse	1																		1.30	1.00	.39	1.50

370 | 371

Inventory & Counterpart 1806

Name	Polls	Oxen	Oxen 3	Cows	2 y o	1 y o	Horses	Colts 3 y o	Colts 2 y o	Colts 1 y o	Orchard	Tillage	Mowing	Pasturing	Buildings	Mills	Stock	Land	Total Amount	Town Taxes	Parish Taxes	Road Tax
Daniel C. Watson	1											1			50				175	1.34	.52	2.01
James Eldron	1		4	3	1	1	1					1	6	18	50			400	850	6.54	2.55	9.91
Wid. Sally Wentworth			2	5	1		1					2	9	16	100				610	4.69	1.84	7.11
Elijah Whitehouse	1			3	0	1						½	1	4	40				265	1.97		3.09
Moses Watson	1	2	2	3		4	1					1½	6	10	40			100	705	5.41		8.21
John [illegible]	1	2	2	2	2	2	1					1½	3	4	40			100	605	4.65	1.81	7.05
Benjamin Wentworth			2	1	2														90	.69		1.05
Thomas Wentworth	1																		130	1.00	.39	1.50
Josiah Wentworth	1			1															150	1.15	.45	1.75
James Woodes	1			1			1								50				245	1.88	.73	2.85
Obediah Whittier Dover																		150	75	.57		.87
Benjamin Wingate	1	4		2		2	1												410	3.15	1.23	4.78
Wid. Elizabeth Wentworth Somersworth												½	4	4					110	.84		1.26
Dudley Watson	1	2	2	4	1	2	1			1	1½	3	2	6	100				670	5.15	2.01	7.80
Aaron Wingate Esq. Farmington												1	6	12				100	250	1.92		2.91
Benjn. Wiggin	1				0		1												200	1.54	.60	2.33
William Warren	1			2	4		1					2	3	6	100				460	3.54	1.38	5.38
Jeremiah Woodman Esq.	1						1												200	1.54	60	2.33
John Whitehouse	1																		130	1.00		1.50
Moses Young	1	2	2	4	4	4				1	1½	3	7	16	150			80	845	6.50	2.53	9.80
Hull Comp Lebanon												2	4						120	.92		
John Jennes	1																		130	1.00	.39	1.50
Samuel Rogers	1																		130	1.00	.39	1.50

Doomages for 1806

	Dol.		Dol.
Joseph Hanson [illegible]	1300	Haven & Smith's Gristmill	2
Jonas C. March Esq. do	1300	Downing & Tebbets do	2
Nathl. Upham do	1500	James Tebbets B. Smith	4.00
Joseph Sherbourn do	50	John Smith do	150
Andrew Peirce do	300	Jacob Hanson do	100
David Barker do	500	Capt. John Osborne Sadler	66
Jabez Dame Jr. do	600	Norway plain upper Sawmill	24
Edward L. Moulton do	200	McDuffee & Dames fulling mill	2.00
Haynes & Ela do	300	John P. Hale Esq.	150
Jabez Dame Esq. Tom	33	Joseph Tilton Esq.	150
Anthoni Whitehouse do	50		
Simon Torr Esq. do	200		
Moses Hale do	650		

Settlement with Collector Benjamin Hayes 14th February 1807 on his List for the year 1806

	$ cts
To pd. State Treasurer	288.30
Cash	25.00
pd. Col. McDuffee school	12.00
pd. Wm. Jennes for road	05.00
pd. Ebenr. Plumer	11.55
pd. Simon Torr order	20.43
Col. Hanson Bridge Repairs	34.50
pd. Daniel Hayes for do	18.94
pd. Francis Meder for road	18.00
pd. County Treasurer	81.55
pd. Jacob McDuffee school	47.00
pd. Joseph Sherburn Teacher	20.00
pd. Cash	44.00
Cash	14.00
Cash	22.49
	$ 632.76
Cash	008.00
	$ 640.76

Recd the above sum of collector Benjamin Ha[yes] and gave him a receipt for the same

State of New Hampshire } To Benjamin Hayes
Strafford ss — } appointed collector of
(LS) taxes for the town of Rochester for the year 1806
Greeting

By virtue of sundry Laws of this state directing Selectmen to raise money for the support of schools and other necessary purposes and in pursuance to a vote of said town directing Selectmen to raise such sum or sums of money as they should Judge necessary And in pursuance to a precept from the Treasurer of said State, And a precept from the Treasurer of said County.

You are hereby required in the name of said state to levy and collect of all persons named in the foregoing list the sums set to their names in dollars and Cents and pay into the Treasury of said state on or before the first day of December next the sum of two hundred and Eighty eight dollars and thirty cents. And pay into the treasury of said county the sum of Eighty one dollars and fifty five cents on or before first day of December next — And three hundred dollars more to the selectmen for the time being by the first day of December next. and the whole of the remainder of said tax by the first day of March next ensuing the date thereof. and if any person or persons shall refuse or neglect to pay the same after legal notice or warning you are to take the same by distraint and sale as the Law Directs. and for your lawful proceeding this shall be your sufficient warrant Given under our hands and seals this 30 day of May 1806.

Jacob McDuffee } Select
James Tebbets } men
Moses Roberts } of Rochester

State of New Hampshire } To Benj.a Hayes appoin-
(LS) Strafford ss — } -ted Collector of Taxes for the
town and Parish of Rochester for the year 1806
Greeting

Pursuant to Sundary Votes of said town for raising money for the support of the Gospel and other necessary purposes and for Collecting the same —
You are hereby required and directed in the name of said State to levy and collect of all persons named in the forgoing List the sums set to their names in dollars and cents under the head parrish Taxes and pay the same to the selectmen for the time being or to their order on or before the first day of march next ensuing the date hereof —
and if any person or persons shall refuse or neglect to pay his or their said Taxes as aforesaid or any part thereof after legal notice or warning you are to take the same by Distraint and sale as the law directs, and for your lawfull proceeding this shall be your sufficient warrant Given under our hands and seals this 30th day of May 1806

Jacob McDuffee } Select
James Tebbets } men
~~Moses~~ } of
} Rochester

373

Town Accounts for the year 1806

Returned in Collector Joshua Holmes list for 1804 —	20
Returned in Colt. Moses Bickford list in 1805	82
Returned in Notes of hand —	46
Raised in Benjamin Hayes list for 1806	120
Rec.d for the sale of Town Lands —	3
Rec.d Cash of Selectmen for 1805 —	122
Rec.d Interest on Several demands	39
	$ 2893

The way said Money is Accounted for

To paid States treasurer for 1806 in full —	286
to paid County treasurer for 1806 in full —	81
To paid Benj.a Meader's School Dist. in full for 1805	28
To paid Capt Daniel McDuffee's dist in full for 1805	40
to pd Simon Torrs district in full for 1804	5
to pd Elijah Otis School District in full for 1805	2
to pd Jacob Hansons School District in full for 1805	17
to pd Hez. Chrisman school dist. in part for 1806	3
to pd Joseph Tebbets School district in part 1803	3
to pd Jonathan Heard for wood for Town school & expenses toward the funeral charge of Wid. Hanson	4
To paid Simon Torr Note one hundred dollars and	100
interest on do —	16
To paid Simon Torr Note thirty five dollars and 25 Cents — and Interest on do. $3.70 —	38
To paid Note at New Hampshire Strafford Bank	175
to paid Interest at N.H. Strafford Bank	4
to paid an execution on indictment on the road between Jacob Hansons & Norway plain	42
to pd Eben.r Plumer for keeping a poor child	10
to pd the support of Wid.o Richards in her sickness —	22
To paid Selectmen for taking Inventory —	4
to paid do for Making town Tax —	6
to paid do for making and giving out school bills	6
to pd do for appoint collector and taking bonds	[illegible]
To pd do for making and giving out surveyor's [illegible]	2
To pd do for recording Inventory and Tax bill	[illegible]
To pd Squam.t Dist. in full for 1805 —	20
to pd Squam.t district in full for 1806 —	25
to paid Jacob McDuffee's district in full for 1806	17
To paid Joseph Hayes district in full for 1806 —	16
to pd Norway Plain district in full for 1806	50
to pd Jacob McDuffee's district in full for 1805 —	1
to paid Joseph Rogers district in full for 1805 —	1
to pd Capt Bickford's District in full for 1806 —	1
to pd Lt. James Place's district in part for 1805 —	1
to pd Joseph Tebbets district in part for 1805 —	2
to pd Joshua Allen's district in full for 1804 —	1
to pd Benjamin Meader's district in full for 1806	2
to paid Col. Joshua Allen's district in full for 1806	2
	122

Town Accounts for 1806

	$	C
To pd Simon Torr's district in full for 1805	31	11
To pd Jonathan Heard for a road through his land in full	61	11
To pd Joseph Sherburn for attending court on behalf of the Town in the year 1803	5	00
To paid Joseph Sherburn Services as town clerk for 1805	15	00
To paid Col David Place for work on brook bridge	34	51
To pd Daniel Hussey for covering Col. Place's bridge and plank for Dunglass Bridge	18	94
To paid Col. McDuffee's district in full for 1805	12	00
To paid Francis Meder for a road through his landing	18	00
To pd James Place's district in full for 1804 and part for 1806	20	00
To paid Col. Joshua Allen's district in full for 1805	33	00
To pd Wm Jarvis for a road through his land to the river, in full	3	00
To pd Samuel Chamberlain's Note	9	9
To pd Dean Samuel Chamberlain's Note	5	75
To pd Lt Timo Corson for erecting a guide post	1	00
To pd Assessors in full for 1806	2	00
To pd Jacob McDuffee for plank for Dunglass bridge	6	94
To pd abatements in Joshua Holmes list for 1804	10	17
To pd Joseph Hanson's Note $58.60 and Interest on do $4.70	63	20
To pd John B Hale for his service in favor of Town	3	00
To pd Selectmen for laying out a road through Jon Heard land	3	00
To pd do for opening a road through Wido Hams land & the land of William Jenness Jun	2	00
To pd Selectmen for meeting the selectmen of Farmington on the petition of the Inhabitants of Milton, Wolfborough and surveying a road over Chesnut hills	3	00
To pd Selectmen for running out the burying ground & Town plan	2	00
To pd do for running out black-water road	2	00
To pd do for dividing the town into school districts and making return and recording the same	9	
To pd do for laying out Col. David Place's bridge to repair	3	00
To pd do for opening a road through Francis Meder's land	2	00
To pd for writing paper through the year	1	00
To pd Selectmen for perambulating the town line with Selectmen of Farmington	5	00
To pd do, for settling with Collectors and school committees paying school masters and arranging town accounts and settling the same with the commissioners	17	00
~~To pd abatement in Benjamin Hayes list of taxes for the year 1806~~	~~00~~	0
To paid abatement in Colt Benjamin Hayes list of taxes for the year 1802	2	00
To pd Col Joshua Allen for work and timber for Garland bridge	9	50
~~To paid abatement in Benj Hayes town bill for the year 1802~~	0	00
To paid Richd Dame's services as Surveyor	6	0
To paid Ichabod Corson for repairing of Garland Bridge	7	68
To paid Daniel Dame's Notes	144	14
and Interest on do	27	16
To paid Richd Hayes district in full for 1804 and 1805 and part of 1806	18	00
To paid Capt Daniel McDuffee School district in full for 1806	18	67
To paid Col. John McDuffee's district in full for 1806	17	71
To pd Simon Torr's district in full for 1806	31	5
	749	31

Town Accounts for 1806

	$
Sum of acct brought up	97[illegible]
To pd abatement in Collector Benjamin Hayes town list for 1806	17
To paid two abatements in Joshua Holmes list for 1804	1
To paid Ebenez Plumer the full Ballance due to him for the support of a poor child Named Mary Heard	11
To paid poors bill	41
To pd Dr James Howe doctoring the poor	5
To paid abatement in Moses Buckford list for the year 1805	13
To paid Moses Buckford for collecting town taxes for the year 1805	16
To paid Richard Hayes poor bill	3
To paid John Plumer Jun Esq for plank for Jonies Bridge	3
To paid commissioners for the year 1806	4
To paid collector Benjamin Hayes for collecting Town Taxes for the year 1806	38
To paid Capt John Odiorne for warning poor people out of Town	1
to paid do for three guide Boards	7
Returned in Notes of hand	425
	$ 2569
Cash remaining in the Selectmens hands	325
	$ 2895

The above statement of accounts of deb[its] and Credit of the town accounts for the year 1806 and as such we exhibit the same to the commissioners

Jacob McDuffee
James Tebbets
Moses Roberts
Select[men] of Roch[ester]

Rochester March 9th 1807
We have cast the Inventory or Tax bill and examined and cast the Town Accounts as above exhibited to us by the Selectmen and find them correct and well vouched

Richd Dame
John Odiorne
Au[ditors]

Parish Accounts for the Year 1806

	$	cts
Returned in Hatevil Knights list for 1803	53	51
Returned in Joshua Holmes Jun. list for 1804	99	20
Returned in Moses Bickfords list for 1805 –	336	37
Raised in Col. Benj.n Hayes list for 1806 —	344	81
	833	89

The ways said money has been laid out

	$	
To p.d the Rev. Joseph Hawens Salary for 1805	00	00
To p.d John Brown for making steps to the Meeting House	1	50
To p.d the abatement of James Place's Tax 1804	3	66
To p.d Selectmen for making parish list	2	50
To p.d Benjamin Hayes for collecting parish tax	0	00
To p.d Joseph Hawens Salary in full for 1806	2[illegible]	66
To p.d Rich.d Cross for taking care of the Meeting house for 1806	6	00
To p.d Selectmen for repairing the Meeting house	3	21
To p.d Abatement in Collector Benjamin Hayes list for the year 1802	0	89
To paid abatement in Collect. Benj.n Hayes parrish list for the year 1806	4	54
To paid an abatement to Benjamin Hayes list of parish Taxes	0	54
Remains in Hatevil Knights list 1803	53	51
Remains in Joshua Holmes Jun. list for 1804	99	20
Remains in Moses Bickford list for 1805	336	37
Remains in Benjn Hayes list for 1806	66	18
	844	76
Which leaves a ballance due to the select men a ballance of	10	87
	833	89

The above accounts of debt and credit is a true statement of the parrish list, and as such we exhibit the same to the Commissioner

Jacob McDuffee } Selectmen of Rochester
James Tebbets }

The above Parish accounts as Exhibited by the Select Men appear to be accurated and well Vouched

John Odiorne } Auditor

Abatement in Collector Benjamin Hayes [list] of Taxes for the year 1806 allowed March 6th 1807

	Town	Parish
Benjamin Dame lost a horse —	$0.53	[illegible]
Stephen Ham lost a yoke of oxen —	0.60	[illegible]
John Heard over taxed —	0.60	0.[illegible]
Joseph Knight lost a cow —	0.15	0.[illegible]
Aaron Jennis lost a cow —	0.15	[illegible]
Moses Jennis do —	0.15	0.[illegible]
Turner Whitehouse pole Tax —	1.00	0.[illegible]
Josiah Wentworth do —	1.00	0.3[illegible]
Daniel Ham lost a horse —	0.53	0.2[illegible]
Josiah Main lost 2 3d horse —	0.23	0.[illegible]
Isaac Wentworth pole tax —	1.00	0.3[illegible]
Capt Daniel McDuffee do —	1.01	0.3[illegible]
Benj. Evans Jr. Tax —	1.19	0.4[illegible]
James Clark's pole tax —	1.00	0.3[illegible]
Joshua Ellis Tax —	1.61	0.1[illegible]
Jacob Heard pole Tax —	1.00	0.3[illegible]
Jonathan Jennes Jun do —	1.15	0.4[illegible]
John Libby pole tax —	1.00	0.3[illegible]
John Plumer 3d pole —	1.15	0.[illegible]
Thomas Wiggin Jun —	1.00	0.0[illegible]
Moses L. Neal Esqr —	1.00	0.3[illegible]
$	16.02	2.5[illegible]

Received the above abatements of Taxes in the town and parrish list for the year 18[illegible] of the Selectmen by me Benj.n Hayes Coll

Second Settlement with Collector Benj Hayes

by ~~Col~~ Joshua Allens Tax — Town 6.54 2.[illegible]

Other abatements allowed to Benjamin [illegible]

Paul Harford lost a horse 53 Town — parish o[illegible]

Samuel Downing over Tax D — 30 Cents

Ebenezer Pearl lost a horse & steer Tax 35 [illegible]

which are allowed to Benj. Hayes & [illegible] other persons —

Jacob McDuffee } Sel[ect]m[en] of Roch[ester]
James Tebbets }
Moses Roberts }

Rochester March 9th 1807 this day [settled] with collector Benj.n Hayes in full for [the] Town taxes for the 1806 and passed receipts [between] him and the Town

Jacob McDuffee } Sel[ectmen]
James Tebbets }
Moses Roberts }

Abatements allowed 1807

In Watteil Knight's list for 1803

	Lands	Moved
Edward Cole Gone out of Town	1.00 —	0.45
Joshua Eller Poor —	1.70 —	0.00
Benja. Evans Jun. Poor —	1.60 —	0.67
from page 266		10.35
	Town 4.30	11.47

Settlement

Rochester, NH

12615-1

Selectmen's Records

1794 – 1806

END

www.ingramcontent.com/pod-product-compliance
Lightning Source LLC
Chambersburg PA
CBHW020535270326
41927CB00006B/585

* 9 7 8 3 7 4 3 4 5 4 7 9 8 *